MEDIA LITERACY: TRANSFORMING
CURRICULUM AND TEACHING

The *Yearbook of the National Society for the Study of Education* (ISSN 0077-5762, online ISSN 1744-7984) is published in April and June by Blackwell Publishing with offices at 350 Main St, Malden, MA 02148 USA; PO Box 1354, Garsington Rd, Oxford, OX4 2DQ, UK; and PO Box 378 Carlton South, 3053 Victoria, Australia.

Society and Membership Office:
The *Yearbook* is published on behalf of the National Society for the Study of Education, with offices at: University of Illinois at Chicago, College of Education (M/C 147) 1040 W. Harrison Street Chicago, IL 60607-7133. For membership information, please visit www.nsse-chicago.org.

Subscription Rates for Volume 104, 2005

	The Americas[†]	Rest of World[‡]
Institutional Standard Rate*	$125	£77
Institutional Premium Rate	$138	£85

*Includes print plus basic online access. [†]Customers in Canada should add 7% GST or provide evidence of entitlement to exemption.
[‡]Customers in the UK should add VAT at 5%; customers in the EU should also add VAT at 5%, or provide a VAT registration number or evidence of entitlement to exemption.
For more information about Blackwell Publishing journals, including online access information, terms and conditions, and other pricing options, please visit www.blackwellpublishing.com.
All orders must be paid by check, money order, or credit card. Checks should be made payable to Blackwell. Checks in US dollars must be drawn on a US bank. Checks in Sterling must be drawn on a UK bank.

Volume 104 is available from the publisher for $40 a copy. For earlier Volumes please contact Periodical Service Company, L. P., 11 Main Street, Germantown, NY 12526-5635 USA Tel: (+518) 537-4700, Fax: (+518) 537-5899, Email: Psc@backsets.com or http://www.backsets.com

For new orders, renewals, sample copy requests, claims, changes of address and all other subscription correspondences please contact the Journals Department at your nearest Blackwell office (address details listed above). US office phone 800-835-6770 or 781-388-8200, Fax 781-388-8232, Email subscrip@bos.blackwellpublishing.com; UK office phone +44 (0) 1865-778315, Fax +44 (0) 1865-471775, Email customerservices@oxon.blackwellpublishing.com; Asia office phone +61 3 9347 0300, Fax +61 3 9347 5001, Email subscriptions@blackwellpublishingasia.com.

The *Yearbook* is mailed Standard Rate. Mailing to rest of world by DHL Smart & Global Mail. Canadian mail is sent by Canadian publications mail agreement number 40573520.

Postmaster: Send all address changes to *Yearbook of the National Society for the Study of Education*, Blackwell Publishing Inc., Journals Subscription Department, 350 Main St., Malden, MA 02148-5020.

Blackwell
Synergy Sign up to receive Blackwell *Synergy* free e-mail alerts with complete *Yearbook* tables of contents and quick links to article abstracts from the most current issue. Simply go to www.blackwell-synergy.com, select the journal from the list of journals, and click on "Sign-up" for FREE email table of contents alerts.

Disclaimer: The Publisher, the National Society for the Study of Education and Editor(s) cannot be held responsible for errors or any consequences arising from the use of information contained in this journal; the views and opinions expressed do not necessarily reflect those of the Publisher, Society or Editor(s).

MEDIA LITERACY: TRANSFORMING
CURRICULUM AND TEACHING

104th Yearbook of the
National Society for the Study of Education

PART I

Edited by
GRETCHEN SCHWARZ
PAMELA U. BROWN

20 NSSE
The NATIONAL
SOCIETY for
the STUDY
of EDUCATION
05

Distributed by BLACKWELL PUBLISHING MALDEN, MASSACHUSETTS

National Society for the Study of Education

The National Society for the Study of Education was founded in 1901 as successor to the National Herbart Society. It publishes an annual two-volume Yearbook, each volume dealing with a separate topic of concern to educators. The Society's yearbook series, now in its one hundred and fourth year, presents articles by scholars and practitioners who are noted for their significant work in critical areas of education.

The Society welcomes as members all individuals who wish to receive its publications and take part in Society activities. Current membership includes educators in the United States, Canada, and elsewhere throughout the world—professors and graduate students in colleges and universities; teachers, administrators, supervisors, and curriculum specialists in elementary and secondary schools; policymakers and researchers at all levels; and any others with an interest in teaching and learning.

Members of the Society elect a Board of Directors. The Board's responsibilities include reviewing proposals for Yearbooks and authorizing their preparation based on accepted proposals, along with guiding the other activities of the Society, including presentations and forums.

Current dues (for 2005) are a modest $40 ($35 for retired members and for students in their first year of membership; $45 for international membership). Members whose dues are paid for the current calendar year receive the Society's Yearbook and are eligible for election to the Board of Directors.

Each year the Society arranges for meetings to be held in conjunction with the annual conferences of one or more of the national educational organizations. All members are urged to attend these meetings, at which the current Yearbook is presented and critiqued. Members are encouraged to submit proposals for future Yearbooks.

Uses and Misuses of Data in Accountability Testing is part II of the 104th Yearbooks. Part I, published earlier, is titled *Media Literacy: Transforming Curriculum and Teaching.*

For further information, write to the Secretary, NSSE, University of Illinois at Chicago, College of Education M/C 147, 1040 W. Harrison St., Chicago, Illinois 60607-7133 or see http://www.nsse-chicago.org

Board of Directors of the
National Society for the Study of Education
(*Term of office expires in the year indicated.*)

Contributors to the Yearbook

v

Reviewers of the Yearbook

MARILYN BINKLEY, National Center for Education Statistics
CAROL SUE BOWMAN, Ramapo College of New Jersey
EDWIN CHRISTMANN, Slippery Rock University
MILLY COWLES, University of Alabama at Birmingham
DANA FUSCO, York College, The City University of New York
SUSIE JANS-THOMAS, Mount Mary College
JERI LEVESQUE, Webster University
JOANN LOONEY, Felician College
CATHERINE LUGG, Rutgers University
SHERRY MCCAUL, University of Wisconsin, Eau Claire
SHARON MCNEELY, Northeastern Illinois University
MICHAEL MELOTH, Albion College
CAROL MELVIN PATE, Chestnut Hill College
MARY REARICK, Eastern Michigan University
FREDERICKA REISMAN, Drexel University
LAURIE RUBERG, Wheeling Jesuit University
ELLEN SANTORA, University of Rochester
MICHAEL SIMKINS, Santa Cruz County Office of Education
LOUANNE SMOLIN, University of Illinois at Chicago
ROBERT TIERNEY, University of British Columbia
SANDRA ZERGER, University of Missouri, Kansas City

Table of Contents

Part One
Understanding Media Literacy

Part Two
Doing Media Literacy in the Schools

Commentaries

Living Within the Media

Media. It has such a relationship with the world today, specifically with teenagers like me. Media gives off so much information that can be valid or invalid, positive or negative. Given the vulnerability of teenagers, the information goes both ways. The relationship that the media does create is so complicated. It is a constant battle back and forth, with all the information that's given. We try to organize it and take it all in—it's just so overwhelming. The media is everything from television to radio stations to newspaper to music to magazines, anything that promotes information publicly. It has played a huge part in politics and education and in our appearance and maturity. Everyone is affected by media in some way or another. Whether the effect is for good or bad is another story.

The media can persuade anyone to do something or to think a certain way. It can promote drugs and violence, or it can preach good education and hard work. We learn from the media and we also get sucked into the media. It covers everything—campaigning, fashion, education, and most importantly, life. When I say life, I mean anything that can ever happen to you, from the clothes you wear to regular days at school to walking home from somewhere.

I would say one of the most effective types of media is music. Music has been a great way for me to deal with life. We have musicians who have lived some of the parts of life that I haven't got to, and other parts that I have. The music I hear today feels like I wrote the lyrics. I hear songs all the time that are telling my personal story—saying the things I was just saying to myself three days ago. The musicians nowadays are just telling the truth. They are explaining the problems they have gone through, realizing kids of this generation are going through them as well.

Hearing those stories, those lyrics, gives me a sense of reassurance; a sense of normality. When I hear them it makes me notice that some-

---

Erin Griffin is a junior at Jones College Prep High School in Chicago, Illinois.

one is going through the same thing I am going through or have gone through. It helps me deal with the issue. I can sing out the song full blast and I feel like I'm cleaning out my soul. When I sing the songs I feel like I'm speaking directly to my problem.

Problems are difficult to deal with. Sometimes the problem you're dealing with isn't even yours. The problem was caused by someone else, or someone brought their problem to you. It is difficult to deal with problems at my age and when I hear someone famous going through the same thing, I have a feeling of acceptance come over me; a feeling of reassurance that what I'm going through is ok and that I will get through it. Adolescence is a difficult stage to be in. There are a mass amount of problems. The media can make those problems more difficult, adding more problems on top of problems with the expectations they present. Being a teenager is very difficult; we are blown away with the amount of opportunities out there, both bad and good.

With every choice a teenager makes, the media has to put their two cents in. The biggest problem I think teenagers go through is identity and individuality. Every single type of media is constantly promoting a perfect teenager or the paradise teenage life. For example, why is it that television or billboards or commercials have skinny, tall, immaculately beautiful girls advertising that they are true beauty?

Who is to say what is beautiful or not? Where is the person who says "let's be realistic here and take actual teenagers from the real world and show their true beauty?" Who says perfect beauty is on the outside? Some of the prettiest people are known for what is inside, rather than their skin type and hair color. Teenagers fight with themselves every morning about how they should do their hair or what to wear because of the promotions of these people they see—these fake, doll-like, mannequin-looking people, who barely know anything about living a true teenage life.

Girls especially have a hard problem with their image. One, they are at the stage where they want boys to notice them. Two, they are growing into young adults, wanting to get rid of that young, girly, and "how cute" look. They don't need the media blowing up this image, this image of perfect and normal and beauty. If they don't look like the people the media are showing, then they feel ugly or horrible, and they try to do as many things as possible to change themselves, their real selves, into the people they see.

I personally had a horrible time with this image of beauty. When I was first becoming a teenager I was so worried of being looked over or being made fun of because of my individuality. I didn't dress in the sexiest outfits or have the prettiest hair but I was a kind, caring, honest, and true person. No one saw that because they were too busy looking at the way I dressed and comparing me to girls on television. The popular girls were the ones saving their lunch money to go buy the expensive make-up. They thought they were killing two birds with one stone. They were using their lunch money for the make-up, and because of that they didn't have money to eat lunch, so they were getting "skinny" too.

Not only has the media presented ideas about beauty; it presents ideas of right and wrong. The media is constantly having society pick sides. It's one or the other in everything. It's either war or no war; God forbid you believe that war is wrong unless as a last resort. There is no in-between. You must have an opinion on something. I believe people who have no knowledge about something should not have the right to pretend to have an opinion on something that they know nothing about—for example, talk show hosts. They are on television with families who are poor or a family with a disabled child who cannot function normally, saying "I know how you feel" or "I understand." They have no idea what it is like. How can they understand when they are not struggling? They have three cars and two houses with a maid; I'm pretty sure that is functioning *better* than normal. Their information would be unreliable and their reactions fake, and there is already enough of that floating around society.

The media provides good information sometimes though, such as public service announcements. I believe one of the most effective commercials out right now is the antidrug announcements. They give real-life situations and real-life solutions, all in a matter of 45 seconds. The newspaper is also a good media format. It has given me plenty of summaries on what is happening in today's world. It gives me a chance to have enough knowledge to have an opinion on something— something that can affect the future of my life, or the person who will run the country I live in, or exposure to transportation, education, and health-related arguments.

The media has affected me in so many ways and I'm only 16. I have plenty of years to come yet, and I don't think the media is going anywhere anytime soon. And the way we handle things we don't really understand isn't either. Do you ever think about pointing the finger about the arguments we hear, health-related and war and all the others? Why are we constantly trying to find the answers to who did it or why it happened? Why can't we just accept things and not worry about where they came from? We're always searching for someone or something to blame things on or to hold responsible. Why? Because if we blame it on someone we have the reason and the cause of it, so that's the end of it?

When I think like that, it's easy for me to blame the media for a lot of things. I blame the media for my junior high years. I blame them for all the comments and names I was called in junior high. I blame them for me not having the cutest boyfriend in school. I blame the media for suicides. I blame the media for weight disorders. I blame the media for informing the neighborhood about transportation changes. I blame the media for allowing us to know about candidates running for office. I blame them for letting musicians sing what they feel like singing and singing what they know. Finally, I have to admit that I blame the media for helping make me the strong independent person that I am today. I can walk with my head held high and my heart filled with love. I can say to myself what I believe is right or wrong. I can say that I have the newspaper from 9/11. I can say that the media has affected me in more ways than I probably know, and I am glad that it has.

CHAPTER 1

Overview: What Is Media Literacy, Who Cares, and Why?

GRETCHEN SCHWARZ

Cell phones ring during college classes and church services. The TV is omnipresent, not only on many hours in most homes, but also gazing down from hotel elevators and at the gas pump. Magazines vie for attention at the grocery checkout. The advertising industry has grown into a multibillion-dollar business. A majority of Americans now have access to the Internet at home. The mass media are everywhere, all the time. Moreover, the influence of the media has become a major topic. After the school shootings at Columbine, for example, newspaper and magazine articles began to decry the negative effects of video games on young people (see Jackson, 1999; Wagner, 2004). Health experts criticize television's connection to increasing childhood obesity (Children who watch TV are at higher risk of overweight, raised cholesterol, 2004). Scholars and pundits question the undemocratic power of the few multinational corporations who own much of the media (Fighting media monopolies, 2003). Moreover, media scholars maintain that the media have become the major storyteller of our culture. Gerbner (1996) declares:

For the first time in human history, children are born into homes where mass-mediated storytellers reach them on the average of more than 7 hours a day . . . These stories do not come from families, schools, churches, neighborhoods, and often not even from the native countries. They come from a small group of distant conglomerates with something to sell. (p. xii)

The United States produces the most media—film, television, and music—in the world; yet, media literacy is still a new concept to most Americans, including educators.

Gretchen Schwarz is a Professor in the School of Teaching and Curriculum Leadership at Oklahoma State University.

What media literacy is, why it matters, and how it can be implemented—especially in the schools—constitute the subject of this yearbook. The answers are diverse, as the chapters will show.

There is a growing sense of urgency about media literacy in K-college education. Although the definition of media literacy remains contentious (Livingstone, 2004), as do different approaches to the field (Tyner, 2003), many scholars, educators, parents, and community activists agree that media literacy is essential in the 21st century. This chapter offers a brief history of the field along with an attempt to define media literacy and offer a rationale for its inclusion in the American public school curriculum. Part I of the yearbook, on the whole, deals with why media literacy can make a difference in American schools. Part II, on the whole, deals with the implementation of media literacy, in and outside the public schools, and the problems facing those who aim to implement it. Media literacy is not without its opponents and its issues. Still, despite differences in theory, focus, and experiences, the contributors to this volume demonstrate their belief in the power of media literacy to transform curriculum, teaching, and even society.

A Brief History

The media, humanity's means of communication, have long concerned thoughtful people, and educators in particular. New media, especially, tend to cause alarm among some at the same time they engender enthusiasm among others. Socrates and Plato declared that writing, for instance, would interfere with memory. Tyner (1998) observes, "Both men condemned the shift away from speech to writing, objecting that writing would disrupt the routine social arrangements—both public and private—of the time" (p. 20). Of course, Plato, unable to resist the new medium, used writing to share the ideas of Socrates. The arrival of new media always demonstrates benefits and drawbacks; the printing press opened the door both to the speedy spread of Luther's and other reformers' ideas in the 16th century, and to the Catholic Church's launch of the Inquisition. Much later, Hitler and Franklin D. Roosevelt both used radio effectively, though for different ends. It is hardly unusual for society to engage in vigorous debate about the implications of new media forms, and sooner or later educators become part of that conversation.

Part II of the 1954 National Society for the Study of Education (NSSE) Yearbook, *Mass Media and Education* (Henry, 1954), acknowledged the growing impact of movies and newspapers on American society and thus on schooling. The preface to this volume references an earlier yearbook on audiovisual instructional materials, noting that in five short years it had become clear that media had expanded to the point that "contents and effects of messages disseminated through the mass media" needed to be "viewed in the light of their social values" (p. vii). Many of today's concerns regarding if and how prolonged media exposure affects sensibilities, changes behaviors, and impacts democratic society were raised by contributors to this volume, who conceded that it was too early to know how television, in particular, would influence young people. Nevertheless, Edgar Dale, chair of the yearbook committee, argued "no teacher in our schools can teach with full effectiveness unless he has a keen understanding of the role of the mass media in the life of his students" (Dale, 1954, p. 8). Concern about the quickly changing mass media, from the new rock music to comic books, grew steadily in the 1950s.

Marshall McLuhan, who remains controversial today for his often unsubstantiated and sometimes convoluted remarks, observed the tremendous power of the mass media, enabled by technology, as television became ubiquitous in the last half of the 20th century. McLuhan, who coined terms like "the medium is the message" and the "global village," seemed especially distressed over the impact of TV; he declared, "For any medium has the power of imposing its own assumption on the unwary" (McLuhan, 1964/2002, p. 15). At the same time, others, including many educators, have welcomed the inclusion of new media, like television and the Internet, in schools, as a means of engaging students and energizing teaching.

Other nations have reacted to the explosion of new media by including media literacy (through media education or media studies) in the school curriculum. Media education has been taught since at least the 1960s in England, and according to Ferrington and Anderson-Inman (1996), "Australia, Great Britain, Norway, and Canada have had extensive K-12 media education programs for years" (p. 668). Aufderheide (1997) reported that media literacy or media competency is a voluntary program in German schools, and Dafna Lemish and Peter Lemish (1997) discussed Israel's struggles to create a national media literacy curriculum. UNESCO (1978) declared that the mass media have an essential part to play in the education of young people—for the purposes of peace, justice, freedom, and progress in general. The work of scholars and educators from the United Kingdom and from Canada (see Pungente, Duncan, & Andersen, Chapter 8, this volume) has been a major influence on the progress of media literacy in the United States, as proponents have struggled to include media literacy in American schools.

Media literacy finally began to thrive in the United States during the 1970s, supported by the U.S. government and the private sector. Tyner (1998) describes this period:

Buoyed by ample funding and a sense of optimism, media education in the 1970s was at its peak . . . The 1970s marked the first concerted and significant effort to involve elementary and secondary students in media studies by focusing on the medium of television, that is, "critical viewing skills curricula (CVS)." (p. 134)

Critical viewing of television was implemented through an approach like film criticism, but the main objective was to protect children from TV junk. Stein (1972), in her chapter on mass media and young children in the 1972 NSSE Yearbook on childhood education, did focus on the more positive socializing effects of such programs as *Sesame Street* and *Mr. Rogers' Neighborhood*. She suggested that mass media could be used effectively as a tool to "provide a social and emotional 'Head Start' as well as a cognitive one" for young children (p. 200).

Part I of the 1974 NSSE Yearbook recognized the growing influence of new media on education. *Media and Symbols: The Forms of Expression, Communication, and Education* included chapters by such media experts as Gavriel Salomon and George Gerbner, and it highlighted the absence of empirical knowledge regarding the connections between the new technology and improved learning. This yearbook called for study specifically into "the structure of the symbols that make up such an important part of our environment, the media that propagate those symbols, and the cognitive consequences of exposing children to them" (Olson, 1974, p. 9). English Language Arts teachers began taking a particular interest in media in the 1970s. For example, Part I of the 1977 NSSE Yearbook, *The Teaching of English* (Squire, 1977), included a chapter by Deborah Dashow Ruth (1977), "The Next Language Art: Views of Nonprint Media." The media have continued to be a focus for many English Language Arts teachers who include various media in the classroom.

Despite considerable enthusiasm by supporters and the involvement of such organizations as the Far West Laboratory for Educational Research/Development, which worked with one television project funded by the United States Office of Education, this movement of the 1970s, along with its support from government, was short-lived. Anderson and Ploghoft (1993) reported, "With the exception of the WNET/

13 project, the federally funded projects were most active during the period 1978–1981, hardly of sufficient duration to provide for broad dissemination of information to schools." (p. 94). School people soon lost interest, and media literacy was one more passing educational fad. Tyner (1998) speculates that this failure may be traced to such culprits as the movement's limited focus on television; the rejection of its protectionist stance that ignored the pleasures of the media and emphasized the problems; the failure to include classroom teachers and students in the design and planning of projects; and the general lack of integration into daily teaching practices (pp. 137–138). Little funding actually ever went to media education, according to Anderson and Ploghoft, who note that career education initiatives, for example, received much more support in the early 1970s (p. 94). By the second half of the 1970s "back to basics" reform ideas were already gaining steam in the schools with the initiation of state-based competency tests, and of course, *A Nation at Risk* (National Commission on Excellence in Education, 1983) underscored the need for a "back to basics" approach at the national level. Conservative school reformers were uninterested in mass media, except for the growing enthusiasm for computers.

Despite these setbacks, media critics like Neil Postman (1986), scholars with more positive attitudes toward the media like England's David Buckingham (2003), and organizations like the Center for Media Literacy in Los Angeles continued to work for media literacy. Part I of the 1980 NSSE Yearbook, *Toward Adolescence: The Middle School Years*, included a chapter by H. Gordon Stevenson (1979) on the importance of media literacy for young adolescents, "The Mass Media and Popular Culture." Stevenson warned that the media viewed adolescents strictly as consumers and ready targets for advertisers, a concern that has only grown. Part II of the 1985 NSSE Yearbook (the last significant discussion of the media in an NSSE yearbook until this volume), *Education in School and Nonschool Settings*, included a chapter by Neil Postman (1985), "Media and Technology as Educators." Ever critical of the media, Postman asserted that television was the enemy of the literate tradition, and the only possible response was for schools to provide youth with a "sense of purpose, meaning, and interconnectedness in what they learn" (p. 193). Postman saw TV as the "other curriculum" against which educators must fight.

Recent Advances

The media literacy movement may have remained dormant if not for the rapid penetration of personal computers into homes, school, and the workplace in the 1990s and the proliferation of media influences, especially those targeted specifically to young people. By the 1990s a new grass roots movement in the United States had emerged. Schechter (1997) described this movement as "bubbling up from below, with parents . . . teachers promoting media literacy, activists asking for corporate accountability, consumers . . . media watchers critiquing news coverage, critics seeking more meaningful program content, producers creating alternative work and independent producers like me agitating" (p. 31). Activists produced such works as *We the Media: A Citizens' Guide to Fighting for Media Democracy* (Hazen & Winokur, 1997). Scholars from a variety of disciplines, such as French sociologist Pierre Bourdieu (*On Television*, 1998), began to publish more about the media. Church groups began to produce media literacy curricula, and individual teachers began to discover media literacy through workshops created by organizations like the New Mexico Media Literacy Project. Considine (2002) captures the recent history of media literacy:

Throughout the 1990's, encouraged to no small degree by the example provided by colleagues in Canada, media literacy proponents in the United States began the process of winning friends and influencing people, including prestigious institutions and individuals. Media literacy was endorsed by U.S. Secretary of Education Richard Riley and by U.S. Secretary of Health and Human Services Donna Shalala. It was featured in the PBS broadcast *Media Literacy: The New Basic?* (1996) and on ABC's evening news with Peter Jennings.

In 1995 the Carnegie Council on Adolescent Development published *Great Transitions: Preparing Youth for the 21st Century*. The report stated that "schools would do well to introduce instruction and activities that contribute to media literacy." (p. 9)

The *Standards for the English Language Arts* (1996) from the National Council of Teachers of English and the International Reading Association include media literacy goals. Literacy educators have been especially interested in media literacy (see, e.g., Alvermann, Moon, & Hagood, 1999). Publications about media literacy for professional educators, crossing curricular boundaries, are appearing more frequently (see, e.g., Ramos, 2001; Schwarz, 2003; Tuggle, Sneed, & Wulfmeyer, 2000). In addition, most states have included media literacy in their state curriculum standards.

Of course, as Johnson (2001) observes, "There are many who believe that media and its institutions are both too ubiquitous and too frivolous to have a place in schools" (p. 6). Not everyone is enthusiastic.

Many parents object to having teachers examine such value-laden subjects, and many teachers believe they are already overburdened by expectations. Moreover, according to Anderson and Ploghoft (1993), the history of media literacy "which is as old as the media themselves, is one of repeated cycles of interest and decline (Anderson, 1980)" (p. 93). Nevertheless, media literacy has arrived in the United States, but it is not yet widely understood, and, indeed, arguments continue over just what the term "media literacy" means.

Diverse Definitions

The most widely agreed-upon definition of media literacy comes from the work of the National Leadership Conference on Media Literacy. Representatives met at the Aspen Institute's Wye Woods (Queenstown, Maryland) in December 1992. Aufderheide (1992) reports that attendees' consensus definition of media literacy was "the ability to access, analyze, and produce information for specific outcomes" (p. v). Later versions include the phrase "to evaluate" and often list diverse types of media through which information is delivered. One of the problems with this definition is that it often results in media literacy being confused with other literacies, such as information, visual, technology, and computer literacy (Tyner, 1998). Each of these literacies has had different advocates in education, from library-media specialists to computer specialists and art teachers. The fragmentation of disciplines in the schools leads to competing terms that emphasize certain media (such as the computer) or certain goals (such as using reference resources well). Media literacy could serve as an umbrella definition, however, as Luke (2001) and others seem to suggest.

Some version of the 1992 definition can be found almost anywhere in the media literacy literature, from journal articles to the websites of media-related organizations and universities. Some would take exception to the definition for not emphasizing media *creation* enough. Masterman (1985), one of England's leading media educators, insists, "Developing a conceptual understanding of the media will involve *both critical reception of* and *active production through* the media. . . . The primary objective is not simply critical awareness and understanding, it is critical *autonomy*" (pp. 24–25). Masterman's definition emphasizes students' ability to make up their own minds about the media. For many educators, media literacy must include the ability of students to express their own voices through diverse media, as well as the ability to "see through" what the mass media currently offer. This interpretation, in addition, reminds us that media can also be positive, creative, and enjoyable.

Clearly, definitions of media literacy vary as the theoretical foundations and educational purposes of media literacy educators vary. Livingstone (2004) says of the "access, analysis, evaluation, and content creation" definition, "Not only does a skills-based definition of literacy focus on users to the neglect of text and technology, it also prioritizes the abilities of the individual over the knowledge arrangements of society" (p. 11). Indeed, many scholars in England and elsewhere, influenced by cultural studies, insist that the definition of media literacy must, in Semali's words (2000), enable "students to investigate injustices, become critical actors committed to combat problems of youth apathy, violence, substance abuse, rampant consumerism, and generate a strong commitment and action to developing a world free of oppression and exploitation" (p. 82). Critical media literacy then includes study of the social, economic, political, and cultural contexts of the mass media, including knowledge of how media corporations work and how the media affect society as well as individuals. Themes of social justice, democracy, power, and voice become paramount.

Considine (2001) has described other approaches to media literacy that alter its meaning. For example, an *aesthetics* approach would treat film or TV as a special kind of literature requiring its own literary analysis, including activities such as evaluating European directors or defining the visual techniques of film noir, for example. For others, the purpose of media literacy is *vocational* education, training in skills like graphic arts or computer programming that lead to employment opportunities (see Hobbs, Chapter 5, this volume). For the growing number of church groups pursuing media literacy; *values education* is a primary purpose. The Catholic Church has produced teaching materials, and some churches are even developing websites devoted to media literacy; for example, the Lutheran Church—Missouri Synod, which sponsors the Christian Media Literacy Institute at http://www.cmli.org to counterbalance messages from the mainstream media.

The Meaning and Aims of Media Literacy

Perceptions of media literacy depend on who is doing the perceiving. Some see media literacy as simply an antidote to or defense against evils like tobacco and drugs or materialism; some see media literacy as primarily empowering students as critical thinkers throughout the curriculum; and some envision media literacy as an active engagement with social justice and equity. These disagreements can be problematic, as we will see in this yearbook. Nevertheless, it is doubtful if anyone would disagree with any of the following observations:

At the heart of all the various elements of media literacy is critical analysis. The media then provide a vast laboratory for helping students to become thinkers in the deepest sense and all that means in terms of character, responsible citizenship, and the other aims of education. Only by recognizing that media literacy represents both a responsibility, as well as an opportunity for educators, will these much needed skills find their way into the curriculum. (Davies, 1996, p. xvi)

[Media literacy is] the ability to create personal meaning from verbal and visual symbols we take in every day through television, radio, computers, newspapers and magazines, and of course, advertising. It's the ability to choose and select, the ability to challenge and question, the ability to *be conscious* about what's going on around us—and not be passive and vulnerable. (Thoman, 1999, p. 50)

Finally, Rubin (1998) says that media literacy "is about understanding the sources and technologies of communication, the codes that are used, the messages that are produced, and the selection, interpretation, and impact of those messages" (p. 3). Given the impact of the mass media on the economy, on politics, on social and cultural practices, on our ways of knowing in all disciplines, and on human identity itself, we must view media as neither irrelevant nor the enemy, and media literacy should have a valued place in American schools.

The Content of the Yearbook

In Part I of this yearbook diverse authors offer their own definitions of media literacy, reasons for its value, theoretical foundations, and descriptions of practice. Although Part I is intended to emphasize theory over practice, theory and practice are difficult to separate among media literacy educators; practitioners are evangelical in their approaches, always arguing for the importance of what they do. Basing his work on cultural studies, critical theory, and semiotic theory, Semali suggests that, in particular, questions about power, privilege, and equity need to be explored by future educators and their students as citizens of a country that professes high ideals. McBrien, with a background in television news, demonstrates the importance of media literacy for American citizens in Chapter 2. Citizens depend on the media for information, but they need to be critical of that information and its sources. Semali, who is an academic, explores the role of a critical media literacy to enable young Americans to ask questions and raise issues (Chapter 3). In Chapter 4 Cortes describes in plain language how the media are influential social teachers, especially when it comes to matters of diversity or "otherness." The media already transmit their own "curriculum," one that should not be simply ignored nor unquestioningly accepted by schools. Together, these authors argue that the success of American democracy requires media literacy. Hobbs, like many authorities in the field, advocates the integration of media literacy across the curriculum. In Chapter 5 she examines the power of media literacy across the curriculum and the potential of media literacy to re-energize the disciplines, using numerous studies of current school practice and calling for more. In Chapter 6, Frechette explores the importance of media literacy and technology in education. Media literacy can no longer be about only TV or movies; Frechette offers a framework that incorporates a critical focus on the Internet, as well. Finally, Brown in Chapter 7 argues that media literacy is also key for teachers themselves, as they are bombarded by additional media messages about teaching, curriculum, and resources. Teachers must now develop media literacy skills and knowledge to enhance their own professional decision making.

In Part II of this volume, we look at various places where media literacy has been developed and implemented and how this has been accomplished. The Canadians, under the leadership of educators like Andersen, Duncan, and Pungente, have been at this project longer than Americans; they have a wealth of knowledge and experience to share. They describe the imagination and hard work required of those who would champion media education in Chapter 8. If media literacy is to be taught across America, teachers will, of course, need training and education. Goetze, Brown, and Schwarz report in Chapter 9 on some of the new university programs and other initiatives involving media literacy that are available to teachers. Notwithstanding the focus on schools, the media movement has been promoted and sustained largely by outside organizations, however. In Chapter 10 Thoman and Jolls trace the history of the influential Center for Media Literacy in Los Angeles, describing its pioneering efforts and sharing some practical teaching materials, as well. Then, Goodman (Chapter 11) describes his work and research in teaching media literacy through after-school programs at the Educational Video Center in New York City, demonstrating that media creation can empower diverse young people in new ways. Schwarz, in Chapter 12, considers the future of media literacy, looking at obstacles and issues for the field, and highlights the potential for media literacy to transform American education, as illustrated by the authors in this volume. Finally, several shorter commentaries reflect the power of media literacy and its impact, from the perspectives of a teacher educator and researcher (Fox), a parent teacher (Crockett), a preservice teacher (Maynard), a library media specialist (Kymes), a science educator (Their), and a media literacy consultant and activist (Rogow).

REFERENCES

Alvermann, D.E., Moon, J.S., & Hagood, M.C. (1999). *Popular culture in the classroom: Teaching and researching critical media literacy*. Newark, DE: International Reading Association, and Chicago: National Reading Conference.

Anderson, J.A., & Ploghoft, M.E. (1993). Children and media in media education. In G.L. Berry & J.K. Asamen (Eds.), *Children and television: Images in a changing socio-cultural world* (pp. 89–102). Newbury Park, CA: Sage.

Aufderheide, P. (1992). *Media literacy: A report of the National Conference on Media Literacy*. Washington, DC: The Aspen Institute. (ERIC Document Reproduction Service No. 365294).

Aufderheide, P. (1997). Media literacy: From a report of the National Leadership Conference on Media Literacy. In R. Kubey (Ed.), *Media literacy in the information age* (pp. 79–86). New Brunswick, NJ: Transaction Publishers.

Bourdieu, P. (1998). *On television*. New York: The New Press.

Buckingham, D. (2003). *Media education: Literacy, learning, and contemporary culture*. UK: Polity.

Children who watch TV are at higher risk of overweight, raised cholesterol. (2004, August 5). *Women's Health Weekly*, 7, 52.

Considine, D. (2001). *Approaches to media education*. Retrieved March 26, 2001, from http://www.medi-awareness.ca

Considine, D. (2002). Media literacy: National developments and international origins. *Journal of Popular Film & Television*, 30(1), 7–15.

Dale, E. (1954). Introduction. In N.B. Henry (Ed.), *Mass media and education. The fifty-third yearbook of the National Society for the Study of Education*, Part II (pp. 1–9). Chicago: National Society for the Study of Education.

Davies, J. (1996). *Educating students in a media-saturated culture*. Lancaster, PA: Technomic Publishing Co.

Ferrington, G., & Anderson-Inman, L. (1996). Media literacy: Upfront and on-line. *Journal of Adolescent and Adult Literacy*, 39, 666–670.

Fighting media monopolies. (2003, July). *Consumer Reports*, 68, 65.

Gerbner, G. (1996). Forward: Invasion of the story sellers. In R. Fox (Ed.), *Harvesting minds: How TV commercials control kids* (pp. ix–xiii). Westport, CT: Praeger.

Hazen, D., & Winokur, J. (Eds.). (1997). *We the media: A citizens' guide to fighting for media democracy*. New York: The New Press.

Henry, N. (Ed.). (1954). *Mass media and education. The fifty-third yearbook of the National Society for the Study of Education*, Part II. Chicago: National Society for the Study of Education.

Hobbs, R. (2005). Media literacy and the K-12 content areas. In G. Schwarz & P.U. Brown (Eds.), *Media literacy: Transforming curriculum and teaching. The 104th yearbook of the National Society for the Study of Education*, Part I (pp. 74–99). Malden, MA: Blackwell Publishing.

Jackson, D.S. (1999, May 24). A room full of doom. *TIME, 153*(20), 65.

Johnson, L.L. (2001). *Media, education, and change*. New York: Peter Lang.

Lemish, D., & Lemish, P. (1997). A much debated consensus: Media literacy in Israel. In R. Kubey (Ed.), *Media literacy in the information age* (pp. 213–228). New Brunswick, NJ: Transaction Publishers.

Livingstone, S. (2004). Media literacy and the challenge of new information and communication technologies. *The Communication Review*, 7, 3–14.

Luke, C. (2001, November). New times, new media: Where to media education? *Media International Australia incorporating Culture and Policy*, 101, 87–104.

Masterman, L. (1985). *Teaching the media*. London: Comedia/MK Press.

McLuhan, M. (1964/2002). *Understanding media: The extensions of man*. Cambridge, MA: MIT Press.

National Commission on Excellence in Education. (1983). *A nation at risk*. Washington, DC: Government Printing Office.

National Council for the Teachers of English and International Reading Association. (1996). *Standards for the English Language Arts*. Urbana, IL: NCTE.

Olson, D. (1974). Introduction. In D.R. Olson (Ed.), *Media and symbols: The forms of expression, communication, and education. The seventy-third yearbook of the National Society for the Study of Education*, Part I (pp. 1–24). Chicago: National Society for the Study of Education.

Postman, N. (1985). Media and technology as educators. In M.D. Fantini & R.L. Sinclair (Eds.), *Education in school and non-school settings. The eighty-fourth yearbook of the National Society for the Study of Education*, Part I (pp. 183–200). Chicago: National Society for the Study of Education.

Postman, N. (1986). *Amusing ourselves to death*. New York: Penguin.

Pungente, J.J., Duncan, B., & Andersen, N. (2005). The Canadian experience: Leading the way. In G. Schwarz & P.U. Brown (Eds.), *Media literacy: Transforming curriculum and teaching. The 104th yearbook of the National Society for the Study of Education*, Part I (pp. 140–160). Malden, MA: Blackwell Publishing.

Ramos, F.P. (2001). "Why do they hit the headlines?" Critical media literacy in the foreign language class. *Journal of Intercultural Studies*, *22*(1), 33–50.

Rubin, A.M. (1998). Media literacy. *Journal of Communication*, *48*(1), 3–4.

Ruth, D.D. (1977). The next language art: Views of nonprint media. In J.R. Squire (Ed.), *The teaching of English. The seventy-sixth yearbook of the National Society for the Study of Education*, Part I (pp. 96–125). Chicago: National Society for the Study of Education.

Schechter, D. (1997). *The more you watch, the less you know*. New York: Seven Stories Press.

Schwarz, G. (2003). Renewing the humanities through media literacy. *Journal of Curriculum and Supervision*, *1*(1), 44–53.

Semali, L. (2000). *Literacy in multimedia America*. New York: Falmer Press.

Squire, J.R. (Ed.). (1977). *The teaching of English. The seventy-sixth yearbook of the National Society for the Study of Education*, Part I. Chicago: National Society for the Study of Education.

Stein, A.H. (1972). Mass media and young children's development. In I.J. Gordon (Ed.), *Early childhood education. The seventy-first yearbook of the National Society for The Study of Education*, Part I (pp. 74–93). Chicago: National Society for the Study of Education.

Stevenson, H.G. (1979). The mass media and popular culture. In M. Johnson (Ed.), *Toward adolescence: The middle school years. The seventy-ninth yearbook of the National Society for the Study of Education*, Part I (pp. 74–93). Chicago: National Society for the Study of Education.

Thoman, E. (1999). Skills and strategies for media education. *Educational Leadership*, *56*(5), 50–54.

Tuggle, C.A., Sneed, D., & Wulfmeyer, K.T. (2000). Teaching media studies as high school social science. *Journalism and Mass Communication Educator*, *54*(4), 67–76.

Tyner, K. (1998). *Literacy in a digital world*. Mahwah, NJ: Lawrence Erlbaum.

Tyner, K. (2003). Beyond boxes and wires: Literacy in transition. *Television & New Media*, *4*, 371–388.

UNESCO. (1978). *Declaration of fundamental principles concerning the contribution of the mass media to strengthening peace and international understanding, to the promotion of human rights and to countering racialism, apartheid and incitement to war*. Twentieth Session of the General Conference of UNESCO, Paris.

Wagner, C.G. (2004, August). Aggression and violent media. *The Futurist*, *38*, 16.

Part One
UNDERSTANDING MEDIA LITERACY

CHAPTER 2

Uninformed in the Information Age: Why Media Necessitate Critical Thinking Education

J. LYNN MCBRIEN

Most psychological theories were cast long before the advent of enormous advances in the technology of communication. As a result, they give insufficient attention to the increasingly powerful role that the symbolic environment plays in present-day human lives. Indeed, in many aspects of living, televised vicarious influence has dethroned the primacy of direct experience. Whether it be thought patterns, values, attitudes, or styles of behavior, life increasingly models the media.

—(Bandura, 1986, p. 20)

We cannot hand ourselves over to the television ready to accept whatever comes. The more we sit in front of it . . . the more we risk being confused about the real nature of the facts. We cannot leave behind our critical conscience.

—(Freire, 1998, p. 124)

Two great thinkers in modern psychology and philosophy, Albert Bandura and Paulo Freire, warned of the effects of contemporary media, specifically, television's ability to recreate the nature of lived experience. Bandura hinted that psychologists need to reexamine their theories in the light of modern mass communications; Freire exhorted his readers to maintain an ability to think critically. Neither Bandura nor Freire anticipated the additional power of the Internet at the turn

---

J. Lynn McBrien is a Ph.D. Candidate in the Division of Educational Studies at Emory University, Atlanta, Georgia.

18

of the century, with its growing reach into American households and its countless pages of unedited information.

Much has been written about the power of media to influence the public through instruments of advertising and a variety of venues (Considine & Haley, 1999; Cortés, 2000; Kilbourne, 1999). In this chapter, I have chosen to use a singular media focus—news—to support the critical importance of teaching media literacy skills to students. I offer analyses of, in particular, news reports about the United Nations World Conference Against Racism (UN WCAR) in 2001 and media representations of terrorism and Muslims since September 2001, to underscore the need for critical thinking skills and media education.

Power of the Press

The phrase "power of the press" is so well known as to be a trite expression about which people do not think carefully. But just how powerful is the press? More than half a century ago, Lazersfeld and Merton (1948/1977) theorized that the media's simple call to attention of an event or topic confers status to that event or topic. Historically, it has been difficult at times to know whether the media was *reporting* an event versus *influencing* it. William Randolph Hearst and Joseph Pulitzer, publishers of well-known daily newspapers, vied for readers by sponsoring sensationalized stunts and exaggerating the news, including events of the Spanish–American War of 1898. Biagi (1999) pointed out that both publishers irresponsibly blamed Spain for the sinking of the *U.S.S. Maine* in Havana, even though the causes of the tragedy were never determined. The media frenzy provoked American hostility toward Spain, and the United States entered into a war that resulted in approximately 3,300 American and many more Spanish lives lost. Orson Welles convinced countless Americans that Martians had landed with his infamous 1938 radio drama *War of the Worlds*. Many believe that the first televised presidential debates between John Kennedy and Richard Nixon were critical to Kennedy's success in the 1960 election, as public opinion reflected negative reactions to Nixon's obvious discomfort, while others claim that attitudes toward the Vietnam War shifted sharply once pictures of the conflict became part of the evening news.

At the same time, Lazersfeld and Merton (1948/1977) also described the "narcotizing dysfunction" of media, meaning that too much information causes the audience to become incapable of critically judging media messages. Morgan's (1989) critique of television viewing and voting behavior reinforces this theory. His analysis of the National

Opinion Research Center polls on voting in presidential elections indicates that those considered heavy viewers of television are less likely to say that they voted, by an average margin of approximately 10%, even when controlling for age, education, sex, income, and political orientation. In this case, Morgan concludes, too much media information correlates with a drop of civic activity.

Media also sets the agenda for the news about which the public thinks. Lieberman (2000, p. 45), in writing about reporters' self-censorship in choosing news to investigate, points out the problem: "You can't report what you don't pursue." By the same token, consumers "can't evaluate what is never reported." If editors and publishers refuse to publish stories because they deem them unimportant or problematic, either due to their political implications or due to their inability to draw an audience, then citizens will not have the opportunity to draw conclusions based on complete evidence. Obviously, everything that might be deemed newsworthy cannot be reported on any given day. News and information selection is an important function of every news media outlet. However, omissions, intended or not, can create a bias in media consumers' social and political opinions. This certainly occurred in the case of the UN WCAR, as I will describe below.

Additionally, "the chicken or the egg?" argument persists as we examine the media's reliance on stereotypes and politically charged phrases. As an example, does the news media's repeated combination of the words "Muslim" with "terrorists" and "extremists" influence the public to equate Muslims with terrorism and fanaticism, or does the social belief that Muslims are terrorists influence the media to repeatedly place those words together? One can find an analysis of the "axis of evil" rhetoric of President George W. Bush in an independent publication such as Z Magazine (Marjaee, 2002), but be hard pressed to find such an exploration in American mainstream media, largely owned by one of nine corporations: AOL-Time Warner, Disney, Bertelsmann, Viacom, News Corporation, TCI, General Electric (owner of National Broadcasting Company [NBC]), Sony (owner of Columbia and TriStar Pictures and major recording interests), and Seagram (owner of Universal film and music interests) (Shah, 2004). Students (and citizens) must learn to ask what corporate ownership of media outlets has to do with news selection and positioning.

Bagdikian (1989) has pointed out that, although more than 80% of U.S. daily newspapers were independently owned at the end of World War II, 72% were owned by 15 corporations by 1986. Ownership of not only newspapers, but also television, radio, and Internet media has continued to become consolidated, with fewer conglomerates owning more of the information media. As Shah (2004) notes, the majority of citizens receive their news and entertainment from these media corporations. When consumers watch NBC programming, is it likely that they know the network is owned by General Electric, a billion-dollar arms dealer (*Columbia Journalism Review*, n.d.)? Students (and citizens) who are made aware of the holdings of media corporations are more likely to reflect critically on the presentation of news than those who do not have this information. Democracy depends on a well-informed citizenry. In order for students to become voters who are able to critically weigh issues, they must be given tools to evaluate the information the media provides.

Does Media Literacy Really Matter?

Behind the argument of promoting or not promoting the examination of media in U.S. classrooms is the fundamental question: What is the purpose of education? In spite of the 200-plus-year history of public education in the United States, leaders and citizens continue to contest whether public education should reinforce age-old national values (citizenship, work, socialization, literacy) or critically scrutinize their legitimacy (Spring, 2002). Media educators tend to promote a critical pedagogy by teaching students to be skeptical of media messages, asking questions such as, What is left out of this message? Who is the creator of the message? What are the media maker's values? Who is paying for this message? Do other sources give similar information? Whether this approach supports or undermines the aims of education in general depends on one's own sense of those aims.

Promoters of media literacy urge educators to engage in media education, noting that all 50 states now incorporate media literacy goals in their educational standards (Butler, 2004; Tugend, 2003). However, at the same time that media education experts are trying to convince teachers to include critical thinking literacy lessons, school districts are being heavily burdened by the ramifications of the Bush administration's No Child Left Behind (NCLB) Act and its emphasis on standardized testing, which has resulted in increased numbers of "failing schools" (Dobbs, 2004). The National Education Association (NEA) has faulted the legislation for narrowing the curriculum and reducing the time teachers have to spend on teaching critical thinking skills (National Education Association, n.d.). Harvard education professor Gary Orfield has criticized NCLB for mandating requirements that cannot be achieved (Archibald, 2003). The sweeping changes required by the legislation leave teachers little room to add media literacy to their curriculum, given the current emphasis on reading and mathematics.

However one addresses the purpose of a public education and how this purpose should be achieved, an additional question for media educators and for American taxpayers remains: Does media literacy really matter? Is it important enough to teach? The main arguments by some teachers, administrators, and parents against media education are that media products are not worthy of study and that there is already insufficient time for teaching the core curriculum. The argument that most media programming is not valuable (unlike, for example, a Shakespeare play) defeats many who want to include media studies in their classrooms, even though most students spend far more hours with the Internet and the television than with Shakespeare. Additionally, one can choose to avoid Shakespeare, but it is nearly impossible to escape the daily onslaught of mass media. Schwoch, White, and Reilly (1992) argued that education must include the teaching of complex skills that enable students to educate themselves throughout their lives, beyond the walls of a school, and suggested that one indispensable component of such learning involves active engagement with the "social, political, and cultural structures and artifacts that comprise the fabric of everyday life. . . . a critical citizenship engaging with media culture is of vital importance" (p. xi).

In spite of (or because of) the fact that media messages inundate our daily lives, the U.S. public is still selective about the media to which it pays attention. For example, millions of Americans tune in to *American Idol*, a reality TV show featuring amateur performers, while newspaper readership is declining (Newspaper Association of America, 2000). Gary Chapman, director of the 21st Century Project at the LBJ School of Public Affairs at the University of Texas, called attention to a 1997 Pew Research release that concluded, "An analysis of public attentiveness to more than 500 news stories over the last 10 years confirms that the American public pays relatively little attention to many of the serious news stories of the day" (Chapman, 2000, p. 3). Chapman also cited Andrew Kohut, director of the Pew Center, as saying, "The ultimate irony of [our] findings is that the Information Age [has] spawned such an uninformed and uninvolved population" (p. 3). Kohut (2000) reported that only 37% of respondents to a Pew poll knew that General Electric owned media, and only 36% of young adults (as compared with 50% of adults aged 65 and older) thought that media were too enmeshed with their owners' business interests. Those teaching media literacy skills can challenge students to consider why both knowledge of media ownership and consideration of their own selection of media can be important in their own lives in terms of the personal and political decisions they will make.

Lack of attention, interest, and involvement create a lack of engagement in critical thinking. But lack of attention does not mean that media messages students are exposed to every day—television shows, advertisements, radio talk shows, billboards, and more—are not being processed at some level. If, as the studies show, media do influence attitudes that affect health, safety, voting, consumerism, and the like, then we do students a disservice if we do not teach them media literacy skills (Considine & Haley, 1999; Cortés, 2000; Duncan, D'Ippolito, Macpherson, & Wilson, 1996).

A Social Cognitive Argument for Media Literacy

One explanation for people's ability to process and be affected by media messages, even those to which they do not carefully attend, comes from social cognitive theory. Social cognitive psychologists Tajfel (1981) and Taylor (1981) explained that people develop cognitive shortcuts, called heuristics, in order to handle the enormous amount of information they need to process on any given day. Unless they perceive that a belief, assumption, or action might cost them in terms of time, money, self-concept, or reputation, people are likely to be "cognitive misers," relying on heuristic tools such as stereotypes to determine their attitudes and responses. Because people tend to think of media such as television, radio, and many magazines as leisure activities, they are less likely to engage critical thinking skills unless they are trained to do so. This is not only the case with media such as television situation comedies, but also with programming such as news.

In the 1970s, Daniel Kahneman, the 2002 Nobel Prize winner in economics, began research with Tversky and others on intuitive judgment and how it differs from the reasoning process. Kahneman (2003) theorized that intuitive processes (the "cognitive miser" mode) are fast, effortless, associative, and often related to affective responses; whereas reasoning processes are slower, deliberate, require effort, and are consciously monitored, and are therefore more flexible than impressions generated by intuition. Intuitive thinking can be highly accurate, as in the case of an expert chess player, or it can result in inaccuracies, such as overgeneralization.

Earlier, Kahneman and Tversky (1973) described several heuristic methods of inferring general beliefs from limited data. Two heuristics relating to stereotypes and prejudice are the "representative heuristic" and the "availability heuristic." People use representative heuristics to draw inferences about probability (Fiske & Taylor, 1991). In cases of social perceptions, a person would draw conclusions about an event or individual based on limited information about that event or individual. The perceiver would determine how likely the perception is to fall into a category based on what is known about the event or individual. In this process, perceivers use stereotypes to compare the limited characteristics they have observed with their general beliefs about a group. This process involves little cognitive effort. News media over the years has offered less and less information about people and events from which consumers will draw conclusions. For example, in 1952, a half-hour television speech was the most common form of advertisement used by presidential candidates. By 1980, the half-hour had been replaced by a 60-second spot ad (Jamieson, 1996).

Perceivers use the availability heuristic process to evaluate the likelihood of a social "truth" based on how quickly similar instances or associations come to mind. Researchers found that when subjects were given a great deal to remember, they tended to generalize a characteristic to a group, even when only a few of its members had that characteristic (Rothbart, Fulero, Jensen, Howard, & Birrell, 1978). Because the social world provides a high volume of information, high memory loads are typical, with the result that stereotyping is common (Hamilton & Rose, 1980). In research I conducted on discrimination experiences of Muslim female adolescents, many participants told me that they had been called "terrorists" or "Hussein's sister" by U.S. classmates (J.L. McBrien, submitted), leading me to conclude that the availability heuristic was in play. U.S. students hear "Muslim" paired with "terrorists" repeatedly in the media to the extent that numerous Islamic groups have posted web pages refuting the stereotype that Muslims are necessarily terrorists (see http://www.cair-net.org/html/911statements.html; http://www.windowonislam.com/misconceptions.htm). The girls' conservative clothing and head coverings indicated to the U.S. students that they were Muslims, so the U.S. students apparently made the association.

Heuristics and information processing theory are highly related as they explain the cognitive processes of making sense of new information. In Lang's (2000) model of processing information generated by mediated messages (into which mass media would fall), perceivers automatically encode a portion of media messages they encounter, based on information that is relevant to the goals and needs of the perceivers, or novel or unexpected information. From there, encoded information is associated with previous memories for storage. Perceivers can retrieve this stored information when the need for it is activated. For instance, if asked, "Who will you vote for in the next election?" a respondent would revert back to stored memories and associations relating to the candidates and how he or she reacted to these stored events. Many factors, including one's purpose for viewing media, the culture of the perceiver, and personal goals, affect the ways in which one selects what portions of messages will be encoded and how they will be stored. Encoding, storing, and retrieving information can each be done in a superficial or a reasoned manner (Lang, 2000). Because of the many perceptions and processes in which people are engaged throughout the day, they must rely on intuitive and heuristic processes.

Heuristics and the United Nations World Conference Against Racism

An example of heuristic inaccuracy based on limited media knowledge and lack of critical thinking occurred on the campus of Emory University in Atlanta in March 2004. Mary Robinson, former President of Ireland and UN High Commissioner for Human Rights, was invited to deliver the keynote address for the spring commencement. Before commencement, the editorials editor of Emory University's campus newspaper, the *Emory Wheel*, wrote an op-ed suggesting that Robinson had been responsible for anti-Semitic literature distributed by some participants at the UN WCAR in Durban, South Africa, in 2001 (Rubin, 2004).

The WCAR was a global attempt, organized by the UN, to redress the wrongs of slavery, colonialism, and other manifestations of racial and ethnic superiority that have resulted in the subjugation of people of color and other minorities. I was at the WCAR as both a delegate and as a Cable News Network (CNN) freelance reporter. Because of my connections with a new nongovernmental organization (NGO), the Unity Project, I was also asked to attend meetings. As a CNN editor at the time, a CNN international editor asked me to file stories that would not be covered by the mainstream reporters for the educational web pages of CNN.

A quick review of news media headlines from August 2001 revealed that mainstream media accused the conference itself of fostering racism: "Israel branded 'racist' by rights forum" (CNN, 2001a); "US, Israel quit forum on racism: Language attacking Jewish state cited" (*Washington Post Online*, 2001); "The racism walkout: US and Israel quit racism talks over denunciation" (*New York Times Online*, 2001). These charges were not true. More accurately, there were criticisms by conference participants of some of Israel's policies, as there were criticisms of policies that contributed to systematic racism in most countries, including the United States. There were also some delegates, particularly at the NGO Forum held in Durban several days before the WCAR, who did voice opinions that Israel was racist. However, UN rapporteurs and Robinson herself would not accept documents that included these comments.

Only one of the six stories I filed on alternative events at the WCAR was published online (on a Youth Summit that occurred just before the meeting of NGOs). The director for the education site at that time said that the WCAR conference was "too controversial" to include. Other reporters and delegates I spoke to in Durban were shocked at the actions taken by the U.S. and Israeli delegations. We saw as many controversial behaviors and materials from Dalits, Roma, Aborigines, Indian Muslims, and indigenous peoples as we saw from both Palestinian and Jewish delegates. The mainstream press simply did not tell the full story (McBrien, 2002a, 2002b, 2003).

The events of 2001 had ramifications three years later at Emory University when Robinson was forced to confront accusations that stemmed from media coverage of the WCAR. Immediately after Rubin's op-ed appeared in the *Emory Wheel*, another student wrote an online response urging students to sign a petition requesting that "this awful woman" be removed as speaker, claiming that Robinson was anti-Semitic. Hundreds of students and parents signed the petition.

In the next issue of the *Emory Wheel*, a front-page story stated that Robinson "has been described as anti-Semitic for her involvement in the World Conference against Racism" and that critics alleged that she "advocated suicide bombers as a legitimate method of pursuing Palestinian statehood" (Gonzalez, 2004, p. 1). Gonzalez quoted one of the drafters of the petition against Robinson as saying that the Durban conference "was known for its anti-Semitic and anti-Zionist literature" (p. 10). The continued use of passive voice allowed the author to avoid stating more specific details of or providing sources for these "known" facts.

Linking a leader to pamphlets handed out by a minority of conference attendees is an example of the availability heuristic, in which social perceivers evaluate the likelihood of a "truth" based on how quickly associations come to mind (Kahneman & Tversky, 1973). On numerous occasions at the WCAR in 2001, I heard Robinson denounce factions at the conference that were handing out leaflets with racist implications. Three years later, many students at Emory assumed that Robinson, by association with not only the conference but also the way in which media represented the conference, was a proponent of anti-Semitism. And can the public be blamed for believing that the UN WCAR was racist? After all, the major news headlines and the news content suggested that the conference had been usurped by Palestinian extremists.

Unless we are specifically taught to analyze media messages, we tend to believe that news reporting is accurate, because we have been taught that journalism is objective and that objectivity is preferable to subjectivity (Schwoch et al., 1992). CNN ran a "Quick Vote" online poll the day after the United States and Israel abandoned the conference, asking, "Do you think that the U.S. and Israel were correct to pull out of the UN World Conference?" (CNN, 2001b). Sixty percent of respondents answered "yes." Had I been a passive reader of the news at that time, I suspect I would have had the same opinion.

The mainstream media depiction of the UN conference is an example of what Bandura meant when he stated that vicarious influence dethrones lived experience. What really happened at the conference was misrepresented by inaccurate media headlines and by the burial of stories in online sections and newsprint. Alternative press reported on the requests of Dalits, Aborigines, and other minority groups, but mainstream U.S. media concentrated on the Palestinian/Israeli conflict. This example of media-transformed reality at the WCAR is just one of countless examples of media distortion, and its implications are immense. Because a conference was dubbed a failure by powerful media companies, Americans replying to a CNN quick vote concluded that it was a waste of time. Yet, given that all governmental delegates aside from the U.S. and Israeli contingents stayed and negotiated difficult compromises, beginning a documented international recognition of the historical legacy of racism, the WCAR could just as easily been reported as a success (Polakow-Suransky, 2001). And repercussions of the limited media analysis of the conference and the public's pat acceptance of that analysis lingered three years later as students accepted this continuing distortion of the WCAR and dubbed Robinson, who was UN High Commissioner of Human Rights at that time, guilty by association.

Heuristics, Terrorism, and Islam

A more recent heuristic association strengthened by both political rhetoric and journalism is a connection between Islam and terror. Approaching two billion members and growing, Islam is the second largest of the world's religions (Huntington, 1996). By all reasonable accounts, only a tiny fraction of Muslims are terrorists, and the majority of Muslim scholars condemn terrorist actions as violations of Islamic teachings (see http://groups.colgate.edu/aarislam/response.htm; http://islam-guide.com; http://muhajabah.com). However, numerous media sources continue to place the word "Muslim" or "Islamic" before "terrorist" or "extremist" (see, e.g., CNN.com, May 27, 2004; MSNBC, August 2, 2004; Rivas & Windrem, September 2, 2004; Sterling, 2004). In contrast, recent attacks in Nigeria that have resulted in the deaths of hundreds of Muslims were attributed to "Christian militia," not "Christian terrorists." A Reuters report on rioting in Kano, Nigeria, provided graphic details about Muslim youth violence that resulted in the deaths of nearly 600 Christians, describing horrific slaughters of children and pregnant women, while noting three-quarters into the article that "Christian militia invaded the remote town of Yelwa, killing hundreds of Muslims in a two-day assault using automatic weapons and machetes. Local community leaders said they buried 630 bodies after the attack" (Ahemba, 2004).

The point is not to diminish the fact that acts of terrorism are being conducted by people who profess an Islamic faith. Clearly, many terrorists claim to be faithful Muslims, and their terrorist activities are horrific. The point is rather that we must consider potential heuristic effects of pairing "terrorist" with any large, diverse population, be it a religion, a culture, a political party, or a nation. The word "terrorist" is usually absent in reporting acts of terror conducted by people who profess to be of other religions, as it should be, with the result that entire populations, Christians, for instance, are not heuristically associated with terrorism. We need to recognize that many hate crimes are perpetrated against law-abiding Muslim citizens after tragedies like the murder of Dutch filmmaker Theo van Gogh by a man professing to be a Muslim in 2004. Since September 11, 2001, Muslims in the United States have been especially vulnerable to stereotypes, prejudice, discrimination, and violence (U.S. Commission on Civil Rights, 2002). The Federal Bureau of Investigation (FBI) reported a 1,600% increase in hate crimes committed against Arab Americans, Muslim Americans, and people perceived to be in one of those groups following September 11, 2001 (FBI, 2001). Might this be partly due to the choices made by the media as to how to present the news?

Historians and media critics have described how media has "demonized" certain populations at various times in America (Duncan et al., 1996). For instance, posters from World War Two carried messages about the need to "wipe out every murdering Jap" and sketches depicting Japanese military carrying naked White women over their shoulders

(*Japanese American Interment Curriculum*), and the government interned Japanese-American citizens in concentration camps in the west. Currently, Muslims and those thought to be Muslims bear the brunt of stereotypes and prejudice. Many radio talk show hosts have stirred the emotions of their listeners with inflammatory remarks. Boston radio host Jay Severin, for example, responded to a caller on his show by saying, "I have an alternative viewpoint. It's slightly different than yours. You think we should befriend them [Muslims]; I think we should kill them" (Jones, 2004).

When youth do not have a space in which they are encouraged to analyze *what is reported*, *how it is reported*, and *what language is used* in reporting on other nations and cultures, they are less likely to do so themselves. The "cognitive miser" mode of thought is more likely to hold sway, as people in general are unlikely to see "the treatment of foreigners" as being of personal consequence.

Media Education for Media Literacy

How can media education contribute to a more informed response to local, national, and world news and to diversity? Lasswell (1948) offered a critical framework for understanding media messages that is similar to the journalist's basic questions, Who? What? When? Where? and Why? For Lasswell, the key questions to be asked by consumers of media were: Who (source) says what (content/ideology) to whom (audience) in what way (style/conventions/technology) with what effect (influence) and why (purpose/profit)? Asking these questions of the above examples, such as the incident at Emory or the UN WCAR or reporting on terrorism and the war in Iraq, would reveal possibilities that would remain unexamined if stereotypes and the cognitive miser processing of information prevailed.

In addition, utilizing the seven principles of media literacy (Considine & Haley, 1999) would necessitate the use of reasoning processes rather than intuition. Without instruction, news viewers and readers tend to accept news stories at face value; they read them as reality. However, the principles of media literacy teach that all media are constructed. The top 60-second story on the evening news has been edited down from a half hour, hour, perhaps hours of videotape. In addition, media is a construction of reality, but not the total reality as it happened. Contending that the UN WCAR was anti-Semitic is one point of view, but it is certainly not a complete picture of the reality of the conference. One must learn to ask what has been left out of a story.

Another principle holds that media constructions have commercial purposes. Even the news is influenced by ratings, as advertisers who pay for programming pay more for ads on the best-rated programs. News programs, too, vie for ratings, and entertainment and information purposes are frequently conflated. Thus, feature stories on entertainment programs such as *American Idol* take up time on television news along with political stories and environmental disasters.

A fourth principle suggests that members of a viewing or reading audience negotiate their own meaning with regard to media messages (Considine & Haley, 1999). As cognitive theories explain, perceivers process information uniquely, based on their personal goals, motivations, beliefs, and values. Some will read talk show host Severin's comments about Muslims as free speech, and some will evaluate his words as hate speech. Further, for any given message, each medium has its own conventions and forms. Televised news relies on the impact of video footage, whereas newspapers rely on the power of language and still photos to convey their messages. Video techniques, such as camera angles and pacing, create different effects. They are designed to construct a particular response in the viewer. Such effects illustrate a sixth principle that media conventions and forms are used to convey values and ideologies. University headlines that indicate that Robinson is anti-Semitic convey particular values, as do national headlines indicating that a UN conference is anti-Semitic. Finally, and perhaps most importantly when determining the importance of media education, media messages can have social consequences. My own research with Muslim students, other researchers' content analyses of texts and films about Arabs and Muslims (Shaheen, 2001; Wingfield & Karaman, 1995), and the pleas of Islamic organizations to stop associating them with terrorism at least suggests a correlation between media representations and societal opinion.

Conclusion

Because contemporary society depends on news media to inform citizens about local and international events, we must be able to decode the messages critically in order to interpret the messages. Because media messages are created, they necessarily have a point of view, even when the creators seek objectivity. The news industry is a profit-making business, so the owners must be attentive to what will sell to consumers. This attention will influence news selection and decisions about how to position news stories. In addition, the political persuasions of media owners can influence what stories command attention; witness the bitterly fought presidential campaign of 2004 and the public controversies over a film like *Fahrenheit 911* or the decision by Sinclair Broadcasting to order affiliates to show an unflattering John Kerry documentary.

Students in a democracy must learn how and why news stories are produced in order to think consciously and critically about information they learn from news media.

Based on the information we receive, we make decisions, determine our voting behavior, and strengthen or question our beliefs. Political scientists and psychologists have concluded that media can change the opinions, attitudes, and behaviors of their readers, listeners, and viewers (Bandura, 1986; Bartels, 1993; McBride, 1998; Robinson, 1976). It is important, even vital to democracy, that students become critical consumers of media messages. The messages are socially constructed products, not mirror images of reality. All media, including this chapter and this book, are constructed for a purpose. Analyzing these messages with a critical conscience requires that we look beyond the text, considering the source of the information, other possible sources (and how those sources might construct the message), and not only what is included, but also what is omitted from the message.

REFERENCES

Ahemba, T. (2004, May 13). Death toll in Nigeria riots 500–600 Christians. *Union Tribune*. Retrieved November 14, 2004, from http://www.signonsandiego.com/news/world/20040513-0836-religion-nigeria-deathtoll.html

Archibald, G. (2003, July 3). NEA rejects outline by Bush for schools. *Washington Times*. Retrieved November 12, 2004, from http://intervarsity.org/lists/arn-l/archives/Jul2003/msg00062.html

Bagdikian, B. (1989). The empire strikes: Mergers in the media world. Retrieved November 13, 2004, from http://www.medialit.org/reading_room/article30.html

Bandura, A. (1986). *Social foundations of thought and action: A social cognitive theory*. Englewood Cliffs, NJ: Prentice Hall.

Bartels, L.M. (1993). The political impact of media exposure. *American Political Science Review*, *87*, 267–285.

Biagi, S. (1999). *Media impact: An introduction to mass media* (4th ed.). Sacramento, CA: California State University Press.

Butler, T.P. (2004, January), Standard procedures. *Cable in the Classroom*, *140*, 7–9.

Chapman, G. (2000, July 17). Well-informed citizens increasingly rare in Information Age. *Los Angeles Times*. Retrieved May 1, 2004, from http://www.interesting-people.org/archives/interesting-people/200007/msg00052.html

CNN.com. (2001a, September 3). Arafat: Summit must condemn Israel. Retrieved January 14, 2002, from http://www.cnn.com/2001/WORLD/africa/08/31/racism.talks/index.html

CNN.com. (2001b, September 6). Quickvote: Are the United States and Israel right to pull out of the UN racism conference?Retrieved January 14, 2002, from http://www.cnn.com/2001/WORLD/africa/09/06/racism.compromise/index.html

CNN.com. (2004, May 27). Abu Hamza: Controversial Muslim figure. Retrieved November 14, 2004, from http://www.cnn.com/2004/WORLD/europe/05/27/uk.hamza.profile/index.html

Columbia Journalism Review. (n.d.). Who owns what?Retrieved November 13, 2004, from http://www.cjr.org/tools/owners/

Considine, D.M., & Haley, G.E. (1999). *Visual messages: Integrating imagery into instruction* (2nd ed.). Englewood, CO: Teachers Ideas Press.

Cortés, C.E. (2000). *The children are watching: How the media teach about diversity*. New York: Teachers College Press.

Dobbs, M. (2004, February 19). More states are fighting "No Child Left Behind" law. *Washington Post Online*. Retrieved April 26, 2004, from http://www.washington-post.com/ac2/wp-dyn?pagename=article&node=&contented=A52720-2004Feb18&notFound=true

Duncan, B., D'Ippolito, J., Macpherson, C., & Wilson, C. (1996). *Mass media and popular culture*. Toronto, Ontario, Canada: Harcourt Brace & Co.

FBI. (2001). *Hate crimes statistics 2001*. Retrieved April 1, 2003, from http://www.fbi.gov/ucr/01hate.pdf

Fiske, S.T., & Taylor, S.E. (1991). *Social cognition* (2nd ed.). New York: McGraw-Hill.

Freire, P. (1998). *Pedagogy of freedom: Ethics, democracy, and civic courage*. New York: Rowman & Littlefield.

Gonzalez, R. (2004, March 26). Petition circulates against Robinson. *The Emory Wheel*, pp. 1, 10.

Hamilton, D.L., & Rose, T.L. (1980). Illusory correlation and the maintenance of stereotypic beliefs. *Journal of Personality and Social Psychology*, *39*, 832–845.

Huntington, S.P. (1996). *The clash of civilizations and the remaking of world order*. New York: Simon & Schuster.

Jamieson, K.H. (1996). *Packaging the presidency: A history and criticism of presidential campaign advertising* (3rd ed.). New York: Oxford University Press.

Japanese American Interment Curriculum. Retrieved November 13, 2004, from http://bss.sfsu.edu/internment/posters.html

Jones, S. (2004, April 28). Muslim group targets talk-show host; plans FCC complaint. CNSNews.com. Retrieved November 13, 2004, from http://www.cnsnews.com/ViewNation.asp?Page=%5CNation%5Carchive%5C200404%5CNAT20040428a.html

Kahneman, D. (2003). A perspective on judgment and choice: Mapping bounded rationality. *American Psychologist, 58,* 697–720.

Kahneman, D., & Tversky, A. (1973). On the psychology of prediction. *Psychological Review, 80,* 237–251.

Kilbourne, J. (1999). *Can't buy my love: How advertising changes the way we think and feel.* New York: Touchstone.

Kohut, A. (2000, March/April). Food for public distrust. *Columbia Journalism Review.* Retrieved April 28, 2004, from http://archives.cjr.org/year/00/2/kohut.asp

Lang, A. (2000). The limited capacity model of mediated message processing. *Journal of Communication, 50,* 46–70.

Lasswell, H. (1948). The structure and function of communication in society. In L. Bryson (Ed.), *The communication of ideas: A series of addresses* (pp. 37–51). New York: Institute for Religious and Social Studies.

Lazersfeld, P.F., & Merton, P. (1948/1977). Mass communications, popular tastes, and organized social action. In W.L. Schramm (Ed.), *Mass communications* (2nd ed.; pp. 492–512). Urbana: University of Illinois Press.

Lieberman, T. (2000, May/June). You can't report what you don't know. *Columbia Journalism Review, 39*(1), 44–49.

Marjaee, F. (2002, May). The Axis of Evil cabal and the case of Iran. *Z Magazine/Znet.* Retrieved November 20, 2004 from http://www.zmag.org/ZMag/articles/may02marjaee.htm

McBride, A. (1998). Television, individualism, and social capital. *PS: Politics and Political Science, 31,* 542–553.

McBrien, J.L. (2002a, Summer). The necessity of media literacy. *Human Rights Education: The Fourth R, 12*(1), 4–5.

McBrien, J.L. (2002b). The need for critical media studies: Post WCAR reflections. In L.A. Allen, D.A. Breault, D. Carter, C. Chargois, R. Gaztambide-Fernández, M. Hayes, & K. Krasny (Eds.), *Curriculum and pedagogy for peace and sustainability* (pp. 75–85). Troy, NY: Educator's International Press, Inc.

McBrien, J.L. (2003). Teaching media literacy to promote cultural understanding. In J. Lasonen & L. Lestinen (Eds.), *Conference proceedings: UNESCO Conference on Intercultural Education: Teaching and learning for intercultural understanding, human rights, and a culture of peace.* Jyväskylä, Finland: Institute for Educational Research. CD-ROM.

Morgan, M. (1989). Television and democracy. In I. Angues, & S. Jhally (Eds.), *Cultural politics in contemporary America* (pp. 240–253). New York: Routledge Press.

MSNBC. ((2004, August 2). Exonerated chaplain resigns from Army. Retrieved November 14, 2004, from http://www.msnbc.msn.com/id/5582324/

National Education Association. (n.d.). No child left behind act: ESEA. Retrieved November 12, 2004, from http://www.nea.org/esea/index.html

Newspaper Association of America. (2000). Leveraging newspaper assets: A study of changing American media usage habits, 2000 research report. Retrieved April 26, 2004, from http://www.naa.org/marketscope/MediaUsage_2000.pdf

New York Times Online. (2001, September 4). The racism walkout: U.S. and Israelis quit racism talks over denunciation. Retrieved December 16, 2002, from http://search.nytimes.com/search/

Polakow-Suransky, S. (2001, October 4). Chronicle of a death foretold: Media coverage of the WCAR. *Black World News and Views on Africana.com.* Retrieved September 18, 2001, from http://www.africana.com/Column/bl_views_68.htm

Rivas, R., & Windrem, R. (2004, September 2). Worldwide-related terrorism deaths on the rise. MSNBC. Retrieved November 13, 2004, from http://www.msnbc.msn.com/id/5889435

Robinson, M.J. (1976). Public affairs television and the growth of political malaise: The case of the "selling of the Pentagon." *American Political Science Review, 70*, 409–432.

Rothbart, M., Fulero, S., Jensen, C., Howard, J., & Birrell, B. (1978). From individual to group impressions: Availability heuristics in stereotype formation. *Journal of Experimental Social Psychology, 14*, 237–255.

Rubin, L. (2004, March 23). Mary Robinson may not be anti-Semitic, but she's close. *The Emory Wheel*, p. 15.

Schwoch, J., White, M., & Reilly, S. (1992). *Media knowledge: Readings in popular culture, pedagogy, and critical citizenship*. Albany: State University of New York Press.

Shah, A. (2004, April 15). Media conglomerates, mergers, concentration of ownership. *Corporate Influence in the Media*. Retrieved May 2, 2004, from http://www.globalissues.org/HumanRights/Media/Corporations/Owners.asp

Shaheen, J. (2001). *Reel bad Arabs: How Hollywood vilifies a people*. Northampton, MA: Interlink Publishing.

Spring, J. (2002). *American education* (10th ed.). Boston: McGraw-Hill.

Sterling, T. (2004, November 14). Dutch officials describe cell of Muslim radicals. *Lexington Herald-Leader*. Retrieved November 14, 2004, from http://www.kentucky.com/mld/heraldleader/news/world/10177971.htm

Tajfel, H. (1981). *Human groups and social categories: Studies in social psychology*. Cambridge, UK: Cambridge University Press.

Taylor, S.E. (1981). A categorization approach to stereotyping. In D.L. Hamilton (Ed.), *Cognitive processes in stereotyping and intergroup behavior* (pp. 88–114). Hillsdale, NJ: Erlbaum.

Tugend, A. (2003, March). Reading between the lines. *American Journalism Review*, 46–51.

United States Commission on Civil Rights. (2002). Briefing on civil rights facing Muslims and Arab Americans in Minnesota post-September 11 before the Wisconsin Advisory Committee to the U.S. Commission on Civil Rights. Retrieved March 28, 2003, from http://usccr.gov/pubs/wibrf/trans.htm

Washington Post Online. (2001, September 4). US, Israel quit forum on racism: Language attacking Jewish state cited. Retrieved September 18, 2002, from http://www.washingtonpost.com/ac2/wp-dyn?pagename=article&node=&contented=A37143-2001Sep3

Wingfield, W., & Karaman, B. (1995, March–April). Arab stereotypes and American educators. *Social Studies and Young Learners, 7*(4), 7–10.

CHAPTER 3

Why Media Literacy Matters in American Schools

LADISLAUS SEMALI

> Any education given by a group tends to socialize its members, but the quality and value of the socialization depends upon the habits and aims of the group.
>
> —John Dewey (1916, p. 62)

Education still means socialization, but since Dewey's time things have changed. Once parents worried about the effect of the peer group; now they worry about the effect of the media. Although families, other children, and schools still influence children and adolescents, the mass media play a significant role in children's lives and their development (Anderson & Huston, 2001; Postman, 1995). The arguments surrounding the socialization power of the mass media have been around for some time (Bronfenbrenner, 1970; Burger & Luckmann, 1972; Danzinger, 1971). Given the changing demographics in American schools and society, ongoing concern over the empowerment of *all* citizens in America, and growing human interconnectedness in the turbulent global village, however, the media's impact on issues of equity, social justice, and democracy grows ever more important. The media are powerful teachers; their lessons should not be ignored if schools want to live up to the presumed ideals of American schooling—the ideals of democracy, increased opportunity (economic, educational, etc.) for each American, honoring the diversity of the population (old and new), and responsible world citizenship.

The media curricula should be examined and questioned in schools, first, because media goals and purposes do not necessarily support the highest ideals America has to offer to its children. For example, Jones and George (2003) report that the NACCP (National Association for the Advancement of Colored People) and Children Now (http://www.childrennow.org) continue to lobby the entertainment industry to

---

Ladislaus Semali is an Associate Professor of Education at the Pennsylvania State University.

increase diversity in entertainment representations, which remain disproportionately whiter and much wealthier than the real United States. Lester (1996) describes numerous ways that media harm through stereotypes. Offering a specific example of media misrepresentation, hooks (1997) declares that the media's "circus" treatment of the O.J. Simpson trial served to hide real and significant issues of domestic violence and sexism. Giroux (1997/1998) pointedly argues that young people, in particular, are at risk:

Unfortunately, the range of possibilities open for youth in the dominant media has become enormously limited. Demonized or trivialized, young people are increasingly portrayed as either a social menace or as groveling dimwits . . . If not demonized, youth are either commodified themselves or constructed as consuming objects . . . Racism feeds this attack on kids by targeting black youth as criminals while convincing working-class white youth that blacks and immigrants are responsible for the poverty, despair, and violence that have become a growing part of everyday life in American society. (pp. 2–3)

Besides television, film, and newspapers, the Internet has expanded rapidly in recent years, saturating today's students with even more information and images. Today, over 92% of elementary and high school classrooms are connected (DOE, 2003). In addition to computers, schools are investing in laptops, wireless networks, digital cameras, and a variety of software and services. Even more striking is the race to acquire the most recent and most sophisticated electronic gadgetry in many U.S. households. Given that the media can, of course, also serve to break down stereotypes, create new understandings among diverse peoples, and promote justice and peace, one would think that the potential infusion of technology into U.S. classrooms and living rooms could lead to increased awareness and greater understanding of the world and its peoples, cultures, and interrelationships, but this is not necessarily the case. Important questions then emerge for educators considering the power, whether for good or ill, of the mass media. Can multimedia technologies be integrated in the K-12 curriculum as a *critical project* without conflict or competition with other courses? What role can teachers play in helping students understand new means of constructing knowledge and disseminating information in ways *that affirm diversity, various forms of public life, equality, and social justice*? Can young people *"talk back"* to media messages that distort differences among people and propagate inequities? Collectively, such questions sum up some of the challenges facing educators, parents, and others who are concerned about the need for developing critical thinking and reflection among media-using students in the 21st century.

To begin to unravel the challenges and dilemmas that these information technologies and media thrust upon parents, teachers, and schools, I present in this chapter arguments to support a school curriculum that might forge a life of justice as well as develop a rational, analytical, and critical understanding of media texts that students use in classrooms and in out-of-school contexts. First, I begin by laying out the rationale for why media literacy matters in schools. Second, I propose that teachers consider teaching critical media literacy as a process of curriculum inquiry or critical pedagogy that permeates the entire school curriculum to address the new languages of the media that have become the lived experience of many young people. Third, I outline examples of established criteria for questioning media texts or what I call analytical frameworks for critical media literacy education, and I offer examples of classroom activities based on these frameworks. In conclusion, I argue that because the majority of our children spend far more time engaged with contemporary culture as it comes from the Internet and over the public airwaves than they will ever again spend reading books, it is imperative that teachers consider taking critical media literacy seriously to facilitate responsible citizenship by helping students produce the knowledge that makes critical "reading" of media texts possible. Our democracy and, indeed, our world demand this new kind of literacy.

Questioning Texts

Questioning texts is the core of media literacy education. Media literacy teaches students to take a critical stance when they read, view, or think about textual or media representations. One broader goal of such critical education is to enable students to understand and critique the curriculum of media in order to conceptualize social/economic justice more clearly. Such understanding leads to opportunities to celebrate demographic diversity, develop a sense of fairness in the distribution of our society's cultural and economic resources, and challenge the exclusionary aspect of the "Eurocentric" one way of seeing the world (Dines & Humez, 1995). Questioning texts of all kinds makes possible a more adequate and accurate reading of the world, on the basis of which, as Freire put it, "people can enter into 'rewriting' the world into a formation in which interests, identities, and legitimate aspirations are more fully present and are present more equally" (cited in Morgan, 1997, p. 6).

For students media literacy becomes the competency to read, to interpret, and to understand how meaning is made and derived from print, photographs, talk radio, and computers. This process involves analyzing, comparing, interpreting, and finding meaning that is different from the usual, routine, and preferred meanings. Typically, *preferred meanings* are found in texts that insist on the existing dominant interpretation or ideology, that explain why things are the way they are as if the status quo were simply natural. When texts with preferred meanings are read or viewed in this noncritical way, their interpretation or meaning tends to coincide with mythical beliefs, clichés, and stereotypical or hidden bias. By applying critical pedagogy to evaluate media texts using established criteria or analytical frameworks that go beyond the myth, cliché, or stereotype, deeper meaning and understanding can be achieved. For example, Koppelman (with Goodhart, 2005) quotes Gabriel (1998) who argues that even "feel good" and widely praised films like *To Kill a Mockingbird* (1962), often shown in high school English classes as the novel is read, may denounce racism but they "present blacks as powerless, requiring white people to save them" (p. 330). Such critical reading of media texts is part of the active and nonpassive reading, viewing, and listening that enable students to think more deeply about issues of prejudice or self-determination. One important aspect of media literacy is, in fact, multicultural education (see Considine, 1994).

To be media literate is to possess the habits of mind needed to critically "read" mass media communications, be they advertisements featuring sophisticated-looking women smoking cigarettes, quick-cut shoot-out scenes in action films, or coverage of far-off wars on the evening news. Rather than being passive consumers of movies, TV shows, and video games, or looking at them as neutral vehicles for information possessing some valid claim to authority or truth, students learn that media "realities" are "constructed"—whether to produce an adrenalin rush, sell a product, or reflect a social or cultural idea (Heins & Cho, 2002; Kellner, 1995; Semali, 2000). Media literacy education is an educational *process* that can inform the way we think about our world and the people in it, and the ways in which we act within it and upon it. It is also about the ways in which a wide range of texts and meanings are produced, as well as the ways in which texts are used, consumed, rejected, embraced, and questioned by all kinds of people. It is through such analytical explorations that we discover the origins of myths we have thought to be true, stereotypes we have never questioned, and the culture of denial (denial of racism, poverty, etc.) that is embedded in our thinking. It is also about understanding our pleasures and questioning them, and about understanding the distribution of power in our societies and in the media world, and questioning these. In a nutshell, media literacy education is not medium specific—though it involves the study of specific media. Media literacy education is a pedagogy of interrogation, necessary to maintain a democratic society and responsible citizenship. Cortes (2000) summarizes:

School education about diversity will always be self-limiting in its effectiveness if school educators do not seriously engage the reality—the inevitability—of students learning about "otherness" through the media. And when I say engage, I mean do more than complain about the media and lament their impact. It does little good to recognize the mass media's multicultural teaching power, particularly, regarding the media treatment of different social and cultural groups, if educators do not also draw upon that recognition to inform and transform their own teaching. (p. xvii)

The Global Village

Media literacy is also necessary for responsible citizenship in the "global village." Global education may not yet have gained as much attention as multicultural education, but in a world of economic interconnectedness, shared environmental concerns, and such troubling issues as terrorism, education about the whole world is needed for all. The media are competing with the family and school to become young people's master storytellers and teachers *throughout the world*. Disney films, books, and spin-off products, for instance, capture the imagination of many children in many societies (e.g., *The Lion King*, *Peter Pan*, etc.). For most Americans, "Disney" is synonymous with entertainment, childhood, and family values. For children, Disney signifies a special place of amusement. However, few people pay attention to the fact that Disney is a media conglomerate in the business of selling products—with the ability to manufacture, sell, and distribute culture on a global scale (Giroux, 1999). We must realize that Disney constructs knowledge of self and the world in part through particular forms of popular visual culture, from animated films to television programs. These representations are ideological texts that provide pleasure, communicate information, influence consumption, and arbitrate power relations (Giroux, 1999; Rogoff, 1998). Many of the representations emanating from Disney, particularly through animated films, are linked to dominant discourses around race, ethnicity, gender, and history.

Disney teaches history, for example, through revised historical narratives that erase complexity, social antagonism, and human agency—any uncomfortable portrayal of colonialism, for example. In *Pocahontas* the main female character is presented as a shapely, contemporary adult who falls for John Smith, who resembles a blond action hero. The real Pocahontas was a child when she first met Smith, and there is no record of her having a romantic relationship with him (Giroux, 1999). In our visual culture, this discourse of constructing visual culture translates to corporations helping to construct a worldview where alternative images and ideas that critique and challenge the dominant culture are relegated to the fringes. The corporations that construct this sanitized perspective are the teachers of the new millennium. For example, Disney characters often use language in the form of racially coded accents and inflections (see *The Lion King*, *The Aristocats*, and *The Lady and the Tramp* for examples). In addition, the setting of many films conveys dangerous or exotic lands where other cultures seem sage and yet underdeveloped (see *Tarzan* and *The Jungle Book* for examples). All of this falls in line with dominant modes of discourse where white Western culture represents "orderliness, rationality, and self-control and non-Western and non-whiteness indicates chaos, irrationality, violence and the breakdown of self-regulation" (Kincheloe & Steinberg, 1998, p. 5). American children's attitudes toward the world outside the United States are influenced by Disney and other media corporations in subtle ways, as are the understandings of young people in the rest of the world.

Media literacy can help students question the "goodness" of sweatshops in poor Asian countries that produce Nike sports shoes grown popular in the United States through their ad campaigns, the genetic engineering of food by transnational corporations who portray themselves on TV ads as purely altruistic, or the power of advertising itself.

In his video, *Advertising and the End of the World*, for instance, media critic Sut Jhally (1998) argues that the advertising industry, such a potent part of the media world, creates greater desires and hence greater consumption among people while natural resources are used at an alarming rate and the environment decays. American consumption of resources, like oil, for example, affects not only America but also the rest of the world.

In short, to understand our own society and to make it better, and to understand the world and make it a better place, media literacy is essential. In fact, Brown and Kysilka (2002) suggest the combining of the major concepts or goals of multicultural and global education. They list five categories below, all of which can be taught through media literacy:

- Understanding of social living in groups
- Understanding of the "other"
- Understanding of interrelatedness and interdependence
- Development of skills in living with diversity
- Adjustment to changes for the future. (p. 9)

Curriculum Inquiry/Critical Pedagogy

In my profession as an educator, I work with preservice secondary teachers to develop analytical frameworks that make media a part of the curriculum for all their students. These analytical frameworks of critical media literacy draw from theories of cultural studies on representation, popular culture, the construction of youth, subjectivity, positioning, and perspectives of critical consciousness that have been made possible by the work of theorists like Hall (1997), Giroux (1988), Kellner (1995), Luke (1999), and McLaren, Hammer, Sholle, and Reilly (1995) and theories of critical literacy from the work of Buckingham (2000), Freire (1997), and others. Conceptualized as a critical literacy project, media literacy uses critical pedagogical tools to help students interpret the layered meanings embedded in the stories they read and the characters they encounter in media texts (fiction or nonfiction). Also, it enables learners to question the intentions of the producer, writer, and distributor, as well as the larger social context—such as history, social economic status, familiarity and comfort with the subject matter, benefits, and one's privileged position in the culture—within which the story is created, read, and interpreted, to uncover the oppressive space in which difference and unequal power exist in relations of inequality and resistance (Semali, 2000).

In this project, critical media literacy education brings a deeper understanding of the languages of the mass media, including the Internet, in all their richness and complexity while bridging the language gap between school and everyday life, including family and play. Doing so, this media pedagogical method enables marginalized youth, in particular, to make it through their difficult journey into adulthood, fully able to speak, represent, and demand recognition for themselves and their community. It empowers students through awareness training and critical pedagogy, deconstructing mass media and creating media of their own. Examples of the latter, described by Tyner (1998), include the work of the Appalachian Media Institute conducted by Appalshop, a "media arts organization in Whitesburg, Kentucky. . . . dedicated to supporting mountain people to tell their own stories" (p. 232), and the

Educational Video Center in Manhattan, an after-school program enabling children to produce documentaries about their lives in New York City (p. 243; see also Goodman, Chapter 11, this volume).

The usefulness of *critical pedagogy* as a media literacy strategy lies in its ability to generate skepticism and analytical frameworks for unpacking assumptions through inquiry methods. Once we are skeptical, we can investigate bias from facts, truths from half-truths, stereotypes from distortions, and the senseless generalizations and manipulations of media spectacles. A critical pedagogy approach is distinguished from other inquiry methods in a variety of ways. For example, critical pedagogy is first contrasted with "protectionist" approaches. A *protectionist* approach aims to shield children from the media through abstentions, such as TV Turnoff Week, or through regulation (rating systems) or censorship (excluding certain objectionable texts). Second, critical pedagogy differs from *interventionist* approaches in that the interventionist method focuses on the negative issues pertaining to the media (e.g., violence, sex-role stereotyping, or manipulation in advertising); this approach interprets media literacy as a strategy to help protect young people from harmful effects, because they are then less likely to be affected by media programs. By drawing distinctions between critical pedagogy, protectionist, and interventionist approaches, I am not suggesting by any means that media literacy education is a panacea for adolescent angst and alienation or school failure. The complexities of school culture, dysfunctional families, and community facilities' serving or ignoring adolescents are beyond the scope of media literacy education. All students can be encouraged to think critically about their media-saturated world, however, and the influence media may play in their choices and perceptions.

In particular, as we seek to prepare children to be productive citizens of a democracy, teaching them to understand and exercise their choices and voices becomes paramount. Brunner and Tally (1999) observe that technologies can support democratic learning in the information age in three ways: (1) as tools for student research; (2) as tools for student production; and (3) as tools for public conversation. As student research tools, the new media can support the values and habits of inquiry learning, giving students wide latitude in shaping their investigations, from posing questions of interest and concern, to locating and analyzing resources, to revising questions and hypotheses and synthesizing findings. Students need guidance and support in this process, however, as they learn to evaluate websites or to use search engines efficiently to locate pertinent information. Teacher knowledge of alternative media sources of information will also help students do thorough research. Students grappling with globalization topics might not otherwise know that they can find organizations, videos, and websites for global justice (see, e.g., Bigelow & Peterson, 2002). As Giroux (2003) states, regarding such processes:

> They also need entry to alternative sources of information, new pedagogical sites to access it, and new tools to historicize and critically engage what they confront. The emerging campus student activist and global justice movements offer fresh pedagogical tools and modes of analysis that might prove invaluable in rethinking both the meaning of a pedagogy of globalization and its implications for working with students and adults within and outside of schools. (p. 67)

In addition, the new electronic media can support students in shaping meaning out of their experiences, expressing meaning in different forms and languages, reflecting on and assessing the value of their work, and sharing it with different audiences, including their own peers. Means of using the new electronic media in production activities include: (1) web-based authoring and publishing tools; (2) multimedia and hypertext tools for creating and annotating reports, newspapers, and nonlinear documents; (3) graphics and animation programs for rendering layered visual representations and even movies; and (4) camcorders and video editors and animators that enable students to create their own dramatic and documentary videos. The goal of encouraging students to create their own media is to engage them in critical authoring, giving them an opportunity to express their ideas and also to critique and evaluate the reading of texts they bring into their authorship or production. When teachers encourage students to become critical authors in a given medium (or a combination of media) they point out the challenges posed by the medium's language, the suitability of the medium to the material, and whether the resulting product will find an appropriate audience beyond the classroom. This type of student-centered research broadens students' academic horizons and promotes their creativity and analytical skills and connects their schoolwork with their everyday experiences. One powerful example is a video students produced on the controversial subject of nuclear power as a project of the Fast Forward Media Lab in Seattle, Washington, in conjunction with the Seattle public schools (Rose, 1996).

Electronic Conversation

As public conversational tools, the new media of the Internet can also link students in dialogue with peers and adults in and beyond the school, and promote the democratic value of communication and mutual understanding in a diverse society. Familiarity with conversational tools helps students think about contacting the author, holding virtual conversations with authors, conversing with peers, and initiating dialogue with students and youth in other states, countries, or cultures. In a semester-long project, my college students in Pennsylvania participated in conversations with students in Sweden and in Minnesota, where they read several newspaper articles to detect bias and exchanged ideas through an electronic discussion board. Similar attempts have involved students at our local high school. In these discussions, student teachers tried to interpret the articles following a rubric provided by instructors. Their interpretations of the articles revealed their own biases about Europe and America, as well as gender bias. These cross-cultural, cross-national conversations open students' minds to issues confronting youth in other locations, and through online discussions they may find solutions or answers to questions they have been thinking about.

With the growth of network technologies like the Internet, computers in schools no longer function simply as storage or communication media, but are broadly reconceived as conversational tools. Through these new media, adolescents can participate in public conversations. By public conversations, I mean reflective exchanges about the meaning and value of the information and knowledge being produced in school. These conversations could be between teachers and parents, or between school administration and the community. Students who sit in a circle and discuss different views of current events are conducting a public conversation. When they interview a local official about waste disposal or other environmental issues, they are conducting a public conversation. When parents help evaluate student portfolios and share their ideas about student work, curriculum, or student involvement in community, they are conducting a public conversation. When students write email or letters to the editor or a television producer about an article or program that presents youth in a bad light, or with gender bias, racial bias, age bias, or ethnicity bias, they are conducting a public conversation par excellence.

Public conversation is necessary for the vitality of democracy and promotes responsible citizenship. When citizens question the actions of their government, they are conducting a public conversation. Public conversations with the school curriculum should be common in a democratic information age school, primarily because through such conversations students put into practice their newly acquired analytical habits of inquiry, reflection, and critical agency. Also, conversations are necessary because through them, students learn democratic habits that are crucial in a pluralistic school system and in a multicultural society in which people can come to very different conclusions about the society they live in and about the world. Learning to listen to and respect arguments that are different from one's own, making oneself understood by others who do not agree, and forging consensus around shared ideas and values are crucial skills in a democratic society.

Using Analytical Frameworks/Questioning Texts

Teachers can guide students in their media literacy work through analytical frameworks that establish textual analysis criteria to be used with print, electronic, or visual texts. Analytical frameworks use processes or structural elements in a systematic way within an identifiable, organizational pattern. An analytical framework establishes focused questions, compares diverse texts, seeks deeper meaning, attempts to connect to the students' own lives, and encourages students to think out of the box. In my media literacy class for preservice teachers, some of the frameworks we use include the following:

- *The Deep Viewing framework*—dissects texts: (1) on a literal level using a variety of responses, including talk, writing, and pictures; (2) through interpretation, including exploring and constructing multiple meanings; and (3) through synthesis, in which participants synthesize, extend, evaluate, and apply information and interpretations made explicit in previous levels to their own social context (Pailliotet, 1999). The Deep Viewing framework helps students through the inquiry process and prompts them with questions to evaluate a text's authorship, point of view, main argument, supporting evidence, relevance to the research questions, and so on. Deep Viewing offers "critical" and "analytical" *frames* that surround media texts, prompting students to analyze and evaluate the contents (see Semali & Pailliotet, 1999).
- *Lester's (1995) framework*—provides a list of questions that probe six levels of analysis: personal, historical, technical, ethical, cultural, and critical.
- *Narrative Analysis framework*—focuses on how the structure of the text—the visual or printed story—is told (e.g., order of events, production, history, circulation, consumption, motives, and values) (Boje, 2001).

To enable students to scrutinize media texts carefully for content, bias, stereotypes, manipulations, relevance, timeliness, accuracy, and omissions, these analytical frameworks provide systematic mental processes to unpack underlying cultural practices embedded in a text. We examine the context as well, particularly in how the context relates to the structure of domination and the forces of resistance presented. History and social contexts that include power and identity are important. For example, reading Shakespeare without dealing with where he was born, his milieu, his contemporaries, and the social order that gave rise to the writing of his plays would be missing a big part of understanding Shakespearean works (e.g., the treatment of Shylock in the *Merchant of Venice*, or *Othello*).

Throughout the semester I engage preservice teachers with activities that they can later modify or use with their future students. We begin by undertaking a personal media awareness survey. The student teachers examine their habits of viewing, listening, reading, and Internet browsing. Through daily journal entries, they document these habits for a period of four weeks. Later on, the data from the journals become the baseline data for comparison with their acquired levels of awareness at the end of the semester. For some students, the change is profoundly insightful.

Then I challenge student teachers to use a web of analytical frameworks, like those listed above, to read texts, including images from advertising and clips from television shows, critically. I teach these teacher candidates how to teach middle school students to use digital cameras and Adobe Photoshop to construct *ADbusters* and alternative messages and images to "talk back" to popular media. The term ADbusters is borrowed from the Adbusters website (http://www.adbusters.org/home), which aims to undermine the effect of advertising and consumerism, often by creating "alternative" ads. Since advertising companies do not always tell the whole truth in their ads (e.g., tobacco ads), it becomes necessary to encourage students to develop their own ads that do the opposite of what advertisers do. As part of the assignment, the preservice teachers can send such ADbusters to the local newspaper and ask for them to be published as public service announcements or as features in the youth section. ADbusters use the same images from advertising to create ads with different messages, creating powerful parodies of tobacco or alcohol or fast food ads. I also encourage students to conduct fact-finding research. This activity involves seeking information from other disciplines (e.g., health education or family consumer science, through research or interviews). This

fact-finding effort and the production of alternative ads aim to coun-
teract the messages created by advertisers to dupe audiences into unbri-
dled consumerism, or if nothing else, make viewers/listeners aware of
what is going on in the advertiser's message.

The assumption behind using ADbusters as alternative messages
and images is to hone in on the idea that the use of *one* text and *one*
framework to analyze a social situation will not get at the deeper meaning of texts to uncover bias, values, oppression, injustice, or pockets of
resistance underlying a given context. Instead, a *web* of analytical frameworks is transactional and penetrates the many layers of the texts. A
critical media literacy framework provides systematic analytical mental
processes to critique existing sociocultural systems. As texts collide with
one another, and interpretations confront one another, deeper meanings can be discovered.

Such a process of critical mindedness generates in teachers and
students habits of questioning, inquiry, reflection, and action to resist
or reject hegemonic practices or ideology. I encourage students to look
at media messages as constructions, just as authors' points of view are
conveyed through writing and reflect the economic, social, political,
historical, and aesthetic contexts in which they arise. The mass media,
like textbooks and trade books, are produced by large corporations;
their content, format, and availability are largely determined by marketing and profit motives (Rogoff, 1998). All texts must be scrutinized
carefully for content, bias, relevance, timeliness, accuracy, and omissions. I propose that such scrutiny ought to take place within the lesson
planning of each unit where reading, writing, viewing, listening, and
thinking take place. Such an integrated approach of curriculum and
instruction can bridge the gap between school and out-of-school, and
the gaps of a fragmented curriculum (Beane, 1997; Bellack & Kliebard,
1971).

Beginning Visually

To initiate the analytical process, I often find it useful to start with
visual texts. I present several ads found in popular print magazines and
at commercial websites as artifacts for analysis. These visual texts are
selected as part of a theme aligned with the school district's reading
guidelines and state standards. Examples of themes that students have
explored include identity, stereotypes, racism/prejudice, women's
rights, and the American dream. Using a list of questions borrowed
from the Narrative Analysis framework, I encourage student teachers
to examine the picture or text carefully to begin to unravel not only its

aesthetic qualities but also the bias and global values portrayed, whether intended or unintended. The guiding questions for such analysis include:

- What characters, motifs, symbols, products, effects, and persuasive devices are used in this picture?
- What values do these elements represent?
- What is your interpretation of messages they are sending?
- Who is pictured as a role model? Who is excluded?
- Who is being targeted as an audience?
- What are the creators really selling?

Because of space constraints, I will not discuss in detail each of these questions. In the classroom, however, students are divided into small groups, and each group selects one of these questions for discussion and writes a paragraph summarizing their response. After their initial analysis, the students come together to compare their responses. Next, I ask them to think of some action to take in light of the biases, values, or injustices revealed by their study of the text. Some of them may choose to create a new slogan, print advertisement, collage, drawing, poem, or script using heroes (local or national) who reflect positive values. These activities generally generate insightful debates and considerable discussion. At the end of the exercise, students usually remark that they will never see ads the same way again. The important lesson to take from this exercise is that we are surrounded by these media presentations every day. We know that media representations of family, interracial relations, and urban youth, for example, are illusions, and yet it is difficult not to compare our own lives with these messages and images or, worse, to let these images define for us what we should believe as truth.

As I teach and guide student teachers to critically read the myths and biases inscribed in the multimedia texts of the information age, they cannot remain assured that messages are innocent and harmless; on the other hand, they should not assume that popular media content is evil and therefore needs to be kept from their future students. Certainly, the media have a place in the quest for equity, social justice, and global peace as, for example, when TV news coverage spurred outrage that helped support the Civil Rights movement in the 1960s.

Often my student teachers are startled when they are presented with texts juxtaposed with unfamiliar images. For example, while a front-page picture in a newspaper like the *Philadelphia Inquirer* is seen as straightforward evidence about the world—a simple and objective mirror of reality—it can be, in effect, evidence of a much more complex but interesting and consequential reality. It reflects as much about who is behind the lens, from photographers to newspaper editors to graphic designers, to the readers who look—sometimes with different eyes—through the newspaper's institutional lens. A photograph can be seen as a cultural artifact because its makers and readers look at the world with an eye that is not universal or natural, but taught to look for certain cues. It can also be seen as a commodity, because a newspaper is concerned with revenue sales.

To challenge my students to read images, I divide them into small groups. I assign each group a different photograph. First, they must describe what is literally occurring in the picture. Students' comments typically focus on the image itself and not necessarily on what it reflects. In the second stage, I ask them to look for unfamiliar symbols. What might this picture evoke in their minds? I pay attention to the role of prior or background knowledge and how such knowledge is put to use in understanding what is occurring in the picture.

Once I used a front-page picture from the *Philadelphia Inquirer*. It was published during the United States' intervention in Haiti several years ago. The picture showed a young man trampled by a mob looting a warehouse full of grain in the capital Port-au-Prince. When I picked up this newspaper, I wondered: Do my students know anything of the history of U.S. intervention in the Caribbean—for example, in Grenada, Panama, and once again Haiti? What preexisting understandings about the United States and the developing world do they hold that allow for their reaction to the picture? What role in forming those understandings was played by the global media, which on this day, as on most others, was uncritical—even celebratory—of American military intervention? At the end of the exercise, there is always the sigh of disbelief: How could such a simple photograph have such profound meaning?

In the debriefing process, students realize that these diverse contexts are in communication with one another to construct a web of meaning of cultural values, purveying and contesting a limited universe of ideas about cultural difference and how they can or should be interpreted. To use television network news, newspaper photographs, novels, or websites as pedagogical sites is to study not a single cultural artifact but a web of meanings—powerful voices in an ongoing cultural discussion of difficult or sensitive issues.

The visual structures represented in photographs and the reading of them rendered by audiences can tell us about the cultural, social, and historical contexts that produced them. A study of visual structures leads us to discover the ways in which meanings are offered to us and, in turn, our part in actively making sense of them. It is important to keep in mind that the assumptions we make, what we consider as common knowledge or common sense, "general" knowledge, widespread beliefs, or popular attitudes are conventions we form as part of our cultural knowledge. My interest in bringing up these examples is to offer a critical perspective on the ways media are constructed, to point out some of the prevailing cultural ideas about others that are portrayed, and to raise questions about what could be done in the classroom and in the curriculum to develop critical thinking.

Conclusion

I conclude this chapter by referring to Slattery and Spehler's (1998) response to the cliché "The youth are our nation of the future." They instead assert that students today are the past, present, and future of the world—not only our nation—all at once. Thus, the future will continue to be elusive if it is not thought of as part of a continuum. The challenges that face us today, with the onslaught of the technologies of the new millennium described in this chapter, must not wait for some future date to be addressed. I am optimistic that analytical frameworks such as those provided in this chapter will empower students to ask questions about the contradictions they see in their present lives and in what they learn, the contradictions between the rhetoric of American democracy and the lives of the poor and marginalized, the contradictions between the good life as portrayed in magazine ads or TV programs and the horrors of disease and famine experienced in other parts of the world. Such questioning must begin now as students read textbooks, view television programs, and surf the Internet, rather than waiting for some future date when they will be "mature enough" to do so (see Kellner, 1990, 2000). Teachers need to start helping their students ask questions now.

The future of our students is here. It is the world of 24-hour news cycles, global markets, and high-speed Internet. Gallup surveys indicate that by the time inner-city students graduate from high school, they have spent 18,000 hours in front of the television, as opposed to 13,000 hours in school. The "average" American will spend in excess of seven years watching television (Kubey & Csikszentmihalyi, 1990). We need look no further than the morning paper to see that our future, and the future of our children, is inextricably linked to the complex challenges of the global community. Media literacy matters in American schools today because, for our children to be prepared to take their place in that world and rise to the challenges that we face today, they must first understand the media.

The situation has been made more complex with the emergence of multimedia, where computers, television, DVD, music files, and Internet technologies seem to converge to provide a limitless data source of information, entertainment, and instant communication. Therefore, the study of one medium or one form of literacy does not make sense. Long-standing assumptions about literacy and language no longer hold true, to the extent that a rethinking of what is implied by *literacy* is urgently needed. As well, media literacy becomes an important curriculum consideration for any school in America when we note with dismay that about half of the three billion documents indexed by Google are corporate pages (a proportion that is expected to grow), with far fewer having to do with any educational organizations (Van Horn, 2002). At the very least we need to help our students understand that they must consider the sources of the information they access every day.

Educators must realize that information technology is redefining literacy and literacy practices in ways not experienced before. Although the development of new technologies may have helped to change literacy practices, as a community of educators and researchers, we still lack much of the information needed to develop grounded research and pedagogy. We need to research, for instance, how the omnipresence of cell phones is changing human relationships, and how readers "read" graphic novels. The theoretical developments that have occurred in the field of literacy in general and in media literacy education, in particular, need to be placed within the broader context of the profound economic, social, political, and cultural changes of our present times rather than in terms of a "postindustrial society." Much study and research remains to be done.

As teachers increasingly integrate the new media into their curricula, they need to establish a set of working criteria or analytical frameworks to evaluate media products for use by their students and to assess the media productions of their own students in a developmentally appropriate fashion. The perils of democracy in a media-saturated society become acutely heightened if students graduating from our public schools cannot question, evaluate information, and analyze how the mass media and the Internet construct images of women and youth, convey meanings about society and the world we live in, and affect one's identity. As I have said before, media literacy will provide tools of criticism to help individuals to avoid media manipulation and to produce their own identities and resistance . . . that will in turn inspire media activism to produce alternative forms or culture and social transformation . . . This means cultivating the ability to ask difficult questions and the self-confidence to reject easy answers—the two fundamental goals of a critical inquiry and what it takes to be an educated person. (Semali, 2000, p. 196)

REFERENCES

Anderson, D., & Huston, A. (2001). Early childhood television viewing and adolescent behavior. *Monographs of the Society for Research in Child Development*, *66*(1). Malden, MA: Blackwell.

Beane, J. (1997). *Curriculum integration: Designing the core of democratic education*. New York: Teachers College Press.

Bellack, A., & Kliebard, H. (1971). Curriculum for integration of disciplines. In L.C. Deighton (Eds.), *The encyclopedia of education* (pp. 585–590). New York: McMillan.

Bigelow, B., & Peterson, B. (Eds.). (2002). *Rethinking globalization: Teaching for justice in an unjust world*. Milwaukee, WI: Rethinking Schools.

Boje, D. (2001). *Narrative methods for organizational and communication research*. Thousand Oaks, CA: Sage.

Bronfenbrenner, U. (1970). *Two worlds of childhood: U.S. and U.S.S.R.* New York: Russell Sage Foundation.

Brown, S.C., & Kysilka, M.L. (2002). *Applying multicultural and global concepts in the classroom and beyond*. Boston: Allyn and Bacon.

Brunner, C., & Tally, B. (1999). *The new media literacy handbook: An educator's guide to bringing new media into the classroom*. New York: Anchor Books, Doubleday.

Buckingham, D. (2000). *After the death of childhood: Growing up in the age of electronic media*. Cambridge, UK: Polity Press.

Burger, P., & Luckmann, T. (1972). *The social construction of reality*. Garden City, NY: Doubleday.

Considine, D. (1994). Media literacy and multicultural education. *Telemedium*, *40*(1), 8–14.

Cortes, C.E. (2000). *The children are watching: How the media teach about diversity*. New York: Teachers College.

Danzinger, L. (1971). *Socialization*. Baltimore, MD: Penguin.

Dewey, J. (1916). *Democracy and education*. New York: Free Press.

Dines, G., & Humez, J.M. (1995). *Gender, race, and class in media*. Thousand Oaks, CA: Sage.

DOE. (2003). *Internet access in U.S. public schools and classrooms: 1994–2002*. Washington, DC: U.S. Department of Education.

Freire, P. (1997). *Critical literacy in the classroom*. New York: Routledge.

Gabriel, J. (1998). *Whitewash: Radicalized politics and media*. London: Routledge.

Giroux, H. (1988). *Schooling and the struggle for public life*. Minneapolis: University of Minnesota Press.

Giroux, H. (1997/1998). *Channel surfing: Racism, the media, and the destruction of today's youth*. New York: St. Martin's Griffin.

Giroux, H. (1999). *The mouse that roared: Disney and the end of innocence*. Lanham, MD: Rowman & Littlefield.

Giroux, H. (2003). *The abandoned generation: Democracy beyond the culture of fear*. New York: Palgrave Macmillan.

Goodman, S. (2005). The practice and principles of teaching critical literacy at the Educational Video Center. In G. Schwarz & P.U. Brown (Eds.), *Media literacy: Transforming curriculum and teaching. The 104th yearbook of the National Society for the Study of Education*, Part I (pp. 206–228). Malden, MA: Blackwell Publishing.

Hall, S. (1997). *Representation: Cultural representations and signifying practices*. London: The Open University.

Heins, M., & Cho, C. (2002). *Media literacy: An alternative to censorship*. New York: Free Expression Policy Project.

hooks, b. (Narrator). (1997). *bell hooks: Cultural criticism and transformation [video]*. Northampton, MA: Media Education Foundation.

Jhally, S. (Producer/Writer). (1998). *Advertising and the end of the world [video]*. Northampton, MA: Media Education Foundation.

Jones, G.R., & George, J.M. (2003). Managing diverse employees in a diverse environment. In *Contemporary management* (3rd ed.; pp. 112–149). New York: McGraw Hill.

Kellner, D. (1990). *Television and the crisis of democracy*. Boulder, CO: Westview Press.

Kellner, D. (1995). *Media culture: Cultural studies, identity and politics between the modern and the postmodern*. New York: Routledge.

Kellner, D. (2000, Spring). Critical perspectives on visual imagery in media and cyber-culture. *Journal of Visual Literacy, 22*(1), 81–90.

Kincheloe, J., & Steinberg, S. (1998). *Unauthorized methods: Strategies for critical teaching*. New York: Routledge.

Koppelman, K.L. (with Goodhart, R.L.). (2005). *Understanding human differences: Multicultural education for a diverse America*. Boston: Pearson.

Kubey, R., & Csikszentmihalyi, M. (1990). *Television and the quality of life*. Hillsdale, NJ: Lawrence Erlbaum.

Lester, P.M. (1995). *Visual communication: Images with messages*. Belmont, CA: Wadsworth.

Lester, P.M. (1996). *Images that injure: Pictorial stereotypes in the media*. Westport, CT: Praeger.

Luke, A. (1999). Media and cultural studies in Australia. *Journal of Adult Literacy, 42*(8), 622–626.

McLaren, P., Hammer, R., Sholle, D., & Reilly, S. (1995). *Rethinking media literacy: A critical pedagogy of representation*. New York: Peter Lang.

Morgan, W. (1997). *Critical literacy in the classroom*. New York: Routledge.

Pailliotet, A. (1999). Deep viewing: Intermediality in preservice teacher education. In L. Semali & A. Pailliotet (Eds.), *Intermediality* (pp. 31–51). Boulder, CO: Westview Press.

Postman, N. (1995). *The end of education*. New York: Alfred A. Knopf.

Rogoff, I. (1998). Studying visual culture. In N. Mirzoeff (Ed.), *The visual culture reader* (pp. 14–26). London: Routledge.

Rose, C. (1996). Media literacy lab: Kid catalyst. *The Independent Film & Video Monthly, 19*(9), 32.

Semali, L. (2000). *Literacy in multimedia America: Integrating media education across the curriculum*. New York: Falmer.

Semali, L., & Pailliotet, A. (1999). *Intermediality: Teachers' handbook of critical media literacy*. Boulder, CO: Westview Press.

Slattery, P., & Spehler, R.M. (1998). Teachers and administrators: A vision of prophetic practices. In J. Kincheloe & S. Steinberg (Eds.), *Unauthorized methods: Strategies for critical teaching* (pp. 254–263). New York: Routledge.

Tyner, K. (1998). *Literacy in a digital world: Teaching and learning in the age of information*. London: Lawrence Erlbaum.

Van Horn, R. (2002). Raw data and news. *Phi Delta Kappan, 8*, 652–654.

CHAPTER 4

How the Media Teach

CARLOS E. CORTÉS

The mass media teach whether or not mediamakers intend to or realize it. And users learn from the media whether or not they try or are even aware of it. This means all of the media, including newspapers, magazines, movies, television, radio, and the new cyberspace media. Such media serve as informal yet omnipresent nonschool textbooks.

This raises an unavoidable challenge for schools. As part of their mission to help prepare young people to become better informed and more astute analytical thinkers, educators should seriously consider making media literacy an essential part of schooling—at minimum, enhancing students' capacity to use media more critically (Leahey, 2004). In particular, students need to develop an understanding of the ways in which the media deal with the theme of diversity.

A necessary step in fostering media literacy is helping students identify the various ways in which the media, as informal educators, teach. In my book, *The Children Are Watching: How the Media Teach about Diversity* (Cortés, 2000), I posit five distinct but interrelated ways through which the media teach:

1. Media present information.
2. Media organize ideas.
3. Media disseminate values.
4. Media create and reinforce expectations.
5. Media provide models for behavior.

Presentation of Information

The mass media deluge readers, viewers, and listeners with information. In his book *Information Anxiety* Wurman (1989) argued that the

---

Carlos Cortés is Professor Emeritus of History at the University of California, Riverside.

amount of information was doubling every five years and that was
before the real cyberspace boom. He noted that a single weekday issue
of the *New York Times* contained more information than the average
resident of 17th-century England was likely to encounter in a lifetime.
Less than a decade later, Shenk (1997) would refer to the Internet-
hypertrophied information overload as *data smog*.

Mediated information may be accurate or inaccurate. It may be
presented in snippets, as factoids, or within a context that fosters greater
comprehensibility. It may be multifaceted or simplistic, nuanced or
stereotypical. It may be packaged as news or presented in the form of
entertainment (consider docudramas).

Consumers may take a jaundiced view of selected sources (e.g.,
certain newspapers or magazines) or mediamakers (selected columnists
or talk radio hosts). Yet, in general, media users rely on newspapers,
magazines, nonfiction books, television news, radio commentary, documentary films, and the Internet as information providers. That information, of course, has been filtered, selected (or rejected), edited,
organized, and contextualized in ways that contribute to its varying
accuracy, comprehensibility, and quality (Gans, 1979).

And what about the entertainment media? Anecdotal evidence
abounds concerning how users have gleaned what they believe to be
reliable information from the fictional media. This evidence sometimes
comes in the form of teacher "war stories." More than two decades ago,
while introducing her students to the study of Nazi Germany, one
Massachusetts high school teacher learned with consternation that
many of them had acquired much of their basic knowledge about that
era from the then popular television World War II comedy series,
Hogan's Heroes (Chartock, 1978).

One day I was reading to my pre-teen granddaughter, Holly, from
Hastings' *The Children's Illustrated Bible* (1994). Suddenly she inter-
rupted Exodus with a stern rebuke: "But, Granddad, that's not the way
it was in *The Prince of Egypt*." The Bible was competing with Dream-
works' 1998 animated film. More recently written scripture has gone
head-to-head with Mel Gibson's vivid, highly personal 2004 screen
interpretation, *The Passion of the Christ*.

Even teachers extract information from the entertainment media.
My head still spins when I recall one of my diversity workshops in which
the tedious subject of Cleopatra's "race" was brought up. In the midst
of the increasingly active give-and-take over whether or not Cleopatra
was Black, one teacher brought the discussion to a stupefying halt with
the seriously uttered question, "How could Cleopatra have been Black?

Elizabeth Taylor played her in the movie!" In short, fictional mass media, as well as nonfictional, serve as sources from which consumers may draw conclusions, reliable or not. Moreover, such "learning" can occur even if recipients are unaware that this media-generated information is becoming part of their knowledge pool (Greenberg, 1988; Rockler, 2001).

True, we also learn by personal experience, in school, and through individual study. However, none of us can develop in-depth knowledge about everything through time-intensive exploration. Nor can we travel into the past. Therefore, we depend upon mediating forms of communication—what historian Daniel Boorstin (1961) termed the "pseudoenvironment"—to provide most of our learning about today's world as well as the past. For example, consider feature films that may take their place as contemporary viewers' primary textbooks on distant historical eras, particularly for those who have never extensively studied these topics (or studied them at all): *Troy* on ancient Greece, *Gladiator* on the Roman Empire, *Cold Mountain* on the U.S. Civil War, *The Last Samurai* on 19th-century Japan, or *Saving Private Ryan* on World War II.

But how accurate is that mediated information? Who knows? Even if we had access to the necessary sources, none of us would have time to cross-check each bit of information disseminated by the media. Paradoxically, even as we criticize the media for their perceived biases and distortions, we rely on them for information.

Moreover, the issue of media information is not simply a question of accuracy (Keever, Martindale, & Weston, 1997). It is also a matter of frequency. Repetition (sometimes referred to as *iterativity*) increases teaching power. In news, even if each and every news story about a topic were factually accurate in and of itself—for example, stories about a religion and its adherents, a state and its residents, a nation and its citizens—the constant reiteration of certain themes when dealing with that subject (combined with the omission of other themes) can create, disseminate, and/or maybe inculcate a distorted public image (Heller, 1992).

Similarly, entertainment media can also contribute to users' pools of "knowledge" through the repetition of a particular set of images about a topic. Now what if news and entertainment treatments of a topic coincide? In that case they would tend to reinforce each other. Once again, the issue is not accuracy, but frequency, particularly when combined with the absence or paucity of alternative media messages about the same topic.

Television's Take on Diversity

So let's look at a few "snapshots" of information about one topic, diversity, in this case presented by one type of media textbook, television. These snapshots are drawn from Graves's (1996) research review in which she highlighted some of the conclusions about television content reached by various scholars. Remember, however, that not all of these conclusions may be as valid today as when the research was conducted.

1. People of color seldom appeared in advertisements as the *only* group endorsing a product. However, commercials regularly showed only White Americans. There was one major exception—during "niche" shows about a specific racial/ethnic group, presumably targeted at that group audience, such as viewers of predominantly Black situation comedies.
2. During the 1980s, Hispanics comprised only 1% of prime-time television families. Yet, during that decade, the Hispanic population rose from 9 to 12% of the United States.
3. Little girl-oriented advertisements for items other than food presented a racially segregated world. White and visibly non-White girls seldom played together with the advertised item.
4. In fictional television between 1955 and 1986, Latinos were twice as likely as European Americans and four times as likely as African Americans to be shown as lawbreakers. Conversely, Asian Americans were shown as victims of violence four times as often as they were depicted as strong and assertive.
5. Various studies revealed that, among visibly racial/ethnic characters, men appeared twice or three times as often as women.
6. Interracial contact among television characters was more likely to occur in job-related situations than in social situations, while race relations were seldom discussed.
7. Most youth conflict occurred *within* a racial/ethnic group rather than *between* members of different racial/ethnic groups.
8. The most continuous, positive TV interracial contact occurred on public television in such children's shows as *Sesame Street*, *Barney and Friends*, and *Reading Rainbow*. In these shows, race relations were sometimes explicitly discussed.

But be cautious. These media textbook snapshots deal with *content*, not with *learning*. Media teaching does not guarantee media-derived learning, just as classroom teaching does not guarantee classroom learning. However, these snapshots suggest the kinds of media-presented information from which consumer learning may occur, much as textbooks suggest what student learning may occur.

The challenge for media literacy is to help students and teachers:

- recognize the information disseminated by the mass media;
- identify the ways that the media present that information;
- hypothesize the kinds of learning that may occur through exposure to both nonfictional and fictional mass media.

Organization of Ideas

Besides simply providing information—a deluge of factoids, data, and images—the mass media also disseminate ideas through the ways that they organize that material (Abt & Seesholtz, 1998; Barnhurst & Mutz, 1997; Dorfman & Woodruff, 1998). Through this process, they influence viewer, reader, and listener cognitive structures—the ways that media users perceive, receive, think about, interpret, and remember. In short, media *transform*, not just *inform*, helping to shape the way consumers themselves process and organize media-disseminated information and ideas (Adoni & Mane, 1984).

This organizing dimension can be seen most clearly in those elements of the media that attempt to directly influence the public's ideas—newspaper editorials, magazine columns, media advertising, television commentators, and radio talk show hosts. By relentlessly bombarding consumers with opinions (along with facts), they attempt to convince the public how to interpret information.

But besides the intentionally idea-organizing aspects of the media, there are more subtle examples of such information framing. In writing a news story, a journalist may attempt to provide a multifaceted interpretation of a complex topic, sometimes by including varieties of perspectives and voices. Yet, even before the reader's eyes reach the story itself, a headline or magazine cover will probably grab the consumer, suggesting the interpretive framework that should be used in reading the story.

In May 1992 rioting broke out in South Central Los Angeles following the jury verdict exonerating the policemen who beat Black motorist Rodney King. The cover of the May 11 *U.S. News & World Report* succinctly framed the event for readers: "After the Rodney King Verdict. RACE AND RAGE, Black vs. White: The New Fears. Cops in the Crossfire." The magazine cover had organized the riot with a "Black–White" slant.

Yet, one week later, the May 18 *Newsweek* cover significantly reorganized the diversity dimensions of that occurrence with the words: "Beyond Black & White: Rethinking Race and Crime in America." What a difference a week makes! The traditional knee-jerk Black–White media convention had given way to a reframing based on the recognition that this incident was, indeed, multiethnic, not biracial.

Narrative structure, too, serves to organize ideas and information (Gregg, 1998). Media narratives, both fictional and nonfictional, perform the traditional roles of folk stories and fairy tales, helping consumers make sense of the world—often the world that they know only through the media pseudoenvironment (Bettelheim, 1976).

Take the theme of social structure. Reporting in 1977 that there had been more than 2,300 research papers on television and human behavior, social psychologist George Comstock concluded:

Several writers have argued that television is a powerful reinforcer of the status quo. The ostensible mechanisms are the effects of its portrayals on public expectations and perceptions. Television portrayals and particularly violent drama are said to assign roles of authority, power, success, failure, dependence, and vulnerability in a manner that matches the real-life social hierarchy, thereby strengthening that hierarchy by increasing its acknowledgement among the public and by failing to provide positive images for members of social categories occupying a subservient position. Content analyses of television drama support the contention that portrayals reflect normative status. (pp. 20–21)

To the degree that fictional media narratives assert the normality of selected social hierarchies, they serve to reinforce the legitimacy of those relationships. News narratives, too, organize ideas and information.

When news broadcasts and newspaper stories repeatedly adopt the same narrative structures when they report on a subject, they help to shape reader and viewer mental and attitudinal frameworks for organizing future information and ideas about those topics (Hartmann & Husband, 1972; Hawkins & Pingree, 1981). When news and entertainment media coincide in their patterns of portraying members of specific groups in limited spheres of action, they create and reify cognitive structures and emotional predispositions for absorbing future images into a meaningful, consistent, if distorted, conceptual framework (Wiegman, 1989).

For example, in a study of the comparative treatment of Blacks and Whites by Chicago local television news, communications scholar Robert Entman (1990) concluded that:

In the stories analyzed, crime reporting made blacks look particularly threatening, while coverage of politics exaggerated the degree to which black politicians (as compared to white ones) practice special interest politics. These images would feed the first two components of modern racism, anti-black affect and resistance to blacks' political demands. On the other hand, the positive dimension of the news, the presence of black anchors and other authority figures, may simultaneously engender an impression that racial discrimination is no longer a problem. (p. 342)

The media, then, go well beyond spreading information (and misinformation). They also influence the organizational schema of viewers, readers, and listeners.

The challenge for media literacy is to help students and teachers:

- learn to recognize the ways media organize different topics;
- identify patterns of organization about individual topics;
- analyze how narrative structures have the potential for influencing the way media users process and interpret future media-disseminated information and images.

Dissemination of Values

Besides organizing ideas and contributing to reception schema, media also disseminate and promote values (Hilmes, 1997; Miller, 1998). In that respect media share a pedagogical space with school textbooks. As Anyon (1979) wrote:

Social agencies, such as the schools, the media, and government, whose functions include the dissemination of information, are major sources of knowledge that is both available and socially approved. If the views embedded in the information disseminated by these agencies predispose people to accept some values and not others, support some groups' activities and not others, and exclude some choices as unacceptable, then they provide invisible intellectual, internalized, and perhaps unconscious boundaries to social choice. (p. 383)

Since their advent, mass media have been lauded for their capacity to shape "positive" or prosocial values and criticized for their threat of fostering "negative" or antisocial values. Hardly a week goes by without some commentator, politician, protest group, advocacy organization, or special interest coalition raising the issue of the media's influence on some aspect of values. These include:

1. *Family values*, usually framed as whether or not the media support or undermine family values, without specifying whose version of family values is at issue
2. *Values about sexual behavior* (at what age, between whom, and the relationship to marriage)
3. *Values about smoking*, particularly with its widespread re-emergence among major characters in motion pictures
4. *Values about abortion*, with different positions trumpeted by headlines, columnists, and talk radio, as well as through visual images of marches and protest groups
5. *Values about marriage*, particularly now that almost every day the media greet newspaper readers, TV news watchers, or radio talk show listeners with some take on the issue of gay marriage, spiced by the overnight popularity of *Will & Grace* and Bravo channel's *Queer Eye for the Straight Guy*.

As far back as 1967, sociologist Herbert Gans likened television to schools and television programs to school courses:

Almost all TV programs and magazine fiction teach something about American society. For example, *Batman* is, from this vantage point, a course in criminology that describes how a superhuman aristocrat does a better job eradicating crime than do public officials. Similarly, *The Beverly Hillbillies* offers a course in social stratification and applied economics, teaching that with money, uneducated and uncultured people can do pretty well in American society, and can easily outwit more sophisticated and more powerful middle-class types. . . . And even the innocuous family situation comedies such as *Ozzie and Harriet* deal occasionally with ethical problems encountered on a neighborhood level. . . . Although the schools argue that they are the major transmitter of society's moral values, the mass media offer a great deal more content on this topic. (pp. 21–22)

Over the years, book titles have suggested concerns about the media's role in disseminating values. For example, the Payne Fund studies of motion picture impact, published during the 1930s, included Forman's (1933) provocatively titled *Our Movie Made Children*. In 1975, media historian Robert Sklar (1975) upped the titular ante in suggesting the movies' role in disseminating values when he selected *Movie-Made America* as the title for his widely read cultural history of U.S. motion pictures. In fact, however, Sklar's seminal work did not adopt the deterministic "hypodermic needle effect" (that media can "inject" beliefs into the consciousness of an audience) position of some of the Payne Fund

Studies (Jarvis, 1991). And the list of those addressing the media as values creators continues to grow. For example, in 1992 movie critic (later radio talk show host) Michael Medved weighed in with *Hollywood v. America: Popular Culture and the War on Traditional Values.*

Sometimes media become the site for a head-to-head struggle over values. On May 3, 1998, the National Broadcasting Company (NBC) aired *The Long Island Incident*, a TV docudrama about the December 7, 1993, one-man shooting rampage on a New York commuter train, which left 6 dead and 19 wounded. Concerned over the show's pro-gun-control values lesson, the National Rifle Association countered with its own pro-gun ownership values textbook. This came via full-page newspaper ads, with the bold-faced heading, "A TERRIBLE PRICE TO PAY FOR RATINGS," consisting of a letter signed by NRA First Vice President Charlton Heston, himself a movie star.

The widespread concern about media as values textbooks emanates from myriad ideological camps. Occasionally, we even find media industry documents that suggest self-awareness of its role in disseminating values. David Black, supervising producer of the long-running hit series, *Law & Order*, was quite direct about this values role when he said, "My dream for every *Law & Order* is that it presents issues the country is trying to deal with, moral issues. It presents both sides equally strongly and when the show goes off the air, people start arguing with each other" (Courrier & Green, 1998, p. 52).

Another revealing earlier example is the Motion Picture Production Code (the Hays Code), adopted by the movie industry in 1934. Ruling Hollywood until beginning its slow decline in the mid-1950s and suffering extinction in 1968, the Code provides a primer on earlier examples of Hollywood's response to public concerns over the motion picture industry's role in teaching values. For example, it banned nudity, "indecent" dance movements, and the ridicule of any religion, as well as mandating the "delicate" treatment of bedrooms, usually enforced by prohibiting scenes with a man and woman in bed together (including husbands and wives!).

One of the Code's most socially revealing values positions was Section II, Rule 6, which read, "Miscegenation (sex relationship between the white and black races) is forbidden." Until that rule was abolished in 1956, Hollywood drummed home the repeated values message that miscegenation should be avoided, mainly between "the white and black races," but also in most cases between Whites and other people categorized as "colored." In those rare screen instances where interracial love or sex occurred or seemed about to occur, disaster followed—failure, punishment, death, or other types of retribution (Cortés, 1991).

To an extent this diversity-related values element of the Hollywood movie curriculum reflected widespread American social mores. At one point in U.S. history, 36 states had some type of ban on interracial marriage. Not until *Loving v. Virginia* (1967), did the U.S. Supreme Court strike down all such antimiscegenation statutes. Only then could all (heterosexual) Americans legally marry the person they loved, regardless of racial background (Moran, 2001).

On the other hand, because not all states had antimiscegenation laws, interracial marriage had long occurred in the United States. Yet Hollywood elevated antimiscegenation values lessons over the presentation of interracial marital realities. In adopting this pattern of portrayals, moviemakers functioned simultaneously as responders (reacting to the presence of such antimiscegenation social mores among many Americans, particularly ticket-buying White Americans), as values educators (following these antimiscegenation "curriculum guidelines" and regularly transmitting this "thou-shall-not" marital lesson to the viewing public), and as profits-at-all-costs commercialists (fearing that movies with interracial love might not "sell" to White audiences, particularly in the South) (Cripps, 1970).

Since the 1967 elimination of antimiscegenation laws, interracial love has developed into a "hot" topic not only in the movies, but also in other areas of the mass media. Hardly a week goes by that some newspaper columnist, wire service, national magazine, or radio talk show host does not feature a story about an explicitly mixed race figure (Tiger Woods), publicize an interracial marriage (see wedding announcements), or discuss the issue of the racial categorization of racially mixed people. Moviemakers now recognize that interracial love, effectively marketed, can actually sell tickets. In some cases, such as *Guess Who's Coming to Dinner* (1967), released in the same year as the *Loving* decision, *Jungle Fever* (1991), and *Monster's Ball* (2001), interracial love provided the focus of the movie. In addition, films like *The Last of the Mohicans* (1992), *Waiting to Exhale* (1995), *Devil in a Blue Dress* (1995), and *Lone Star* (1996) featured interracial love as an important subtext (see Gates, 2004 for example).

Yet possibly the most revealing dimension of the fictional treatment of interracial love has been the growing number of films and TV shows, including daytime soap operas (Bramlett-Solomon & Farwell, 1996), in which such love simply occurs, with little or no mention of the issue of race. The image and the physical presence of the actors send the values message. Intentionally or unintentionally, such shows disseminate the value that interracial love is normal, or at least not as abnormal as was taught in the past. This values lesson parallels the declining, although still existent, societal opposition to interracial dating and marriage.

The challenge for media literacy is to help students:

- learn to discern the various kinds of values messages being disseminated by the media;
- identify the many ways that media can package those messages.

Creation and Reinforcement of Expectations

In *Hollywood v. America*, Medved (1992) argued, "If nothing else, repeated exposure to media images serves to alter our perceptions of the society in which we live and to gradually shape what we accept—and expect—from our fellow citizens" (p. xxiii). I agree. Mass media do help to shape expectations.

Take, for example, the perception of aging. What expectations do media reinforce about what it means to get older? It is axiomatic that producers of local television news shows prefer anchor people with pretty faces. Yet, when it comes to the television personification of "pretty," there is a striking gender gap. Male newscasters are allowed to age. With gray hair and wrinkles they become wiser and more distinguished. But, as female newscasters age, they become—how can I put it with subtlety?—more expendable. For female newscasters, turning 40 can mean heading over the hill. That is why local news anchor teams have sometimes been described as looking like an overage playboy and his third wife.

This gender gap is equally obvious in movies. When "senior" men have affairs with (much) younger women, sometimes half their age, it usually passes with little note. Take, for example, the films *Entrapment* (1999), which pairs Sean Connery with Catherine Zeta-Jones, 39 years his junior, and *The Human Stain* (2003), which links Anthony Hopkins and Nicole Kidman, with a 30-year difference in their ages.

But when genders are reversed, every decade or so, they become grist for widespread comment, analysis, and even celebration of how Hollywood has made a huge breakthrough. *Harold and Maude* (1972) is still a cult film for its nontraditional age pairing. Jump ahead more than a quarter century. *Something's Gotta Give* (2003) inspired analysts to repeatedly call attention to the fact that Diane Keaton had an affair with Keanu Reeves, 18 years her junior, before restoring order by dumping him in favor of an older Jack Nicholson.

The age gender gap even makes its way into casting. In the 1967 classic, *The Graduate*, Dustin Hoffman's Benjamin, just graduated from college, has an affair with an older woman, Mrs. Robinson (played by Anne Bancroft), one of his parents' generation. Yet, in real life at that time, Hoffman was only six years younger than Bancroft.

The diversity-related visual media curriculum on gender expectations is clear. Women, beware of growing older.

The Hays Code, too, provides examples of the creation of expectations. It specified that crime could not pay in American films; all screen criminals ultimately had to receive their just desserts. So it came as a shock to audiences when a criminal mastermind (played by Steve McQueen) flew away to Europe to enjoy the fruits of his brilliantly engineered bank robberies at the end of the 1968 film, *The Thomas Crown Affair*.

With the 1968 burial of the Hays Code, Hollywood moved from a crime-cannot-pay to a crime-may-or-may-not-pay position of expectation shaping. Ironically and unfortunately, this more permissive instructional position regarding the potential results of criminality paralleled the rise of ethnic theme films spurred by the civil rights movements of the 1960s and the revival of ethnic consciousness of the early 1970s. This resulted in a flood of movies with ethnics as the principal perpetrators of crime.

Italian Americans on Screen

Since the late 1960s, for example, Italian Americans have become nearly synonymous with screen crime, particularly since *The Godfather* (1972). That iconic film reinvigorated the Italian American crime genre and launched a multidecade stream of Italian American large- and small-screen mobsters, including the HBO hit series, *The Sopranos*.

Recognizing that audiences are now preconditioned to "expect" (or at least entertain the idea) that Italian American characters are likely to be involved in some aspect of violence or criminality (Tomasulo, 1996), makers of movies and television shows now often slap Italian surnames on criminal characters, even when their ethnicity has no plot significance. Simultaneously it has fostered a predisposition among news media consumers to expect—or, more temperately, to consider the possibility—that Italian-surnamed public figures just might have criminal connections. For example, Democratic Vice-Presidential candidate Geraldine Ferraro faced this problem during the 1984 presidential election, in this case suffering from the media-highlighted focus on the business dealings of her husband.

One of the most bizarrely revealing illustrations of Italian American media expectations came in an April 20, 1998, *Sports Illustrated* story about a young African American high school student who had decided to enter the National Basketball Association draft. His name was Korleone Young. Given his first name, *Sports Illustrated* could not resist writing an article entitled "Young Guns" (1998), featuring a chart comparing the basketball player with Michael Corleone, the fictional mob boss of *The Godfather* series. Among the comparisons: that both of them shot with their right hands, and that while Korleone Young's ambition was "to bury jumpers in the Meadowlands," Michael Corleone's ambition was "to bury stoolies in the Meadowlands" (p. 26).

Even the entertainment media themselves give grudging recognition of their power to foster public expectations. Before the network showing of *The Godfather Saga* (the re-edited and chronologically reordered TV version of the first two *Godfather* films), the following warning appeared on the screen, simultaneously intoned by a solemn voice: "*The Godfather* is a fictional account of the activities of a small group of ruthless criminals. It would be erroneous and unfair to suggest that they are representative of any ethnic group." Of course, this warning was followed by hours of characters speaking Italian and bearing names like Tataglia, Barzini, and Clemenza.

Moreover, the "Godfather disclaimer" has become the prototype for filmmaker posturing prior to other ethnic gang films—for example, *Scarface* (1983, Cuban Americans) and *Year of the Dragon* (1985, Chinese Americans). By dutifully warning audiences—*don't you dare learn anything about ethnic groups while watching these ethnic gang films*—they try to absolve themselves of any responsibility that their viewers may possibly develop negative perspectives about ethnic groups from watching their motion pictures.

The War in Iraq

In some respects, the current war in Iraq has become a litmus test for media expectation setting. Take two 2004 controversies: the release and publication of photographs of flag-covered coffins of U.S. armed services personnel, and Ted Koppel's April 30 *Nightline* reading of the names of American soldiers who had died in Iraq, accompanied by their photos.

This is not the place to hypothesize the motives of Russ Kick who sought, acquired, and put the flag-covered coffins on his Memory Hole website, of the newspapers and magazines that published the photos, or of the *Nightline* team. Nor is it the place to try to wade through all of the palaver about whether or not such actions were "respectful" or "appropriate." Rather it is to call attention to the fact that the many responses, by both opponents and supporters of the war, concurred because of their recognition of the expectation-setting potential of those media events. Those with diverse positions on the war concurred that these two media events *could* feed into and hypertrophy expectations that Iraq *might* become increasingly viewed as another Vietnam.

The concern with those images was not that they might contribute to evidentiary analysis: do the facts of the war in Iraq (assuming anyone has sufficient factual basis on which to base a firm conclusion) support or reject a conclusion that this war is becoming a Vietnam-like phenomenon? No. The concern (by some) and hope (by others) was that the emotion-packed images of flag-covered coffins and emotion-packed names of dead soldiers might foster such a media-driven expectation.

The challenge for media literacy is to help students:

- recognize how their media experiences might have shaped their own expectations;
- identify expectation-forming dimensions of the media;
- analyze the techniques that media use to shape expectations.

Models for Behavior

Finally, mass media provide models for behavior (Kniveton, 1976). The Motion Picture Production Code demonstrated this concern with its injunction: "The techniques of murder must be presented in a way that will not inspire imitation."

Contemporary mediamakers recognize and market the power of behavioral modeling. That is why there is "product placement," as companies and advertising agencies try to promote sales by having their goods used by movie and TV celebrities and fictional heroes and heroines onscreen. Even comic books now integrate commercial products into their stories. Likewise, numerous public health projects have focused on inserting health messages—from antibullying to the importance of immunization to information on the risk of HIV—into prime-time TV programming (Kaiser Family Foundation, 2004).

There is ample anecdotal evidence concerning the impact of media role modeling. Television and movies provide myriad examples of how entertainment media have influenced verbal behavior. They have added to the American vernacular ("Go ahead, make my day," "Show me the money," "Make him an offer he can't refuse," or Donald Trump's "You're fired" on his 2004 TV "reality" show, *The Apprentice* (Naughton, Peyser, Gimbel, & Juarez, 2004). Talk radio has also gotten into the verbal role modeling act. Rush Limbaugh has enriched the American English language with various terms, among them "ditto heads" and "feminazi." The use of the latter is at the center of a free speech debate in academia (see, e.g., Facente, 2002; Rauch, 1999).

Do actions speak louder than words? Well, you don't need to take it to the extremes of the gentle gardener of the novel and film *Being There* (1979), who learned almost everything he knew from TV. Consider the following.

Applications for forensic psychology and forensic anthropology degree programs have skyrocketed since the advent of television programs like *CSI: Crime Scene Investigation*, *Crossing Jordan*, and *Law & Order: Criminal Intent* (see, e.g., CBS News, 2002). When *Happy Days'* Fonzie took out a library card, real-life library card applications leaped 500%. The book and later 1976 film, *All the President's Men*, galvanized young journalists to become investigative reporters (Bowden, 2004). Maybe most fascinating is the fact that all-star first baseman Jim Thome of the Philadelphia Phillies altered his batting stance after watching Robert Redford in the 1984 movie, *The Natural* (Hagen, 2004).

Many critics focus on what they perceive as the media's role modeling of inappropriate sexual or violence-related behavior (or, more recently, smoking by Joe Camel and, increasingly, by lead characters in feature films—according to some estimates, at four times the national smoking rate). Many young people now suffer from what has been termed "Slight Trigger Disease," the tendency to do physical battle over minor bumps or perceived "wrong" looks. According to Kauffman and Burbach (1997), they may be doing what they see adults do, often transmitted to them through the media:

They see popular sports figures who seem to be always on edge, talking trash, scowling at close calls, and flashing intimidating looks at their opponents . . . politicians reflexively demeaning each other . . . television talk show hosts encouraging guests to abuse each other verbally, often over trivial issues. (p. 322)

The issue of media-taught behavior has even made it into the courtroom. For example, when 12-year-old Lionel Tate was tried for the 1991 killing of 6-year-old Tiffany Eunick by body slamming her, the

defense argued that he was unduly influenced by watching World
Federation Wrestling on television (Cable News Network, 2004).

However, both critics and defenders of the media often address the
wrong proposition when debating the media's behavioral role modeling.
It is difficult, generally impossible, to prove that the media have actually
caused something to happen (after all, millions may watch the same
movie or television show without imitating that behavior). Rather, the
question should be tweaked in the following manner. If it were not for
the media, would this have happened? For example, how likely is it that
Lionel Tate would have dreamed up the particular body slams that killed
Tiffany Eunick?

But consider some dimensions that are not framed as potential
cause-and-effect provocation to action. Some critical theorists argue
that media fostering of "nonchange"—or at least a reduction in the
speed of change—may constitute the most important behavior-related
aspect of the media. From this perspective, interracial buddy movies
and desegregated TV news teams may actually retard the process of
social change. Rather than role modeling integration, they may surrep-
titiously suggest that social change is occurring so rapidly and normally
that additional special efforts are unnecessary.

Then there is the issue of disinhibiting effects. Instead of asking
whether or not media model behavior by guiding and provoking people
into action, we also need to consider their potential for removing
inhibitions to previously repressed actions. Do movies that celebrate
vigilantism (e.g., the *Death Wish* series) contribute to societal violence
by removing inhibitions to imitative behavior? Or do they reduce violence by providing viewers a catharsis for pent-up frustrations? Do
films with teenage sex disinhibit such activity by making it appear
normative or "safe," thereby contributing to teenage promiscuity (as
well as pregnancy)? Or do they provide a vicarious substitute for the
real thing?

The challenge for media literacy is to help students:

- learn to hypothesize the possible relationships between media
  behavior and things that occur outside of the media
- determine what kinds of evidence they would need to draw solid
  conclusions about such relationships.

Conclusion

Media teach. And consumers learn from the media. Decades of
research and unobtrusive evidence have demonstrated these two indis-

putable realities. Increasingly we live in a media-deluged world, in which people draw much of their knowledge, form many of their ideas, develop values and expectations, and even model some of their behavior as a result of interacting with the media. In preparing students to be analytical thinkers in such a world, school educators should seriously consider making media literacy an essential part of their curriculum.

REFERENCES

Abt, R., & Seesholtz, M. (1998). Talking us down: The shameless world revisited. *Journal of Popular Film & Television, 26*(1), 42–48.

Adoni, H., & Mane, S. (1984). Media and the social construction of reality: Toward an integration of theory and research. *Communication Theory, 11,* 323–340.

Anyon, J. (1979). Ideology and the United States history textbooks. *Harvard Educational Review, 49*(3), 361–386.

Barnhurst, K.G., & Mutz, D. (1997). American journalism and the decline in event-centered reporting. *Journal of Communication, 47*(4), 27–53.

Bettelheim, B. (1976). *The uses of enchantment: The meaning and importance of fairy tales.* New York: Knopf.

Boorstin, D.J. (1961). *The image or whatever happened to the American dream?* New York: Atheneum.

Bowden, M. (2004). When the front page meets the big screen. *The Atlantic Monthly, 293*(2), 146–150.

Bramlett-Solomon, S., & Farwell, T.M. (1996). Sex on the soaps: An analysis of Black, White, and interracial couple intimacy. In V.T. Berry & C.L. Manning-Miller (Eds.), *Mediated messages and African-American culture* (pp. 146–158). Thousand Oaks, CA: Sage.

Cable News Network. (2004, January 29). *Lionel Tate pleads guilty to second-degree murder.* Retrieved February 23, 2004, from http://www.cnn.com/2004/LAW/01/29/wrestling.death/

CBS News. (2002, November 7). *Mad about forensics.* Retrieved December 7, 2004, from http://www.cbsnews.com/stories/2002/11/06/earlyshow/living/parenting/main528385.shtml

Chartock, R. (1978). A holocaust unit for classroom teachers. *Social Education, 42,* 278–285.

Comstock, G.A. (1977). *The impact of television on American institutions and the American public.* Honolulu: East–West Communication Institute, East–West Center.

Cortés, C.E. (1991). Hollywood interracial love: Social taboo as screen titillation. In P. Loukides & L.K. Fuller (Eds.), *Plot conventions in American popular film* (pp. 21–35). Bowling Green, OH: Bowling Green State University Popular Press.

Cortés, C.E. (2000). *The children are watching: How the media teach about diversity.* New York: Teachers College Press.

Courrier, K., & Green, S. (1998). *"Law and Order": The unofficial companion.* Los Angeles: Renaissance.

Cripps, T. (1970). The myth of the southern box office: A factor in racial stereotyping in American movies, 1920–1940. In J.C. Curtis & L.L. Gould (Eds.), *The Black experience in America: Selected essays* (pp. 116–144). Austin: University of Texas Press.

Dorfman, L., & Woodruff, K. (1998). The roles of speakers in local television news stories on youth and violence. *Journal of Popular Film and Television, 23*(2), 80–85.

Entman, R.M. (1990). Modern racism and the images of Blacks in local television news. *Critical Studies in Mass Communication, 7,* 245–332.

Facente, S. (2002). The free speech debate: What crosses the line? *The Ithacan Online, 69,* 26. Retrieved December 7, 2004, from http://www.ithaca.edu/ithacan/articles/0204/11/opinion/3the_free_spe.htm

Forman, H.J. (1933). *Our movie made children.* New York: Macmillan.

Gans, H.J. (1967). The mass media as an educational institution. *Television Quarterly, 6*(2), 20–37.

Gans, H.J. (1979). *Deciding what's news.* New York: Pantheon.

Gates, P. (2004). Always a partner in crime: Black masculinity in the Hollywood detective film. *Journal of Popular Film and Television, 32*(1), 20–29.

Graves, S.B. (1996). Diversity on television. In T.M. MacBeth (Ed.), *Tuning in to young viewers: Social science perspectives on television* (pp. 61–86). Thousand Oaks, CA: Sage.

Greenberg, B.S. (1988). Some uncommon television images and the drench hypothesis. In S. Oskamp (Ed.), *Television as a social issue, Applied Social Psychology Annual 8* (pp. 88–102). Newbury Park, CA: Sage.

Gregg, R.W. (1998). *International relations on film.* Boulder, CO: Lynne Rienner.

Hagen, P. (2004). Thome's natural swing result of Manuel training. *Philadelphia Daily News, June 11 [Electronic version].* Retrieved from http://www.philly.com/mld/philly/sports/baseball/8896203.htm?1c

Hartmann, P., & Husband, C. (1972). The mass media and racial conflict. In D. McQuail (Ed.), *Sociology of mass communications* (pp. 435–455). Baltimore, MD: Penguin.

Hastings, S. (1994). *The children's illustrated Bible.* London: Dorling Kindersley.

Hawkins, R., & Pingree, S. (1981). Using television to construct social reality. *Journal of Broadcasting, 25*, 347–364.

Heller, M.A. (1992). Bad news. *Hispanic, 5*(10), 18–26.

Hilmes, M. (1997). *Radio voices: American broadcasting, 1922–1952.* Minneapolis: University of Minnesota Press.

Jarvis, A.R.J. (1991). The Payne Fund reports: A discussion of their content, public reaction, and effect on the motion picture industry, 1930–1940. *Journal of Popular Culture, 25*(2), 127–140.

Kaiser Family Foundation. (2004, April 15). Entertainment education and health in the United States: Issue Brief. Retrieved from http://www.kff.org/entmedia/7047.cfm

Kauffman, J.M., & Burbach, H.J. (1997). On creating a climate of classroom civility. *Phi Delta Kappan, 79*(4), 320–325.

Keever, B.A.D., Martindale, C., & Weston, M.A. (Eds.). (1997). *U.S. news coverage of racial minorities: A sourcebook, 1934–1996.* Westport, CT: Greenwood.

Kniveton, B.H. (1976). Social learning and imitation in relation to television. In R. Brown (Ed.), *Children and Television* (pp. 237–266). Thousand Oaks, CA: Sage.

Leahey, C.R. (2004). Examining media coverage: A classroom study of Iraq war news. *Social Education, 68*(4), 280–284.

Loving v. Virginia, 388 U.S.1. (1967).

Medved, M. (1992). *Hollywood v. America: Popular culture and the war on traditional values.* New York: HarperPerennial.

Miller, T. (1998). *Technologies of truth: Cultural citizenship and the popular media.* Minneapolis: University of Minnesota Press.

Moran, R.F. (2001). *Interracial intimacy: The regulation of race and romance.* Chicago: University of Chicago Press.

Naughton, K., Peyser, M., Gimbel, B., & Juarez, V. (2004). The world according to Trump. *Newsweek, 143*(9), 48–55.

Rauch, J. (1999). Earthquake in P.C. land. *National Journal, 31*, 594–595.

Rockler, N.R. (2001). Messages between the lions: The dominance of the transmission paradigm in student interpretations of *The Lion King. Journal of Communication Inquiry, 25*(1), 6–21.

Shenk, D. (1997). *Data smog: Surviving the information glut.* San Francisco: Harper Edge.

Sklar, R. (1975). *Movie-made America: A cultural history of American movies.* New York: Random House.

Tomasulo, F.P. (1996). Italian Americans in the Hollywood cinema: Filmmakers, characters, audiences. *Voices in Italian Americana, 7*(1), 65–77.

Wiegman, R. (1989). Negotiating AMERICA: Gender, race, and the ideology of the interracial male bond. *Cultural Critique, 13*, 89–117.

Wurman, R.S. (1989). *Information anxiety.* New York: Doubleday.

Young Guns. (1998, April 20). *Sports Illustrated. 88*(16), 26.

CHAPTER 5

Media Literacy and the K-12 Content Areas

RENEE HOBBS

Educators have diverse and conflicting perspectives about the mass media. Most have a love–hate relationship with the mass media that is complex and multidimensional, and these attitudes and beliefs shape teachers' instructional practices in the classroom. As a result, many approaches to media literacy are emerging simultaneously in the 15,000 school districts in the United States, as educators begin introducing students to instructional practices of media analysis and media production. Media literacy education has been rising in visibility in K-12 schools throughout the 1990s, and while still proportionately small, a growing number of school-based programs are in place at the elementary, middle, and high school levels. Defined generally as "the ability to access, analyze, evaluate, and communicate messages in a wide variety of forms" (Aufderheide & Firestone, 1993), media literacy education emphasizes the twin dimensions of analyzing media and creating media (Buckingham, 2003; Kellner, 1995). Drawing upon 15 years of rich tradition in the United Kingdom, Canada, and Australia (see Alvarado & Boyd-Barrett, 1992 for review), there has been substantial progress in the United States as educators have developed key concepts and principles that unify the field, formed two national organizations, and held regular conferences (Action Coalition for Media Education [ACME], 2004; Alliance for a Media Literate America [AMLA], 2004).

Media literacy education is being explored by scholars in many different fields (including education, literature, media studies, psychology, and public health) but there is less evidence of implementations occurring in K-12 settings. With more than 1.3 million teachers in U.S. public schools, it is impossible to estimate the extent to which the instructional practices described in this chapter are widespread or rare.

Renee Hobbs is an Associate Professor in the Department of Broadcasting, Telecommunications and Mass Media at Temple University and is a cofounder of the Alliance for a Media Literate America.

Given the pressures on educators generated by state testing, differential access to technology, and other significant obstacles, it is reasonable to assume that only a small proportion of American students receive any systematic application of media literacy concepts within the context of subject area instruction (Kubey, 1998).

Many factors may lead a teacher to begin incorporating media analysis and media production activities into the curriculum. Motivations for incorporating media literacy into the curriculum range widely, including efforts to creatively integrate technology (Brooks, 2003; Brunner & Tally, 1999); to motivate and inspire student learning (Hunt, 2001); to minimize exposure to media violence (Levin, 1998); to expand appreciation for social and cultural diversity (Fox, 2002); to reduce the power of U.S. media corporations to control culture (ACME, 2004), to strengthen students' recognition of how film and visual media work as forms of expression and communication (Krueger & Christel, 2001; McCarthy & Ondaatje, 2002); or to enable students to explore the constructed nature of culture, identity, and values (Alvermann, Moon, & Hagoon, 1999; Pacatte, 2000). Others view media literacy as a response to the postmodern condition of education and society (Giroux & Simon, 1989), a method of promoting critical thinking (Considine & Haley, 1999), or an application of constructivist principles of education (Tyner, 1998). Still others see media literacy as a dimension of critical pedagogical theory (Giroux & Simon, 1989; Kellner, 1995). These differences in motivations lie at the heart of some of the arguments and debates that have characterized the media literacy movement's growth and development in the 1990s (Hobbs, 1998). Is the diversity of perspectives now in place among content-area practitioners a source of strength and vitality, or has it polarized and paralyzed the development of the field?

To address this question, this chapter reviews ongoing educational initiatives in media literacy documented in the emerging body of case study and practitioner literature and identifies those (few) empirical studies that have measured the effects of media literacy instruction on students' knowledge, attitudes, and behaviors, with particular focus on health education, social studies, English language arts, communication arts, and the fine and performing arts. These subject areas have been identified as having the most frequent reference to media literacy in state curriculum documents (Kubey & Baker, 1999). From this, recommendations are presented that may help scholars and practitioners to develop this emerging field by exploring questions deserving of further research.

Health Education

Health educators, perhaps more than any other subject area teachers, are more likely than educators in other disciplines to have embraced media literacy as a promising practice. Some kinds of media literacy activities are ubiquitous in health education state frameworks. For example, analyzing tobacco and alcohol advertising is a component of most state education curricula (Kubey & Baker, 1999). Physicians and health educators may embrace the perspective that media consumption poses a health risk to children and youth and that media literacy can build resiliency to fight the onslaught of negative messages featuring violence, sexuality, and substance abuse (Strasburger, 1995). A large-scale study of over 3,000 children aged 2–17 shows that children spend nearly eight hours per day, outside of school, in watching television, listening to music, playing videogames, using the Internet, and reading books or magazines (Kaiser Family Foundation, 1999). As one of the primary agents of socialization, television and other media can shape attitudes about health and lifestyle in many ways. Nutritionists, for example, recognize that the mass media have a powerful influence in shaping the food choices of American consumers (Nestle, 2002). Representations of violence and aggression make up more than 57% of all television programming and have effects that may include inducing fear, increasing desensitization and decreasing empathy, changes in attitudes about unknown others, and behavioral imitation (American Academy of Pediatrics, 2000).

Media literacy curriculum materials have been created to address the problem of media violence (Thoman, 1995), the marketing of alcohol and tobacco and illegal drug use (Doba & Doukoullos, 2001), and other health-related topics. Hundreds of regional health conferences between 1995 and 2000 featured presentations and workshops in integrating media literacy into health education, and health educators are a major subgroup of the membership of the Alliance for a Media Literate America (F. Rogow, personal communication, April 24, 2001). Major organizations including the Centers for Substance Abuse and Prevention (CSAP), the White House Office of National Drug Control and Prevention (ONDCP), and the National Institute for Child Health and Human Development (NICHD) have supported media literacy by hosting conferences or providing funding for programs (see Kubey & Hobbs, 2001, for review).

Researchers have studied the efficacy of media literacy in promoting healthy behaviors using evaluation methodology typical to health intervention studies. Austin and Johnson (1997) examined the effect of media literacy instruction on elementary school students' attitudes about alcohol, finding that a media literacy intervention significantly reduced intention to drink alcohol among children and adolescents. A study of media literacy incorporated within an antidrug life skills education curriculum showed that media analysis activities can be effective in building knowledge and changing attitudes about the intention to use illegal drugs (Eisen, 2001). Other research has shown that media literacy can reduce susceptibility to tobacco use (Austin & Pinkleton, in press); increase skepticism about perceptions of the thin ideal in beauty and fashion magazines (Irving & Berel, 2001; Irving, DuPen, & Berel, 1998); and increase body acceptance and encourage reasonable dieting behaviors (Neumark-Sztainer, Sherwood, Coller, & Hannan, 2000; Wade, Davidson, & O'Dea, 2003).

This research is beginning to demonstrate the efficacy of media literacy education by assessing short-term measurable effects on attitudes and behavior. However, there is not yet a solid base of case study, practitioner-focused, or qualitative evidence that documents what actually happens in health classrooms when media literacy is used as an instructional tool. What instructional practices are used to introduce media literacy in health education settings? How do students respond to media literacy when it concerns topics related to health and wellness? Qualitative research will help foster an understanding of how children and young people respond to media literacy when explored in the context of health education.

Because some health educators may bring a protectionist (antimedia) stance to this work, research should also examine the extent to which current efforts to integrate media literacy in health education focus on overt persuasion, knowledge acquisition, or the development of critical reasoning skills. Are media literacy programs that increase students' negative attitudes about tobacco and alcohol more effective than those that emphasize the acquisition of knowledge about media industries and influence or the development of critical reasoning and analysis skills? If media literacy is simply a vehicle to send persuasive messages about "good behavior," adolescents may rapidly learn to tune out, as they already do with so many of their parents' and teachers' exhortations.

Social Studies

It is likely that media literacy is so embedded in social studies education as to be hidden from view. Students are often asked to use information from newspapers, the Internet, and television, studying cartoons, ads, pamphlets, and other resources that provide primary source information about historical and current events. But while these texts are common to the work of social studies educators, less is known about *how* materials are used. Do social studies teachers encourage students to reflect upon the ways in which media genres, forms, and representations shape message content? Do social studies educators help students to understand that media texts do not offer transparent reflections of events or people, but interpretations, presented with varying degrees of reliability and power? According to Scholes (1998):

The point is not to pretend to offer students some magic talisman that will enable them to tell truth from falsehood in the media, but rather help them understand "mediation" (the pouring of raw data through the sieve of any particular media) as a textual process that requires interpretation. (p. 140)

While little is known about the presence (or absence) of critical discourse concerning the constructed nature of the message forms, secondary social studies teachers have long been among the most prominent users of audiovisual material in the classroom (Martorella, 1997). While at one time TV and films were a motivational treat for students, historical fiction films (including often popular, mass culture fare) and nonfiction documentaries are now common resources in American classrooms (Cuban, 1986). Some teachers even design their curriculum around the screening of specific films (Duvall, n.d.). Other teachers bring in material they have taped off the air from television news or documentary programs. At conferences, audiovisual and multimedia materials are widely available for sale and occasionally educators may attend a seminar or workshop that demonstrates active viewing procedures, including innovative approaches to note-taking, the use of library research and reading, critical analysis of visual images, or follow-up activities involving oral presentation or role-playing.

To many social studies educators, the focus is on content and knowledge acquisition, with an emphasis on the mastery of key ideas, facts, names, and dates (Loewen, 1995). Media history and content related to media issues may come into the curriculum, for example, when learning about the freedoms protected by the Bill of Rights or when studying the changes in the American presidential election system. But since many social studies teachers avoid discussion about controversial issues and as many as half of these teachers lack a BA or MA in history or even a major with "some history" in it (Loewen, 1995), media issues (when they are included at all) tend to be predictable. Media violence and the role of TV in presidential elections are the usual topics in a content-focused social studies program, and there are a number of videos, curriculum materials, and other resources that teachers may use to promote media literacy when exploring these issues.

But other social studies educators emphasize instructional strategies that promote critical thinking skills, not rote content-area learning, which is precisely why professional organizations in the social studies are urging that media literacy education be integrated into social studies curriculum frameworks, viewing it as a strategy for bringing principles of constructivism to the traditionalist's classroom (Considine & Haley, 1999). For example, in Texas, social studies skills are defined broadly in state standards as the ability to apply critical thinking skills to organize and use information acquired from a variety of print and nonprint sources (Texas Education Agency, 1998a). When media literacy is integrated as a method of inquiry for the social studies, specific objectives for student performance may include: 1) identifying ways that social scientists analyze limited evidence; 2) locating and using primary and secondary sources, including media and news services, biographies, interviews, and artifacts; and 3) analyzing information by sequencing, categorizing, identifying cause-and-effect relationships, comparing and contrasting, finding the main idea, summarizing, making generalizations and predictions, and drawing inferences and conclusions (Texas Education Agency, 1998b).

In Oyster River, New Hampshire, a social studies teacher used newsmagazines in a current events activity around the time of the 1996 presidential election. The class examined a *Time* magazine issue featuring the furrowed face of Bob Dole, analyzing the editorial position offered by the visual dimensions of the photo, including the use of color, contrast, facial expression, and lighting. Additional activities included tracking a candidate's issues, slogans, and sound bites and seeing how the media covered these. As a class, students kept track of how much time the media spent reporting on who was ahead and behind in the polls (the "horse-race" style coverage) as compared with providing information on candidates' policies on controversial issues (Hobbs, 1998c). It is hoped that many social studies educators engage in instructional practices like these in the context of a presidential election. But given the enormous diversity of potential interactive technology tools and media texts available to social studies educators and the lack of research on how these resources are used, we have little knowledge of the instructional processes that teachers draw upon when they employ media and technology in the classroom.

Renewed interest in civic education has helped draw attention to the relevance of media literacy as a tool for instruction in K-12 social studies. However, the Civic Mission of Schools report, issued by the Carnegie Foundation and the Center for Information and Research on Civic Learning and Engagement at the University of Maryland (2003), did not directly identify media literacy as a key dimension of social studies education. The key elements endorsed for effective civic education in schools in the report were: instruction in government, history, law, and democracy; class discussion of current local, national, and international issues and events; community service and service learning linked to curriculum and class instruction; extracurricular opportunities to get involved in the school and community; participation in school governance; and simulations of democratic processes and procedures. Certainly, media analysis can be included as a component of any discussion of current events, and perhaps media production might be relevant to some of the above-listed areas as well. However, the absence of media literacy, which is not explicitly identified as a promising practice, does suggest that, in contrast to English teachers, social studies educators are aiming to reform instructional practice through active learning that connects directly to the school and community; it does not appear that there is (as a central goal) an emphasis on the kind of critical thinking and inquiry processes about the representations of social reality that are central to media literacy education.

Future research should establish a body of evidence that documents the range of postviewing instructional strategies used by social studies teachers, particularly at the secondary level. How frequently do social studies teachers use critical questions to analyze historical fiction and documentary films as constructed texts that carry an ideological message and point of view? What kinds of postviewing instructional experiences are most likely to activate media literacy skills? Research exploring these issues would strengthen an appreciation for the value of audiovisual materials in the content area of social studies and provide well-needed documentation of an underresearched and often invisible component of instruction in secondary education.

English and Language Arts Education

An increasing number of literacy scholars and practitioners recognize that films, websites, television programs, magazines, newspapers, and even popular music are "texts," and as such, they communicate and carry meaning to "readers." Indeed, literacy educators are finally responding to the social and cultural changes brought about by the increasing dominance of visual and electronic media in the culture. According to this view, including a range of diverse narrative and expository texts from the realms of film, television, popular print media, radio, and the Internet helps create authentic learning environments that can connect the classroom to the living room (Foster, 1998; Fox, 2002; Krueger & Christel, 2001; Teasely & Wilder, 1997; Worsnop, 1994). One publication from the International Reading Association included more than 60 research articles about the relationship between visual and communication media as tools in the development of literacy skills (Flood, Heath, & Lapp, 1997). Literacy educators with interests in media literacy generally adopt perspectives of textual analysis and sociocultural critical theory from the disciplines of the humanities, semiotics, and cultural studies, and some make use of psychological research in learning theory.

Methods of instruction emphasize the process of critical analysis, discussion, and the representation of ideas in verbal, visual, and graphic forms. Using *critical questions* to stimulate students' active reading response is increasingly a common classroom practice, and this instructional strategy has been extended to include the texts of popular culture, including television, movies, and popular music (Alvermann, Moon, & Hagood, 1999).

Media literacy activities generally involve active small- and large-group *discussion* concerning the analysis and interpretation of media messages. Yates (2002) found that discussion of television and mass media was used by two-thirds of teachers in a small southeastern city. As Nystrand (1997) has shown, the quality of students' overall literacy achievement and academic performance is highly correlated with the quality and duration of class discussion. Teachers who use popular culture to motivate students report that, as expected, students are indeed more talkative when television, film, the Internet, and popular music are connected to classroom lessons. In a case study published in the *Journal of Adolescent and Adult Literacy*, Stevens (2001) writes about the use of clips from the television show *South Park* in the classroom:

This lesson benefited from the inclusion of popular culture clips. Students' demeanors were visibly transformed as the movie clips were introduced, leading to a higher level of engagement that was maintained throughout the lesson. While the topic could have been explored without the inclusion of the clips, the lesson took on dynamic dimensions as students engaged in discussions and writing responses. (p. 550)

Of course, this is no surprise to a classroom teacher: as students activate prior knowledge, they take pleasure in learning. As many have specific information, ideas, questions, and theories to share, teachers can more easily step into the role of facilitating inquiry (Sommer, 2001). For many teachers, the use of popular culture in the classroom is valuable primarily for its motivational function; it is possible that some teachers do not use popular culture texts to promote critical thinking per se. As a result, some scholars fear that talking about media and popular culture "dumbs down" the curriculum and that replacing literature with popular culture impoverishes the quality of classroom discourse (Applebee, 1996).

In recent years, these fears have been partially alleviated by the work of Robert Scholes from Brown University, the current president of the Modern Language Association, whose work on the Pacesetter English program helped bring media literacy into the Advanced Placement curriculum in high school English (Scholes, 1998). In this program, English educators are urged to incorporate a wide range of texts beyond the traditional literary canon, including film, television, advertising, the Internet, and popular media (College Board, 2000).

Finally, an increasingly prominent method of instruction in English education emphasizes the use of media and technology tools for *representing ideas in verbal, visual, or graphic forms* for the purpose of self-expression and communication. Educational technology specialists, who emphasize the need for students to have opportunities to use visual and electronic tools to create as well as analyze media texts, support English teachers in these efforts. This alliance is finding considerable support in school districts and in national professional organizations. For example, in 2003, the Board of Directors of the National Council of Teachers of English approved a resolution stating that they will: (1) encourage preservice, in-service, and staff development programs that will focus on new literacies, multimedia composition, and an expanded conceptualization of literacy; (2) encourage research and develop models of district, school, and classroom policies that would promote multimedia composition; and (3) encourage integrating multimedia composition in English language arts curriculum and teacher education, and in refining related standards at local, state, and national levels (NCTE, 2003). This resolution provides further evidence that, among mainstream K-12 educators, the concept of literacy is being broadened to include multimedia forms of expression and communication alongside print media.

Little empirical work has been conducted to measure the impact of media literacy on the development of students' academic skill development. Preliminary evidence shows that media analysis and media production activities may affect the growth of literacy skills for older adolescents. In some high schools, media literacy has been shown to create an instructional context that measurably strengthens students' critical thinking skills (Quin & McMahon, 1995) and a recent evaluation of a year-long program integrating media literacy into Grade 11 English showed statistically significant increases in students' reading comprehension strategies and writing skills compared with a matched control group that received no media literacy instruction (Hobbs & Frost, 2003). Further research is needed to understand how media literacy education affects the differential development of speaking, listening, writing, and reading among high- and low-ability students, in particular. It will also be necessary to determine whether and how family media use habits (including reading, computer use, and viewing behaviors) interact with classroom instructional practices to promote the development of critical thinking skills.

Fine and Performing Arts

The media arts are now often included along with the visual arts, music, dance, and drama in both secondary and university education programs. The media arts—defined as art that is produced using some combination of technology or incorporating media objects as an essential component of the work—includes narrative, documentary, and experimental films; videos and digital products; and installation art that uses media and computer-generated and displayed art (McCarthy & Ondaatje, 2002). While it is not common for drama, music, visual arts, or dance teachers to engage in formal media analysis activities, many use video production to record performances, and some teachers even weave the key concepts of media literacy into their existing arts curriculum. In some high schools, media arts are positioned as one of the many tools for self-expression and creativity; in other schools, media arts courses are housed within a technology program. This may have an impact on the instruction provided to students. Some high school media arts programs rely on graphic design and media professionals for staffing. In these programs, the curriculum (even though housed in the arts program) may revolve around the mastery of specific technology tools (i.e., learning to use Photoshop for graphic design, Adobe Premiere for video editing, and Reason for music composition and sound). Other media arts education programs sniff at the technology and commercial-sector focus of such programs and instead bring the artist-in-residency model into schools, involving practicing artists from the community on short-term media projects with a small group of youth.

Artists may bring with them a particular interest in demythologizing mass media and promoting students' interest in independent media (Goldfarb, 2002), but the focus of these programs may emphasize the relationship between the artist and the youth (Tyner, 1998). Often, the programs link a media production activity with a political, social, or community issue that has high levels of perceived relevance to youth (Goodman, 2003).

The rapid increase in the number of youth media programs nationwide is testament to the willingness of artists and activists, generally working outside of formal K-12 institutions, to provide creative opportunities for children and young people to explore the artistic and social potential of media and technology. For example, Art Start is a nonprofit organization in New York City that runs a number of programs for youth, including the Media Works Project, launched in 1994, which works with teens who are struggling in "last chance" high schools, living on the street, or who have recently been released from prison. Through Art Start's inquiry-based approach to teaching media literacy, students learn how to decode the media by analyzing the messages of advertising, music, television, and film. Participants then cultivate their ideas and learn strategies to counter the stereotypes around them by creating their own media projects. To help students develop their ideas, guest artists and mentors conduct special workshops on a regular basis and students meet with media professionals for intensive research and hands-on guidance. In 1995, the students produced their first public service announcement (PSA) campaign, Protect Your Child Against Racism. In 2003, they designed an antiviolence campaign called Visualizing Violence, displayed on billboards and bus shelters in New York City (S. Fulford, personal communication, October 20, 2003). Similar programs exist in a number of large urban areas (including Los Angeles, San Francisco, and Philadelphia) that have high concentrations of artists and media professionals.

Some states have addressed the intersection of media arts and media literacy in a systematic way. At the Perpich Center for Arts Education (PCAE), a state arts agency in Minneapolis, Minnesota, the Media Arts Program teaches students and teachers to use tools of current and emerging technologies to create works that express feelings and ideas. At the Arts High School, a magnet school, students are challenged to appreciate, analyze, and create works through photography, cinema, sound, digital arts, and interactive media. Developed by veteran teacher and artist Nancy Norwood and her faculty colleagues, the curriculum covers key concepts such as sequencing, montage, sound and image relationships, and the elements of time and motion. Students are also introduced to a variety of genres and approaches to subject matter, basic technology, and criticism in an historical and cultural context. Finally, students develop critical and creative thinking skills by creating works that convey their own ideas, and work on an independent senior project of their choice as they develop a personal vision. The PCAE also offers a menu of staff development programs for art teachers in the state. The media arts program weaves together five focus areas: 1) creativity, which includes the development of ideas, aesthetics, skills, techniques, forms, genres, and exhibition; 2) criticism, which involves description, analysis, interpretation, and judgment; 3) history of film, photography, digital imaging, animation, radio, video art, and documentary; 4) a career focus, developed through field trips, guest artists, and college planning; and 5) an emphasis on multimedia technology, including the use of photography, film, video, and sound. Media literacy is incorporated as a component of all five focus areas, particularly criticism (Perpich Center for Arts Education, 2004).

Future research should seek to better understand the ways in which art teachers strike a balance between critical analysis and creative production when they incorporate popular media "texts" or media technology tools into their work. Because of their unique training that incorporates intensive exposure to both analysis and production, art educators often strike this balance with exquisite grace (Goldfarb, 2002). However, at the present time, there are few case studies that demonstrate how experienced teachers integrate media analysis and media production into the arts curriculum. Such work could help identify "best practices" across the disciplines of drama, dance, music, the visual arts, and the media arts.

Vocational Education and Communication Arts

Another permutation of media literacy in K-12 education emphasizes students not as artists, but as professional communicators. In Australia, student media production has long been emphasized as central to media education; an earlier perception that media education was a low-status vocational subject, characterized by an emphasis on production skills, nonwritten outcomes, and students' engagement in physical rather than mental activities, seems to have diminished (Quin, 2003). In the United States, there are more than 10,000 high school journalism teachers (who often take this assignment in addition to a primary teaching responsibility) and 1,500 media/communications specialists in K-12 schools (Market Data Retrieval, 2003). Simple one-camera studios are not uncommon in the library/media centers of some newly built elementary schools, where students make daily or weekly newscasts. Journalism education and media production at the high school level have long been approached as a preprofessional skill leading to a career (Blanchard & Christ, 1993).

Not surprisingly, at the same time that many high school journalism programs have been eliminated or have struggled for survival since the 1980s, video production facilities have expanded to include more than half of American high schools, with a variety of elective courses offered to students. Often these courses are part of a vocational education or nonacademic track, designed as electives or for noncollege bound students. In high school, students can learn how to operate media production equipment, including cameras, switching and sound equipment, and editing and image manipulation software. These courses often (overtly or covertly) draw from the pool of students with low grade point averages (GPAs) or learning disabilities, racial minorities, or students of low socioeconomic status (Hobbs, 1994). Of course, many schools have ambitious, outstanding programs with a diverse group of participating boys and girls including high-ability students (with many of these schools now routinely posting their students' work on the Internet). In some communities, high school video production courses are taught by former media professionals, who may or may not emphasize the development of critical thinking about the media, message analysis, or social or political activism (Goldfarb, 2002). Conversely, other districts assign video production classes to teachers who may have little expertise or prior experience with media production, teaching, or classroom management, ensuring a rapid staffing turnover that may limit the effectiveness of programs.

In fact, it is important to note that media literacy educators have long felt ambivalent (and even hostile) about the value of vocationally oriented media production as an end in itself. Masterman (1985, pp. 26–27) notes, "Practical activity does not, in itself, constitute media education," warning about the technicist trap—the tendency to see media education as a series of purely technical operations, which can lead to student media production functioning as "busywork, and in its more advanced manifestations, a form of cultural reproduction in which dominant practices become naturalized." According to this view, print and visual media production activities should support the development of critical thinking skills about the media, and an emphasis on vocationalism should be discouraged.

But preprofessional experiences in media production may offer opportunities to explore elements of media analysis, embedded in real-world decision making and consequences. The production of a high school newspaper, still the most common media production activity in American public schools, affords many informal and formal learning experiences that can advance media literacy among students, teachers, and the whole community. Delfino (2004) describes a case where administrators criticized the faculty advisor to a student newspaper for printing a letter to the editor that complained about the texts being used in English classes. It was assumed that the advisor agreed with everything printed in the student newspaper. The criticism demonstrated a lack of understanding of the purpose of letters to the editor, but the complaint served as a vehicle to educate the faculty about the role of the press in a free society, and particularly as to how a newspaper can provide the opportunity for students and community members to air their views and opinions.

There has been some support of K-12 media literacy efforts on the part of university media and communication programs. The National Communication Association (NCA, 1998) has developed educational standards for speaking, listening, and media literacy in elementary and secondary education. Future research should address the role of the university in supporting media literacy education initiatives at the pre-college level. What are the most appropriate forms of support that universities could provide to K-12 educators? Do students who enroll in vocationally oriented communication arts courses in high schools pursue communication majors in college or get entry-level jobs in media fields? Critics charge that vocationally oriented communication arts programs (whether at the secondary or postsecondary level) are outdated and irresponsible, given the highly competitive employment climate in broadcasting and media production fields (Blanchard & Christ, 1993). According to this view, students with broad training in the liberal arts are more likely to be successful media professionals; strong communication and critical thinking skills, coupled with a broad general knowledge base, are deemed more valuable than narrow occupational training using a switcher, sound mixer, or editing or graphics software (Kyker & Curchy, 2004).

Some secondary educators have modified communication arts programs to emphasize this broad humanities focus, instead of a narrow vocational specialization. Some of these schools balance technology skills with a substantial emphasis on critical thinking and an appreciation of the complex processes involved in the communication of meaning through symbolic forms. For example, the Communications Arts High School in San Antonio, Texas, emphasizes a humanities-focused, multimedia literacy approach, and unlike some magnet schools, it does not limit recruitment; students do not have to submit a portfolio or focus only on communications careers. Learning and instruction is based on the premise that the 21st century will demand strong communication skills in reading, writing, speaking, listening, and thinking (Communications Arts High School, 2004).

Since 1988, educators at Montgomery Blair High School in Silver Spring, Maryland, have offered the Communication Arts Program (CAP), a highly selective (application-based) integrated humanities program for students who wish to explore connections between the humanities and the study of media and communication. This program provides numerous opportunities for students to develop critical thinking and communication skills through activities that link coursework in social studies, language arts, media analysis, and media production. Students engage in formal debates, analyze press coverage of political campaigns, produce documentaries, write scripts, analyze films, perform in plays, design websites, and conduct interviews and complete community service projects. In their senior year, students demonstrate their communication competencies in a formal, public interview where they present a portfolio of work they have completed to document their progress (D. D'Angelo, personal communication, November 10, 2003). The program has been so successful that in 2004–2005, the district offered a "Media Literacy Academy," which was open to all students in the district. It includes two required interdisciplinary courses in media literacy (one thematically focused on health; the other focused on media's role in social/political issues) along with a wide range of electives in communication arts.

There is little research evidence that describes instructional practices in high school journalism or video production courses and even less that explores the short-term impact of communication arts education for students now enrolled in such courses. Researchers should investigate the impact of such educational programs on students' attitudes, knowledge, and media use habits and explore how participation in such courses may affect the postsecondary education and career choices of students.

Informal Learning with Media Production

While media production teachers once had a school-wide monopoly with their vocational, nonacademic media production classes, today, more and more students have access to video camcorders, digital cameras, and editing and image manipulation software in the home. Secondary teachers from the subject areas of the humanities, foreign languages, and the physical sciences are also more likely to give students the opportunity to create messages in nonprint forms (Brooks, 2003; Bruce, 2002; Gardner, 2003). With the rapidly decreasing costs of video camcorders and editing software, the skills of composition using edited visual images, language, and sound will eventually become routine experiences for adolescents. But because schools change so slowly, and because the emphasis on K-12 educational technology has placed the Internet and computers (and not digital cameras or video production) at the center of the curriculum, it is probably likely that many young people will first encounter media production experiences as a spontaneous recreational or optional homework activity.

Future research should document the use of media production projects and activities by content-area teachers who may not formally embed media literacy into their curriculum but who may offer alternative assessments including student-produced media projects. What do students learn when, as part of their coursework, they are given the option of producing a short film, designing a web page, or writing a script to document their learning in the content areas? Such activities may enhance students' perceptions of the meaningfulness of learning, arouse curiosity, and encourage them to see connections between ideas (Bruce, 2002; Callahan, 2001). Case studies of project-driven assignments and documentation of student progress and performance in the construction of multimedia projects would provide a clearer, more detailed portrait of some of the benefits and drawbacks of using multimedia production as an assessment of student learning in the content areas.

After-school programs in media production are another growing area of media literacy education. These programs are now common in hundreds of American cities, as exemplified by the Digital Media Training Lab in Philadelphia, a program for low-income African American teen males where students write scripts, design storyboards, and create videos. The Listen Up network (http://www.listenup.org) provides a valuable distribution function for similar youth media programs, allowing people to view online streaming video clips of youth-produced work. And new forms of media production are emerging, as Jenkins (2004) describes participants in a GlobalKidz workshop in New York, for example, who worked with videogame professionals to construct a game about racial profiling at airports. Students encountered important ethical issues in the process. How were they going to represent racial differences? Were they going to perpetuate or challenge stereotypes? These experiences contribute enormously to building critical thinking and communication skills that, according to Jenkins, lead youth to view commercial media content with a more self-conscious perspective.

Misuses of Media in the Classroom

Anyone who visits an American high school and observes classroom activities will see an array of instructional practices involving media and technology that do not appear, on first blush, to be "educational." Some teachers will mistakenly describe any use of media in the classroom as "media literacy." What actually happens in classrooms when teachers use fiction films or documentaries? What attitudes and beliefs are emphasized when teachers use newsmagazines or newspapers? What are students learning when they surf the Internet in a school technology lab? Educators have long recognized that teaching with and about media and popular culture is both subversive *and* conservative, and that technology use in K-12 classrooms can be less innovative and instructionally valuable than suggested by all the hype about the wonders of educational technology (Oppenheimer, 2003). But for all the dynamic, engaged, and effective teaching going on in American schools, teachers can and do use film, television, and music in the classroom in sometimes inappropriate ways—as a substitute for poor preparation, to reward students for good behavior, or to prop up students who lack print literacy skills (Hobbs, 1994). School districts have adopted policies to minimize the possibility of parental disapproval and to encourage teachers to reflect carefully on their specific educational goals when using contemporary media forms in the classroom (Zirkel, 1999). In response to misuses of media, school districts across the nation have instituted policies that limit teachers' use of popular films, television programs, and music. Some districts have a "controversial learning resource" policy that defines such materials as those "not included in the approved learning resources of the district and which are subject to disagreement as to appropriateness because they relate to controversial issues or present material in a manner or context which is itself controversial" (Zirkel, p. 70).

Researchers should examine and evaluate the range of district-level policies (and actual implementation of these policies) that now define the appropriate uses of film, video, or popular media in the classroom. Some school districts have highly restrictive policies, as in the example described by Stevens (2001), who reports that to use a clip from a PG-rated film with middle-school students, district policy required permission slips from all students' parents. In other districts, teachers report that requirements may include submitting video clips for classroom use for the principal's approval 20 days before screening, or providing copies of videos to be used to a district-level administrator for approval at the beginning of each semester. In some schools, principals communicate their disapproval of district policies and do not require teachers to adhere to video use policies; in other communities, principals establish and enforce even more stringent informal policies (including no use of videotape or popular music) than district-level policies dictate. Research could explore the question of how video and popular culture material is conceptualized as educational fare by teachers who use these materials, how students react to the use of popular culture texts, and how faculty colleagues and school leaders respond when they learn of the use of media "texts" as a component of instruction in the subject areas.

Conclusion

Despite differences in motivations, there is the emergence of some consensus concerning the process of instruction, particularly in the areas of social studies and English language arts, where a richer body of evidence makes it possible to attempt some generalization. The inquiry model seems to be one of the shared practices evident in the work of educators in English language arts and social studies, and less clearly dominant in communication arts education. This four-step inquiry process is a common model:

- encouraging students to reflect on their own beliefs and attitudes about the mass media in society and about their media use habits and behaviors in the home;
- helping students learn how to gather information from different source materials, media types and genres, and points of view;
- developing skills of critical thinking to analyze and evaluate messages, and, in particular, learning to subject visual evidence to critical inquiry through close analysis of media "texts";
- creating messages for authentic audiences using a wide range of media production tools.

Through these methods, teachers aim to provide learning experiences in which students reach their own understandings about how to fully participate as individuals, citizens, and consumers in a media-saturated society.

Media literacy in the United States is not emerging primarily from statewide or school district initiatives, but from the bottom-up energy of individual teachers who value the way that using media, technology, and popular culture improves the quality of their interaction with students or who are passionate about helping young people understand, challenge, and transform media's cultural dominance. Educators with interests in media literacy are individuals who may not have any allegiance to a shared professional organization. Typically, these educators work in relative isolation without much day-to-day contact with professional colleagues who share their interests. Reviewing the diverse array of approaches that are currently being used in K-12 education vis-à-vis media, technology, and literacy, it is easy to see why the "great debates" (Hobbs, 1998a) are still underway about the appropriate way to bring media literacy to students in American public schools. The diversity of motives and approaches (coming from diverse aims and goals along with so many distinct content areas and approaches) is a source of strength, even though it may increase the cacophony of voices in this emerging field.

It is appropriate to review another question that relates to the application of media literacy as integrated within existing subject areas: should media literacy be taught as a specialist subject or integrated within the context of existing subjects? More and more, media literacy is being taught as a course, often within communication arts or English, because of an individual teacher's enthusiasm for the specialty. Taught as a specialist subject, few students will be reached in a given school or school district. Taught within existing content areas, more students will be reached, but it is likely that shallow and superficial understandings may result because of the difficulty in providing meaningful, ongoing staff development for large numbers of people who, because of the absence of media literacy in undergraduate teacher education programs, may lack the background tools and knowledge to implement this instruction thoughtfully and with sufficient depth.

Scholars and practitioners should explore some of the following research questions that stem from the proliferation of approaches that have blossomed across the content areas during the 1990s, some of which extend from the debates that have long highlighted focal questions for this emerging field (Hobbs, 1998a). These include:

1. *How does media literacy improve students' academic development in the content areas?* There is a pressing need for a more systematic theoretical formulation of how media literacy may affect students' growth of knowledge and skills. Does media literacy instruction increase student interest in learning and motivation for school achievement? How does the inquiry process strengthen critical thinking skills, creativity, or communication skills? What kinds of instructional experiences lead to student growth? What psychological and learning theories best enable us to examine how media analysis and media production experiences can contribute to students' intellectual, social, emotional, and personal development? Media literacy should be conceptually aligned with appropriate theoretical formulations, which may include multiple intelligences, critical pedagogy, and the emerging scholarship in learning for understanding and multiliteracies.

2. *How does professional development support growth in teacher competencies?* While there are numerous seminars, conferences, and workshops available for K-12 teachers on media literacy in the content areas, there is little evidence that demonstrates that such programs are effective in transforming instructional practice beyond evaluation data collected at the conclusion of a staff development program. Some scholars suggest that three years of ongoing work with staff are required in order to fully integrate media literacy within the K-12 subject areas (Hobbs, 1998b). Bazalgette, Bevort, and Savino (1992) have asserted that fully half of the teachers who receive exposure to media education concepts will never implement it with their students. We still know relatively little about the factors that enable teachers to make changes in their instructional practices in order to incorporate media literacy. What is needed most to address these issues is a wide range of longitudinal case studies examining school-based implementations (involving groups of teachers) that includes teacher observational data and measures of student performance. This would help provide evidence that could strengthen the design and implementation of teacher education programs.

3. *Should media literacy education focus on after-school and community education programs instead of K-12 education settings?* The growth of youth media and media arts programs, combined with increas-

ingly inexpensive access to computers, digital cameras, and editing software, plus the voluminous resources of the Internet, invite wonder about potential transformations to education that may be happening from innovations occurring outside the K-12 system. Should media literacy education be focused on transforming conservative school cultures that generally resist innovation? On this score, philanthropies have placed their money squarely *outside* the schools, preferring to fund technology or arts-based community programs in youth media and media literacy (Campbell, Hoey, & Perlman, 2001). Although some researchers have begun to evaluate school-based media literacy programs, few studies have been published. One of the challenges faced by most evaluators is the question of conducting research that takes into account the complex real-life characteristics of the school environment. For example, many factors encourage (or discourage) K-12 teachers from implementing curriculum materials in the way that they are intended to be used. While funding agencies place a premium on scientifically evaluated curriculum, teachers rarely (if ever) implement instructional materials according to the teachers' manual. Not only does this limit the validity of research evidence, according to Hollis, Kileen, and Doyon (2003, p. 1), but "much of what might make a curriculum valuable to a teacher, such as the flexibility to teach it in whatever way they want, may be exactly the factor that hinders the ability of a curriculum to achieve its greatest effect." Further research should examine how educators actually use media literacy materials (including videos and lesson plans) in the classroom.

Sadly, many teachers are still teaching more or less the same way as they did when they started in their profession more than 25 years ago. With the average American teacher now aged 46 and likely to stay in education until retirement (Keller & Manzo, 2003), there are still many thousands of schools in the United States where most students get little meaningful time over the course of 12 years of public schooling to engage in critical thinking about media messages or to create messages using technology tools. In many schools, the only meaningful relationship between literacy and technology is the use of word processing software. Most teachers simply have not had the time (or the perceived need) to become fluent in using media tools or the training to understand how to use media texts or media issues to promote critical thinking. By and large, schools of education have not yet discovered media literacy. Because even young teachers are often not experienced with how to analyze visual or electronic messages, and do not themselves know how to create messages using media and technology, strengthening young people's media literacy skills in the 21st century will continue to be an enormous challenge. If media literacy is to continue to develop as a promising practice in K-12 education, the first generation of innovative educators who have helped integrate media literacy into the context of existing curricula must now begin to create systemic, institutional change that moves beyond the classroom to influence educational leaders and educational institutions.

REFERENCES

Action Coalition for Media Education (ACME). (2004). Why ACME? Retrieved February 28, 2004, from http://www.acmecoalition.org/about.html

Alliance for a Media Literate America (AMLA). (2004). About the AMLA. Retrieved February 28, 2004, from http://amlainfo.org/about.html

Alvarado, M., & Boyd-Barrett, O. (1992). *Media education: An introduction.* London: British Film Institute.

Alvermann, D., Moon, J., & Hagood, M. (1999). *Popular culture in the classroom: Teaching and researching critical media literacy.* Newark, DE: International Reading Association.

American Academy of Pediatrics. (2000). Media education in the practice setting. *Media matters.* Retrieved February 28, 2004, from http://aap.org/advocacy/mmguide.pdf

Applebee, A. (1996). *Curriculum as conversation.* Chicago: University of Chicago Press.

Aufderheide, P., & Firestone, C. (1993). *Media literacy: A report of the national leadership conference on media literacy.* Queenstown, MD: Aspen Institute.

Austin, E., & Johnson, K. (1997). Effects of general and alcohol-specific media literacy training on children's decision making about alcohol. *Journal of Health Communication, 2,* 17–42.

Austin, E., & Pinkleton, B. (in press). Evaluation of American Legacy Foundation/ Washington State Department of Health media literacy pilot study. *Journal of Health Communication.*

Bazalgette, C., Bevort, E., & Savino, J. (1992). *New directions: Media education worldwide.* London: British Film Institute.

Blanchard, R., & Christ, W. (1993). *Media education and the liberal arts: A blueprint for the new professionalism.* Hillsdale, NJ: Lawrence Erlbaum Associates.

Brooks, J. (2003). Technology in the real world. Retrieved October 26, 2003, from http://www.ciconline.com/Enrichment/Teaching/learningwithtechnology/expertadvice/default.htm##Jim

Bruce, D. (2002). Thinking visually: The process of video composition in peer-production groups in a language arts classroom. Unpublished doctoral dissertation, Kent State University, OH.

Brunner, C., & Tally, W. (1999). *The new media literacy handbook.* New York: Anchor.

Buckingham, D. (2003). *Media education.* London: Polity Press.

Callahan, J.M. (2001). Teaching and learning of critical media literacy in secondary English classrooms. Unpublished doctoral dissertation, State University of New York, Buffalo.

Campbell, P., Hoey, L., & Perlman, L. (2001). Sticking with my dreams: Defining and refining youth media in the 21st century. Unpublished paper. Retrieved January 12, 2002, from http://www.campbell-kibler.com/youth_media.html

Center for Information and Research on Civic Learning and Engagement at the University of Maryland. (2003). The civic mission of schools. Retrieved May 14, 2004, from http://civicmissionofschools.org

College Board. (2000). Pacesetter English. Retrieved February 28, 2004, from http://www.collegeboard.com/about/association/pace/pace_english.html

Communications Arts High School. (2004). Home page. Retrieved May 10, 2004, from http://www.nisd.net/comartww/

Considine, D., & Haley, G. (1999). *Visual messages: Integrating imagery into instruction* (2nd ed.). Englewood, CO: Libraries Unlimited.

Cuban, L. (1986). *Teachers and machines: The classroom use of technology since 1920.* New York: Teachers College Press.

Delfino, C. (2004). State of scholastic journalism: Preparing students to be critical consumers of media. American Society of Newspaper Editors. Retrieved May 24, 2004, from http://highschooljournalism.org//teachers/stateofjournalismprincipalsguidech6.htm

Doba, S., & Doukoullos, S. (2001). *Media literacy for drug prevention: A unit for middle school educators.* New York: *New York Times.*

Duvall, A. (n.d.). Teaching U.S. history through feature films. A Massachusetts Department of Education curriculum frameworks project. Retrieved May 20, 2004, from http://hub1.worlded.org/docs/hampden/yourpage.html

Eisen, M. (2001). Intermediate outcomes from a life skills education program with a media literacy component. In W. Crano & M. Burgoon (Eds.), *Mass media and drug prevention.* Claremont Symposium on Applied Social Psychology (pp. 187–214). Mahwah, NJ: Lawrence Erlbaum Associates.

Flood, J., Heath, S.B., & Lapp, D. (1997). *Handbook of research on teaching literacy through the communicative and visual arts.* International Reading Association. New York: Macmillan.

Foster, H. (1998). Reading and writing in the shadow of film and television. In J.S. Simmons & L. Baines (Eds.), *Language study in middle school, high school, and beyond* (pp. 167–189). Newark, DE: International Reading Association.

Fox, R. (2002). Images across cultures: Exploring advertising in the diverse classroom. In K. Fleckenstein, L. Calendrillo, & D. Worley (Eds.), *Language and image in the reading-writing classroom: Teaching vision.* Mahwah, NJ: Lawrence Erlbaum Associates.

Gardner, T. (2003). Novel news: Broadcast coverage of character, conflict, resolution and setting. Read, write, think: Lesson plans for K-12 educators. National Council of Teachers of English. Retrieved February 28, 2004, from http://www.read-writethink.org/lessons/lesson_view.asp?id=199

Giroux, H., & Simon, R. (1989). *Popular culture, schooling and everyday life.* Granby, MA: Bergin and Garvey.

Goldfarb, B. (2002). *Visual pedagogy: Media cultures in and beyond the classroom.* Durham, NC: Duke University Press.

Goodman, S. (2003). *Teaching youth media.* New York: Teachers College Press.

Hobbs, R. (1994). Pedagogical issues in U.S. media education. In S. Deetz (Ed.), *Communication Yearbook 17* (pp. 453–466). Newbury Park, CA: Sage Publications.

Hobbs, R. (1998a). The seven great debates in media literacy education. *Journal of Communication, 48,* 9–29.

Hobbs, R. (1998b). Media literacy in Massachusetts. In A. Hart (Ed.), *Teaching the media: International perspectives* (pp. 127–144). Mahwah, NJ: Lawrence Erlbaum Associates.

Hobbs, R. (1998c). Building citizenship skills through media literacy education. In M. Salvador & P. Sias (Eds.), *The public voice in a democracy at risk* (pp. 57–76). Westport, CT: Praeger.

Hobbs, R., & Frost, R. (2003). Measuring the acquisition of media-literacy skills. *Reading Research Quarterly, 38,* 330–355.

Hollis, C., Kileen, M., & Doyon, M. (2003). Evaluating media literacy for health curriculum: Lessons learned. Unpublished concept paper. University of New Mexico.

Hunt, C. (2001). Must see TV: The timelessness of television as a teaching tool. *Journal of Management Education, 25*(6), 631–647.

Irving, L., & Berel, S. (2001). Comparison and media-literacy programs to strengthen college women's resistance to media images. *Psychology of Women Quarterly, 25,* 103–111.

Irving, L., DuPen, J., & Berel, S. (1998). A media literacy program for high school females. *Eating Disorders, 6,* 119–132.

Jenkins, H. (2004, January 2). Media literacy goes to school. *Technology Review.* Retrieved February 1, 2004, from http://www.technologyreview.com/articles/wo_jenkins010204.asp?p=1

Kaiser Family Foundation. (1999). Kids and media @ the new millennium. A report of the Kaiser Family Foundation. Retrieved January 20, 2000, from http://kff.org

Keller, B., & Manzo, K. (2003, September 10). Teachers: White, female and middle-aged. *Education Week, 23*(2), 10.

Kellner, D. (1995). *Media culture: Cultural studies, identity and politics between the modern and postmodern.* New York: Routledge.

Krueger, E., & Christel, M. (2001). *Seeing and believing: How to teach media literacy in the English classroom.* Portsmouth, NH: Boynton Cook.

Kubey, R. (1998). Obstacles to the development of media education in the United States. *Journal of Communication, 48,* 58–69.

Kubey, R., & Baker, F. (1999). Has media literacy found a curricular foothold? *Education Week,* October 27. Retrieved May 15, 2000, from http://edweek.com/ew/ewstory.cfm?slug=09ubey2.h19&keywords=media%20literacy

Kubey, R., & Hobbs, R. (2001). Setting research directions for media literacy and health education. Center for Media Studies, School of Communication, Information and Library Studies. New Brunswick, NJ: Rutgers University. Retrieved from http://www.mediastudies.rutgers.edu/mh_conference/index.html

Kyker, K., & Curchy, C. (2004). Maybe it's time to have "the talk." Video Viewfinder. SchoolTV.com. Retrieved May 24, 2004, from http://schooltv.com/vidview17.htm

Levin, D. (1998). *Remote control childhood? Combating the hazards of media culture.* Washington, DC: National Association for the Education of Young Children.

Loewen, J. (1995). *Lies my teacher told me.* New York: New Press.

Market Data Retrieval. (2003). *The education market. Catalog.* Shelton, CT: Dun and Bradstreet.

Martorella, P. (1997). *Interactive technologies and the social studies.* Albany: State University of New York Press.

Masterman, L. (1985). *Teaching the media.* London: Routledge.

McCarthy, K., & Ondaatje, E.H. (2002). *From celluloid to cyberspace: The media arts and the changing arts world.* New York: Rand.

National Communication Association (NCA). (1998). The speaking, listening, and media literacy standards and competency statements for K-12 education. Retrieved November 14, 2000, from http://www.natcom.org/Instruction/K-12/standards.pdf

National Council of Teachers of English (NCTE). (2003). Position statement: On composing with nonprint media. Approved by the Board of Directors at the 2003 business meeting, San Francisco. Retrieved February 28, 2004, from http://www.ncte.org/about/over/positions/category/media/114919.htm

Nestle, M. (2002). *Food politics: How the food industry influences nutrition and health.* Berkeley: University of California Press.

Neumark-Sztainer, D., Sherwood, N., Coller, T., & Hannan, P. (2000). Primary prevention of disordered eating among preadolescent girls: Feasibility and short-term effect of a community-based intervention. *Journal of the American Dietetic Association, 100,* 1466–1473.

Nystrand, M. (1997). *Opening dialogue: Understanding the dynamics of language and learning in the English classroom.* New York: Teachers College Press.

Oppenheimer, P. (2003). *The flickering mind.* New York: Random House.

Pacatte, R. (2000). Riding the wave of media literacy in the USA. Pauline Center for Media Studies. Retrieved February 28, 2004, from http://www.daughtersofstpaul.com/mediastudies/articles/articlemlusa.html

Perpich Center for Arts Education. (2004). Arts High School. High school resources for media arts. Retrieved May 15, 2004, from http://www.pcae.k12.mn.us/school/media/resources.html

Quin, R. (2003). Questions of knowledge in Australian media education. *Television and New Media, 4*(4), 439–460.

Quin, R., & McMahon, B. (1995). Evaluating standards in media education. *Canadian Journal of Educational Communication, 22*(1), 15–25.

Scholes, R. (1998). *The rise and fall of English.* New Haven, CT: Yale University Press.

Sommer, P. (2001). Using film in the English classroom: Why and how. *Journal of Adolescent and Adult Literacy, 44*, 485–487.

Stevens, L. (2001). South Park and society: Instructional and curricular implications of popular culture in the classroom. *Journal of Adolescent and Adult Literacy, 44*, 548–555.

Strasburger, V.C. (1995). *Adolescence and the media: Medical and psychological impact*. New York: Ballantine Books.

Teasely, A., & Wilder, A. (1997). *Reel conversations: Reading films with young adults*. Portsmouth, NH: Heinemann/Boynton Cook.

Texas Education Agency. (1998a). Texas essential knowledge and skills for English language arts and reading. Subchapter C: High school. Grade 10. Retrieved February 28, 2004, from http://www.tea.state.tx.us/rules/tac/chapter110/ch110c.html#m;110.42

Texas Education Agency. (1998b). Texas administrative code, Title 19, Part 2. Texas essential knowledge and skills for social studies. Retrieved May 10, 2004, from http://www.tea.state.tx.us/rules/tac/chapter113/index.html

Thoman, E. (1995). *Beyond blame: Challenging violence in the media*. Los Angeles: Center for Media Literacy.

Tyner, K. (1998). *Literacy in the digital age*. Mahwah, NJ: Lawrence Erlbaum Associates.

Wade, T., Davidson, S., & O'Dea, J. (2003). A preliminary controlled evaluation of a school-based media literacy program and self-esteem program for reducing eating disorder risk factors. *Journal of Eating Disorders, 33*, 371–387.

Worsnop, C. (1994). *Screening images: Ideas for media education*. Mississauga, Ontario: Wright Communications.

Yates, B. (2002). Media education's present and future: A survey of teachers. *Studies in media and information literacy 2, 3*. Retrieved November 22, 2004, from http://www.utpjournals.com/merchant.ihtml?pid=4180&step=4

Zirkel, P. (1999, May). Showing R-rated videos in school. *NASSP Bulletin, 83*(607), 69–73.

CHAPTER 6

Critical Thinking for the Cyberage

JULIE D. FRECHETTE

Technology and education are two issues critical to the future of our country. Technology will continue to play a bigger role in the education of our children, whether through electronic libraries or computers

—in the classroom or at home.

—Chairman William F. Goodling, U.S. House Committee on
Education and the Workforce (1998)

As we enter the 21st century, few would question the growing importance of telecommunications technology in the classroom. Over the past decade, schools have focused their attention on acquiring the necessary technology for computer and especially Internet access. Estimates from the report on *School Investments in Instructional Technology* (2001) document the total technology expenditures for the K-12 system at $7.2 billion during 1998, a number that has increased exponentially with the rise of Internet use in schools. In a study by the National Center for Education Statistics (2001), almost all public schools in the United States were reported to have access to the Internet: 98% were connected, a significant increase from 35% in 1994 (Cattagni & Farris Westat, 2001). As impressive as these advances in educational technology *acquisition* are, most school resources for technology are devoid of relevant curricula designed to foster intellectual learning.

As McKinsey & Co. (1995) explain, "to date, the vast majority of school technology-related expenditures have been devoted to building up the hardware infrastructure of computers, peripherals, and network connections. Estimates of K-12 spending on educational technology during the early 1990s found that nearly two-thirds of all investments on technology have been for this technical infrastructure" (cited in Anderson & Becker, 2001). Accordingly, those who have been assessing

---

Julie D. Frechette is Associate Professor of Communications at Worcester State College in Worcester, Massachusetts.

the impact of computers and telecommunications technology in schools have argued that technology alone is not enough if students are to be challenged as critical learners. The 2001 report on *School Investments in Instructional Technology* summarizes findings from the U.S. Congress, the Office of Technology Assessment (OTA) Report on Teachers Technology (1995), The President's Committee of Advisors on Science and Technology & Panel on Educational Technology (1997), the CEO Forum (1999), and the Department of Education's (2000) National Technology Plan, all of which underscore the need for instructional support to accompany technology.

At the same time, with the growing use of the Internet in schools, many educators see the need for integrating critical literacy skills, or "information literacy," into the curriculum so students are properly trained for global electronic travel. Today's youth must learn not only how to acquire the information they desire, but more importantly, how to make sense of it. As Leverenz puts it, the focus should *not* be to wire schools for instant access to this electronic marvel; rather, students must first pass "their driving tests . . . on the Internet" (cited in Bundy, 1997).

One means of teaching students "driver education" on the information superhighway is to employ a media literacy curriculum framework. Popularly defined as "the ability to access, analyze, evaluate, and produce communication in a variety of forms" (Leveranz & Tyner, 1993, p. 21), media literacy is the exploration and critical examination of the deluge of mediated messages we receive daily in visual and/or textual form. Media literacy offers us a way to become "literate" in visual and popular texts, giving us the tools through which to examine the political, cultural, historical, economic, and social ramifications of the media (Frechette, 1997, p. 2). As Leverenz and Tyner explain, media literacy, or media education, begins "when the reader mentally questions mediated information in books, on television, and in all sorts of pop culture messages" (p. 21). The time has come to provide the means for media literacy in cyberspace so that students can become "critically autonomous" in this millennium.

This chapter will allow us to address questions centered on the integration of new telecommunications technology in the classroom by responding to concerns over Internet access and content through media literacy initiatives. While much research about online computer technology focuses on the communication *end*-goal of accessing the "Information Superhighway," we will explore the *means* through which technological access is deployed, essentially asking the questions: what does it means to be literate in the information age, how can information literacy be initiated, and how can the learning process be transformed? Ultimately, the main objective of this chapter is to enable educators to develop curricula that encourage students to judge the validity and worth of Internet content as they strive to become critically autonomous in a technological world.

The Need for Media Literacy with Technology

Embedded within scholarly debates about the pros and cons of computer and telecommunications technology in schools lays a body of literature, though modest in size, that ventures toward the articulation of transformative possibilities within cyberspace. Lankshear, Peters, and Knobel (1996) champion the potential for critical pedagogy to expand and develop within cyberspace environments, advancing several supportive arguments for the utilization of cyberspace to transform classroom practices. First, they contend that cyberspace environments have the potential for making students aware of the historical and contingent nature of discourse. This comes partly as a result of Net users' experiences as creators, refiners, and sustainers of social practices through the act of encoding and decoding symbols and images. Second, interactions, experiences, and information within cyberspace environments point to the complexity, diversity, and multiplicity of human subjectivities, the highly fluid nature of identity, and the enormous possibilities for creating personal identities (all of which challenge modernist notions of subjectivity). Third, conceptualizations of pedagogy can shift from teaching to learning within cyberspace. This results from the fact that, in many instances, students know more about computer-mediated communications technology than teachers, which displaces traditional power dynamics between the educator/educated. This does not mean that the teacher imparts irrelevant information or knowledge, but that student proficiencies in this area should be considered integral aspects of the learning process and tapped. Furthermore, students can access a variety of information/sources that allows them to go beyond teacher and textbook knowledge and curriculum details. As a result, learning can potentially become more collaborative between students and teachers (Garner & Gillingham, 1996). Without giving up claims to authority or valuable information, teachers can deploy knowledge by becoming interrogators, conceptualizers, and facilitators of student-generated questions and ideas in a classroom more attuned to change and human diversity.

Given the techno-optimism (the belief that technology will improve teaching and learning) that many educators share, technology can and should do more than drill basic skills or aid efficiency in communications and research. Various thoughtful educators propose approaches to technology in the classroom that raise questions, require deeper study, and even problematize technology itself (and its products, such as Channel One or broadcast news) (Apple, 1993; Freire, 1998; Giroux, 2000). For example, Paulo Freire (1989) and Henry Giroux (1998) contend that more often than not, for-profit mainstream media reproduce stereotypes due to the imbalance between those who wield cultural, economic, political, and technological power and those who do not. Apple and Weis (1983) made similar claims when arguing that the reproduction of knowledge through rigid curricula, pedagogy, and school structures perpetuates societal inequities. Regardless of the form of technology, educators/sociologists committed to educational and progressive change must always examine who controls technology and how it will be used, especially given that these important decisions affect the educational choices made in schools about technology. Additionally, as argued by Marshall McLuhan (1964), each technology/medium has specific traits that set it apart from other communication contexts and interactions. Thus, it is vital that we analyze and understand the relationship between technology and power, especially within educational environments.

For Larry Cuban, researching the effectiveness of computer use in classrooms is one means to assessing its impact. In his 2001 analysis, Cuban discovers that computer use in classrooms is sporadic at best, and that most teachers use computers to support traditional pedagogy and curricula. This leads him to conclude that gains in academic achievement are not necessarily the result of contemporary uses of computers in schools. Such findings resonate with research by Means, Haertel, and Roberts (2004) as they explore the implications of technology within schools and classrooms. Like McLuhan, they argue that social and educational uses of technology determine its use and effectiveness.

Given the need to better address the impact of media and technology on learning in the information age, scholars and educators have begun to stress the need for media education programs that promote critical thinking. Alvermann and Hagood (2000) argue, "As a result of the greater demands that students face in new times, they must acquire the analytic tools necessary for critically 'reading' all kinds of media texts—film, video, MTV, the Internet, and so on" (p. 203). Building on the struggle to move literacy, in general, beyond the mere acquisition of skills to critical thinking about texts and society, Luke (2001) advocates the combining of media studies with information and communication technology (ICT). She asserts:

many kids of this generation of cybernauts are already literate in the *skills* of hypertext navigation and production—but not necessarily skilled in the application of critical analytic tools . . . In short, we should be getting students to ask the same questions of dot.com culture and cybertextuality that we expect them to ask of broadcaster static print-based texts. (p. 93)

While learning to access and evaluate information online, students need also to ask questions about the human impacts of the very technology they are using. For instance, what are the benefits and disadvantages of globalization, as the world continues to connect technologically; what about privacy issues online; how does increased use of technology for communication affect human socialization; and how can the Internet serve democracy?

The Internet is not a neutral tool any more than TV is a window on reality. Technology education must include media literacy or vice versa. Perhaps Postman (1995) says it best:

Technology education is not a technical subject. It is a branch of the humanities. Technology education aims at students' learning about what technology helps us to do and what it hinders us from doing; it is about how technology uses us, for good or ill, and about how it has used people in the past, for good or ill. It is about how technology creates new worlds, for good or ill. (pp. 191–192)

Developing a Curriculum Framework

In documenting the obstacles to the development of media education in the United States, Kubey (1998) contends that there is a lack of support from parents, as well as teachers and administrators, who want their children to be "computer literate" rather than "media literate." Traditionally, computer literacy has referred to one's technological proficiencies using particular software or hardware components or computer applications. Computer literacy prioritizes skills-based learning that emphasizes the technological medium over the process and objective of learning. Obtaining computer skills has often been associated with upward mobility within the realm of commerce and business. As Kubey explains, "parents believe that computer expertise can equal a leg up in the job market" (p. 60). While workplace concerns have long dominated American education, the merging of computer, information, and media literacy skills is long overdue. With the proliferation of computer-mediated information technologies in schools, students are faced with the challenge of learning not only how to acquire useful information through new technologies, but more importantly, how to critically analyze and evaluate information once it has been retrieved and deciphered. This critical learning process is only becoming more arduous with the proliferation of information forms and sources.

A curriculum framework for media literacy with technology can be built using the three multiple literacies offered by Meyrowitz (1998)— media *content* literacy, media *grammar* literacy, and *medium* literacy. Teachers can "help students become critical consumers of information through an experiential learning process that teaches both 'about' and 'through' media" (Quesada & Lockwood Summers, 1998). This requires teaching methods that encourage group dialogue through the use of questioning strategies aimed at encouraging the higher levels of cognitive learning outlined in Bloom's taxonomy. In order for critical autonomy or independent critical thinking to be attained, students must be motivated to learn for the sake of personal empowerment, rather than acquisition of marketable skills, through analysis, reflection, synthesis, and evaluation of media. Although Bloom developed these cognitive measures well before the widespread use of computer and the Internet in education, their relevancy remains. As Gilster (1997) explains, digital literacy requires "the ability to read with meaning and to understand" (p. 33) as it applies to the Internet. Just as Bloom established measures for learning competencies that enable learners to make informed judgments after a series of cognitive development processes, Gilster believes that cyber-cognition demands similar measures. He explains that making informed decisions about what is found online requires knowledge acquisition through developing and applying online search skills; that analysis and synthesis come from assembling knowledge "from diverse sources" using Internet tools; and that critical thinking must be developed "using the model of the electronic word— hypertext and hypermedia" (pp. 2–3).

Media Content Literacy

One of the most important elements of Internet access involves not only how much information we can acquire, but the quality of the information we receive. When using the Internet, three essential questions need asking in order to evaluate what we stand to gain with this new technology: (1) how well can we make discerning judgments about what we receive? (2) what ideas and issues are available on the Internet? and (3) what absences and silences exist, in other words, what is *not* to be found? Unfortunately, while there is accurate and important information accessible through the Internet, there is also much that is inappropriate for learning purposes. This is especially troubling for teachers. Crossman (1997) explains:

> [Many] teachers whose students use the Web are concerned about the question of authenticity and reliability of information on the Internet in general and the Web in particular. Even the most casual evening of Web surfing reveals incredible amounts of trivia, misinformation, bad manners, hostility, stupidity, and other vagaries of humankind. (p. 31)

Using Meyrowitz's (1998) media-as-conduits metaphor, Internet *content* literacy carefully considers the value and reliability of information acquired online. While few education models apply content literacy to the Internet, library media specialists have been in the forefront of devising content literacy skills enabling students to question the veracity of the information they receive online. Drawing from Grassian's University of California, Los Angeles, College Library online resource (2000), there are many analytical questions to be asked when thinking critically about discipline-based Internet resources. The majority of these questions are center on content and evaluation.

The information source. One of the first evaluative questions for web resources investigates the information provider or source. By asking who the originator, creator, or author of a website (or email) is, students can determine if a website represents a group, an organization, an institution, a corporation, or a governmental body. At the root of this question are concerns regarding the reliability and representativeness of the information acquired. Teachers would want their students to look at the URL address provided on the home or front page of the site in order to get clues as to whether the information comes from a trustworthy institution, such as a school or university, or whether it is from an anonymous individual whose credibility would need verification. It would be advisable for students to verify the qualifications of content authors, sponsors, or supporters. Students would want to find out if the website is officially or unofficially endorsed or sponsored by particular groups, organizations, institutions, and the like, as this again impacts the credibility of the information acquired.

Influences on content. The next set of evaluative questions aims to discover if the website or email describes or provides the results of research or scholarly effort. In terms of basic research skills, it makes sense for teachers to instill in their students a curiosity regarding whether or not there are sufficient references provided to other works to document hypotheses, claims, or assertions. By asking if there is enough information to properly cite the document, students can decide if the information they have found is appropriate for a research report. Students would want to know if the website/email combines educational, research, and scholarly information with commercial or non-commercial product or service marketing, as this affects the underlying goals or objectives of the site.

By inquiring into the economic or political influences of Internet content, students should question whether the ratio of useful information to superfluous information is adequate. They would want to pay attention to the amount of advertising, as well as unrelated graphics or links, as these factors necessarily impact the content. For instance, if information on oral hygiene is provided by a toothpaste manufacturer seeking to influence brand-name loyalty, students should be more skeptical of the claims being made within the site. Other profit motives include fees for the use of access to any of the information provided at a site. Naturally, students would want to determine whether such fees are warranted or whether similar information could be found for free on other sites, or through other research tools. In terms of politics, students would want to discover the motives, values, and ideas influencing the content so that they can better sort through and evaluate the claims and assertions projected on a website.

Ideally, the purpose of a website should be clearly indicated. Since this is not always the case, further investigation through the use of evaluative questions helps students better determine the motivations of the content providers.

Timeliness. Finally, the timeliness of online information would need to be fathomed so that students could discern whether or not the study or research on the website/email is up to date. If the date of the information is not easily located within the content, students could look for the last update to the page or to the site, at the bottom of the front or home page. This enables students to judge the accuracy of the information presented based on their knowledge of recent scholarship, discoveries, or perspectives that would affect previous findings.

As Meyrowitz explains, content literacy skills are not exclusive to any medium per se, but are easily applicable from one medium to another. Students can employ these same evaluative questions in studying books, newspapers, magazines, television programs, and other texts. Certainly, Internet content presents some unconventional circumstances that set it apart from other research tools. Vast amounts of information are available on any given topic, allowing students more flexibility in conducting research than a school library might offer. Nevertheless, students must first figure out how to find the type of information they are looking for, which requires skills in conducting effective online excursions using various search engines. Whereas students can always go to a librarian or teacher for search tips or strategies, it is not always easy to figure out which Internet sites are worthy of perusal and which ones should be avoided. Librarians and teachers will still need to offer students online resources that help students find educational sites that are reliable and useful.

Media Grammar Literacy

While there is nothing prodigious in applying critical evaluative questions to the Internet, the critical study and utilization of the Internet is distinctive in terms of its media grammar and form. For this reason, media literacy in cyberspace must go beyond online *content* literacy by addressing the peculiarities of the Internet as a communication technology. Media *grammar* literacy for the Internet requires an understanding of the production elements used to alter people's understanding of messages communicated electronically. As such, teachers would want their students to learn graphic design principles so that they better understand how web pages are created or infused with carefully crafted signifiers. Vibrant colors, large or unusual fonts, flashing text, striking visuals, and music, used to draw or divert attention, need to be decoded so that students ascertain the function, intention, or goal served by the graphics, icons, and design elements.

Subsequently, the basic elements of graphic design, usually reserved for art or vocational curricula, need to be integrated across the curriculum so that students can better comprehend how various production elements work to signify or connote particular meanings in cyberspace. Since the Internet is necessarily nonlinear in form, there are many design elements used to feature certain areas, visuals, or links. Whether these elements are used for business, educational, or civic means, students would want to evaluate the creativity and effectiveness involved in the structural design of the message by examining: (1) what media elements are being used for communication (i.e., words, pictures, sounds, videos, animations, etc.) and (2) how content is organized (i.e., through user-controlled hypertext or hypermedia links).

As a component of media *grammar* literacy, visual literacy theory has been used to encourage students to produce and interpret *visual* messages. In *Visual Messages: Integrating Imagery into Instruction*, Considine and Haley (1992) explain that like traditional literacy, visual literacy embraces what might be termed a reading and writing component (p. 15). Students can be taught to recognize, read, recall, and comprehend visual messages. Accordingly, students who understand the design and composition of visual messages can better communicate through visual means. With the rapid increase in student-designed web pages, design elements converged around Internet technology are becoming more necessary. By using the components of visual literacy that have been applied to audio, moving images, and still graphics, students can better think *about* and *through* the images and multisensory components of the Internet.

Medium Literacy

Media grammar literacy, or visual literacy, includes an understanding of the *medium* and the message, the form as well as the content. In terms of the Internet, *medium literacy* would require students to examine the variables previously described in Meyrowitz's (1998) multiple literacies model, and those extrapolated from Meyrowitz's sample medium variables. In particular, Internet technology impacts: (1) the multisensory types of information conveyed, as it conveys messages through visual, aural, and textual means; (2) the uni/bi/multidirectionality of the communication, which is affected by Internet postings, email correspondence between individuals, and chat-room discussions between two or more people; and (3) the speed and degree of immediacy in encoding, dissemination, and decoding, which are altered by the Internet's instantaneous message transmission and its ability to bring otherwise disjointed individuals or groups together in non-face-to-face encounters. One of the most important applications of medium theory would lead students to examine how message variables, both content and visual, are uniquely acquired and represented in cyberspace. Students must learn to question whether the information they find is unique to the Internet or is available through print and other non-Internet resources. This inquiry leads students to understand the potential of the Internet as a decentralized form of technology, because it greatly increases the amount of information and perspectives (both dominant and nondominant) available on any given topic. This presents creative opportunities for students to find ideas and messages that infrequently unfold in mainstream media. Moreover, through user-controlled hypertext or hypermedia links, students can "interactively" determine what informational course they want to navigate. Educational prospects such as these can only unfold in the critical thinking classroom whereby students are encouraged to discover, compare and contrast, and critique the messages communicated through computer information technology.

Cyberliteracy Lessons in Critical Thinking

According to Richard Paul and Linda Elder, directors of the Center and Foundation for Critical Thinking, "critical thinking is the kind of thinking—about any subject, content, or domain—that improves itself through disciplined analysis and assessment" (Paul & Elder, 2001, p. 6). In their guide to developing and using critical thinking concepts and tools, they explain that if students are to gain skills in logic and critical thinking, they will need to: (1) identify important questions and problematize knowledge; (2) conduct research and analyze information and their sources; (3) make important judgments based on well-reasoned and tested conclusions and solutions; (4) examine the relationship between their methodology and biases in order to test their claims, inferences, and outcomes; (5) impart their findings through effective communication; and (6) address the implications of their research within the greater realm of ideas (p. 6).

Similarly, McPeck (1981) explains that:

critical thinking requires the judicious use of skepticism, tempered by experience, such that it is productive of a more satisfactory solution to, or insight into, the problem at hand. At least, this is why it is invoked . . . Learning to think critically is in large measure learning to know when to question something, and what sorts of questions to ask. (p. 7)

Most educators would agree that effective cyber-learning demands pedagogical and curricular approaches that foster critical thinking. However, as most employment of technology in the classroom prioritizes the medium over the message, or the means to online data over the purpose and method of information retrieval and assessment, critical thinking skills are not always fully developed or applied. As Roszak (1994) remarks, most educators treat the computer primarily as a means of instruction:

What they may overlook is the way in which the computer brings with it a hidden curriculum that impinges upon the ideals they would teach. For this is indeed a powerful teaching tool, a smart machine that brings with it certain deep assumptions about the nature of mentality. Embodied in the machine there is an idea of what the mind is and how it works. The idea is there because scientists who purport to understand cognition and intelligence have put it there. No other teaching tool has ever brought intellectual luggage of so consequential a kind with it. A conception of mind—even if it is no better than a caricature—easily carries over into a prescription for character and value. When we grant anyone the power to teach us *how* to think, we may also be granting them the chance to teach us *what* to think, where to begin thinking, where to stop. (p. 241)

These concerns are especially relevant given the vast changes that have taken place in educational learning and research. As more students learn through computers and conduct research online, whether at school or at home, the need for a systematic approach to establishing educational foundations like critical thinking remains essential. Subsequently, cyberliteracy demands the development and application of critical learning lessons that go beyond merely using technology for its own sake. Few resources have been devised to help students understand the constructed nature of Internet communication. As Quesada and Lockwood Summers (1998) explain, students need to realize that:

information presented in various print and electronic sources can have commercial, ideological, and political implications. This is critical awareness in American society where major television and publishing networks are controlled by a handful of corporations and more than half of the sites on the Internet are commercial. Of the Websites created other than for commercial purposes, many have their own agendas that motivate their designers to spread the word electronically.

In response to these concerns, Quesada and Lockwood Summers (1998) offer some important suggestions and strategies in critically engaging students with Internet technology. First, students need to understand that all media are symbolic sign systems that re-present (not reflect) reality (Masterman, in Quesada & Lockwood Summers). In order to better comprehend this concept, students can brainstorm the multiple sources of information about a particular event or issue by categorizing, reflecting upon, and discussing both the form (the format, such as TV) and the content (the actual text, images, sounds, and substance) of the message. By separating the variables of print and electronic sources, students can more readily understand how form and content are related in each medium. Once students have created a list of information sources, teachers should ask questions that help them deconstruct the production elements or media *grammar* used to create meaning. They would want to consider what media variables (words, pictures, sounds, video, animation, etc.) are used to communicate the message, and how the content is organized (linear or nonlinear, mass communicated or decentralized, interactive or noninteractive). Through small- and large-group discussions, students would want to discuss which media elements (words, pictures, animations, special effects, etc.) or combination of elements have the most impact, and why.

After expressing their media viewpoints and the experiences that impact their feelings and emotive responses, teachers would want to address *medium* literacy by having students think about the benefits and drawbacks of different forms of print and electronic communication. Quesada and Lockwood Summers (1998) offer a useful lesson in which students match the content of various informational sources to practical research situations. If they are looking for up-to-the-minute data, students should be asked if they are more likely to find it in a daily newspaper, a monthly magazine, or on the World Wide Web. If they want a historical view, are they more likely to find it in a book, print encyclopedia, CD-ROM reference tool, video documentary, or on web TV? Which sources provide local data? Which ones are more international in scope?

Taking Quesada and Lockwood Summers's lesson one step further, it would be important for students to consider which sources go beyond the mainstream, providing them with nondominant, alternative information that challenges the ideological, political, and economic motivations of data sources. Because students are not always aware of nonmainstream alternatives, teachers would want to provide students with multimedia resources allowing them to critically question and (re)engage with those sources they most frequently encounter. This leads to many useful lessons designed to encourage students to analyze and evaluate the significance and credibility of media forms. Students should be encouraged to go back to their comprehensive list of information sources in order to identify which resources (e.g., the nightly news) contain information that is prefiltered by experts, authorities, sponsors, and advertisers, and which ones are unfiltered (i.e., Internet chat rooms). Teachers would want their students to consider the validity of sources such as infomercials in which "experts" endorse a particular product (Quesada & Lockwood Summers, 1998).

One new resource for cyberliteracy lessons comes through the Center for Media Literacy—*Media Literacy: Thinking Critically about the Internet* (Paxton, 2004). This book includes units on the history and future of the Internet, the Internet and society, the Internet and business, and the Internet's affect on individuals. Specifically, Paxton examines the issues of cybercrime, hate sites, parental controls, blogs, and more, all useful in grades 6–12.

Another scholar who addresses literacy goals for the information age is Gunther Kress, who offers his own vision about the future of literacy programs through innovative curricula designed to help children excel at a time when social and economic changes abound. By paying close attention to visual imagery and multimodal approaches to communication, Kress explores the "semiotic disposition" of children in assessing how they respond to changes within our contemporary mediated environment (Kress, 1997). Likewise, Len Unsworth (2001) sets out to help educators improve student literacy skills through various texts by offering specific curricula designed to help students learn to analyze images, web pages, tables, and charts.

Not only is it important for students to learn to raise vital questions about visual imagery, signs, and meaning; they must be encouraged to harness the potential of cyber-learning, given the uniqueness of the Internet as a distributed network and information source. For many, the Internet has been influential in supplying otherwise unavailable data or knowledge in limited circulation. In the medical field, the Internet has been especially useful in connecting doctors, patients, and concerned family members within and across nations in efforts to share information about and advocate for alternative medical treatments. Concerned groups and citizens examining political and economic issues or controversies can find cyber-subcultural groups aiming to provide different narratives or explanations of events, perspectives, and historical documentation. For consumers, the Internet has been influential in helping people discover the wholesale prices of automobiles, appliances, furniture, and other consumable goods, as well as the best mortgage rates and real estate prices. Moreover, people can participate and interact more freely in cyberspace than in top-down, linear, mass modes of communication, through Internet postings, cyber-chat rooms, email, and web page design. In these capacities, the equation of "who knows what about whom through what media" is altered so that the public is theoretically able to access the same information as private corporations or institutions. Of course, proficiencies in computer skills and access to computer terminals affect access. But as Internet access continues to rapidly grow in schools, students need to go beyond cyber-savvy skepticism by learning to make use of the creative and informed possibilities provided by Internet technology and by contributing to the knowledge base themselves.

The Future of Educational Technology

With the growing interest in confronting the challenges presented by the emergence of new information technologies in schools and other learning environments, serious thought needs to be devoted to the multidimensional opportunities and obstacles presented by digital technology. Through media literacy centered on technological access *and* critical evaluation, this chapter has provided evidence for, and strategies designed to deal with, educational technology. Teachers, educational administrators, and students are in need of a theoretical and pragmatic foundation that provides hands-on learning lessons encouraging knowledge *about* and *through* new information technologies.

Moreover, while much communication and educational research focuses on the effective (or ineffective) application of new information technologies to the improvement of reading or writing comprehension, as well as other standard competencies, we need to continue to challenge the very essence of the learning process by critiquing those institutional forces aiming to offer a packaged curriculum through marketable skills rather than through creative and effective curricular applications. Roszak (1994) reminds us that we are deceiving ourselves if we believe that getting children to use computers at an early age necessarily leads to the mastery of knowledge. Rather, children need to learn to think in scientifically sound ways (p. 242).

In the 1998 special media literacy issue of the *Journal of Communication*, Christ and Potter highlighted the importance of posing three main questions associated with curriculum, all of which apply to both K-12 and higher education. They are: (1) What is the purpose of the curriculum? (2) How should media literacy fit into the curriculum? and (3) What are the key elements or principles of media literacy that should be taught? It is through the questioning of school culture that pedagogical models will be designed to restructure the learning process as well as the curricular content. By encouraging teachers to be more flexible in determining the process and outcome of the learning experience, the methods herein allow teachers to guide students through the effective use of group dialogue and questioning strategies, thereby encouraging students to: "a) be pensively deliberative; b) synthesize concepts and ideas; and c) critically interrogate the political, economic, and symbiotic factors impacting media and society" (Christ & Potter, 1998, p. 8).

Similarly, while the field of educational technology has emerged in response to the growing realization that teachers are using more audio-visual and information technology, related research delineates a hybrid area of study through its focus on the critical uses of electronic forms of literacy, not for the sake of technology alone, but for the purposes of providing students with lifelong literacy skills (Tyner, 1998, p. 58). Among the limited resources delineating a web-based curriculum, too few have considered the curricular ideas and strategies espoused in this chapter, or addressed the higher levels of cognitive development that lead to an understanding of the signification of meaning. Tyner (2003), advocating the inclusion of "digital literacy" in the curriculum, concludes,

In the best possible world, learners will be "power users" who can strategically manipulate the full complement of communication tools to access information, to create and amplify their own messages, and to participate fully and dynamically in the social arena. (p. 384)

Despite the findings and gains supported by the present research, further excursions are necessary to continue to address the importance of developing media literacy in cyberspace. Hence a comprehensive account of the current uses of educational technology is necessary in order to discover additional local, national, and global media literacy approaches and practices. As Tyner (1998) explains, many more perspectives are needed to shape the debate about the specific uses of new and emerging communication technologies if teaching and learning are to be responsive to students who live in a world awash with information (p. 71). Accordingly, coalitions and alliances between educators, public leaders, and citizens are needed in order for some consensus to evolve about the role of technology within and outside education. Moreover, as Nixon (2003) suggests, researchers need new topics and new methods for inquiry into literacy in a digital world as young people participate in live chats, play computer games with others, and engage in video-conferences over the web.

If computer technologies are to live up to their potential, more people must learn about, and learn about effectively using, the Internet while there is freedom to do so. If teachers, administrators, parents, and citizens care deeply about the future of the medium that enables us to assemble worldwide through computer conferencing and homepages, we will need to reconsider educational theories and practices designed to include new technologies in schools. To exclude philosophical and pedagogical reforms in the ways we teach about and use technology is to ignore the deep human implications that come from privileging media rather than content, and style over substance. Basic social, political, philosophical, and moral questions remain, questions that will affect the quality of human life. Can we have freedom of information and still protect children from online predators? How should we respond to racist hate groups on the Internet? Whose information on which websites is reliable and useful? At a time when students need to become empowered citizens concerned about the implications of technology for accessibility, privacy, democracy, and globalization, we must ensure that children understand not just how, when, and why to use technology, but perhaps more importantly, the differences between their connections with machines and their connections with humanity and the world.

REFERENCES

Alvermann, D.E., & Hagood, M.C. (2000). Critical media literacy: Research, theory, and practice in "new times." *The Journal of Educational Research, 93*(3), 193–205.

Anderson, R.E., & Becker, H.J. (2001). *School investments in instructional technology* (Report No. 8). Irvine and Minneapolis: University of California, Irvine and University of Minnesota, Center for Research on Information Technology and Organizations.

Apple, M. (1993). *Official knowledge: Democratic education in a conservative age.* New York: Routledge.

Apple, M., & Weis, L. (1983). *Ideology & practice in schooling.* Philadelphia: Temple University Press.

Bundy, A. (1997, August 3). *Pedagogy, politics, power: Preaching information literacy to the unconverted.* Keynote address on Information Literacy to the Catholic Teacher Librarians, New South Wales. Retrieved from http://www.library.unisa.edu.au//papers/infolit1.htm

Cattagni, A., & Farris Westat, E. (2001). *Internet access in U.S. public schools and classrooms: 1994–2000* (Report No. 2001–071). Washington, DC: U.S. Department of Education.

CEO Forum on Education & Technology. (1999, February 22). *School technology and readiness report: Professional development: A link to better learning* [Electronic version]. Washington, DC: CEO Forum.

Christ, W.G., & Potter, W.J. (1998). Media literacy, media education, and the academy. *Journal of Communication, 48*(1), 5–15.

Considine, D., & Haley, G. (1992). *Visual messages: Integrating imagery into instruction.* Englewood, CO: Teacher Ideas Press.

Crossman, D. (1997). The evolution of the World Wide Web as an emerging instructional technology tool. In B.H. Khan (Ed.), *Web-based instruction* (pp. 27–42). Englewood Cliffs, NJ: Educational Technology Publications.

Cuban, L. (2001). *Oversold and underused: Computers in the classroom.* Cambridge, MA: Harvard University Press.

Frechette, J. (1997). The politics of implementing media literacy into the United States: A look at the objectives and obstacles facing the Massachusetts public school teacher. Unpublished masters thesis, University of Massachusetts, Amherst.

Freire, P. (1989). *Pedagogy of the oppressed.* New York: Continuum.

Freire, P. (1998). *Pedagogy of freedom: Ethics, democracy, and civic courage.* Lanham, MD: Rowman & Littlefield.

Garner, R., & Gillingham, M.G. (1996). *Internet communication in six classrooms: Conversations across time, space, and culture.* Mahwah, NJ: Lawrence Erlbaum Associates.

Gilster, P. (1997). *Digital literacy.* New York: Wiley Computer Publishing.

Giroux, H. (1998). Race and the trauma of youth. In H. Giroux (Ed.), *Channel surfing: Racism, the media, and the destruction of today's youth* (pp. 1–17). New York: St. Martin's Press.

Giroux, H. (2000). *Stealing innocence.* New York: St. Martin's Press.

Grassian, E. (2000). *Thinking critically about World Wide Web resources.* UCLA College Library Online Resources: Retrieved from http://www.library.ucla.edu/libraries/college/help/critical/index.htm

Kress, G. (1997). *Before writing: Rethinking the paths to literacy.* London: Routledge.

Kubey, R. (1998). Obstacles to the development of media education in the United States. *Journal of Communications, 48*(1), 58–69.

Lankshear, C., Peters, M., & Knobel, M. (1996). *Critical pedagogy and cyberspace.* In H. Giroux, C. Lankshear, P. McLaren, & M. Peters (Eds.), *Counternarratives: Cultural studies and critical pedagogies in postmodern spaces* (pp. 149–188). New York: Routledge.

Leveranz, D., & Tyner, K. (1993, August/September). Inquiring minds want to know: What is media literacy? *The Independent,* 21–25.

Luke, C. (2001, November). New times, new media: Where to media education? *Media International Australia Incorporating Culture and Policy*, 101, 87.
McKinsey and Company. (1995). *Connecting K-12 schools to the information superhighway*. Retrieved October 12, 2004 from http://cavern.uark.edu/mckinsey/
McLuhan, M. (1964). *Understanding media: The extensions of man*. New York: McGraw-Hill.
McPeck, J. (1981). *Critical thinking and education*. New York: St. Martin's Press.
Means, B., Haertel, G., & Roberts, L. (2004). *Using technology evaluation to enhance student learning*. New York: Teachers College Press.
Meyrowitz, J. (1998). Multiple media literacies. *Journal of Communication, 48*(1), 96–108.
Nixon, H. (2003). New research literacies for contemporary research into literacy and new media? *Reading Research Quarterly, 38*, 407–413.
Paul, R., & Elder, L. (2001). *How to study and learn a discipline: Using critical thinking concepts and tools*. Dillan Beach, CA: The Foundation for Critical Thinking.
Paxson, P. (2004). *Media literacy: Thinking critically about the Internet*. Lincoln, NB: GPN Educational Media.
Postman, N. (1995). *The end of education*. New York: Alfred A. Knopf.
Quesada, A., & Lockwood Summers, S. (1998). Literacy in the cyberage: Teaching kids to be media savvy. *Technology & Learning, 18*(5), 30–36.
Roszak, T. (1994). *The cult of information*. Berkeley: University of California Press.
The President's Committee of Advisors on Science and Technology & Panel on Educational Technology. (1997, March). *Report to the president on the use of technology to strengthen k-12 education in the United States* [Online]. Retrieved from http:// www.whitehouse.gov/WH/EOP/OSTP/NSTC/PCAST/k-12ed.html
Tyner, K. (1998). *Literacy in a digital world: Teaching and learning in the age of information*. Mahwah, NJ: Lawrence Erlbaum Associates.
Tyner, K. (2003). Beyond boxes and wires: Literacy in transition. *Television & New Media, 4*, 371–388.
Unsworth, L. (2001). *Teaching multiliteracies across the curriculum: Changing contexts of text and image in classroom practice*. Buckingham, UK: Open University Press.
U.S. Congress, Office of Technology Assessment. (1995). *Teachers and technology: Making the connection (OTA-HER-616)*. Washington, DC: U.S. Government Printing Office.
U.S. Department of Education. (2000). *e-Learning: Putting a world-class education at the fingertips of all children*. Retrieved November 2, 2004 from http://www.ed.gov/ Technology/elearning/e-learning.pdf
U.S. House Committee on Commerce and Committee on Education and the Workforce. (1998). *Education and technology initiatives* (ISBN Publication No. 0-16-057671-7). Washington, DC: U.S. Government Printing Office.

CHAPTER 7

The Shadow Curriculum

PAMELA U. BROWN

The common thinking about the meaning of *curriculum* is simple. The average person, having been to school, is comfortable using the word and in doing so probably equates curriculum with planned content to be covered in a school setting. If asked, Americans would likely agree that elementary curriculum includes reading, arithmetic, and perhaps science and social studies; some may add physical education and fine arts. The notion of secondary curriculum is even more straightforward with its demarcation of specific courses, most falling into the basic areas of language arts, mathematics, science, or social studies. Though this accepted usage of *curriculum* is contested by curriculum scholars who seek both to deepen and to broaden its meaning, the scholars often— after carefully articulating their own views regarding the meaning of *curriculum* and pointing out logical fallacies or weaknesses in other possible definitions—fall into the habit of using the term themselves, at least occasionally, to mean *a course of study*.

When academics in curriculum studies or the social foundations of education use modifiers for the word "curriculum," we begin to acknowledge a more complex understanding of curriculum itself. Phrases such as *the hidden curriculum*, *the null curriculum*, or *the lived curriculum*, once considered, begin to make sense to those who ponder the lives of teachers and students in school. Using such modifiers describes curriculum more precisely through what is missing: that which is not a part of the public plan, or the way in which the planned curriculum is always altered by the presence of and interaction with students.

Another descriptive phrase to pinpoint an aspect of curriculum, only recently coming into use, is *the shadow curriculum*. Environmentalists on college campuses first used the term to differentiate universities' stated positions regarding renewable resources from their actual practices, which are often in opposition to the institutions' public statements (see, e.g., Kelly, 2003). *Shadow curriculum* has also been adopted by some in the field of media literacy (Media Education Foundation, 2003) to describe an aspect of the hidden curriculum centering on marketing to students in school. The underlying message of those who support commercialism in schools is that such marketing is both acceptable on its face and desirable for making direct connections between business enterprises and public schools. The term *shadow curriculum* is used by those who question the assumption that direct selling to students who are compelled to attend school is questionable on several levels—ethical, moral, and democratic.

This chapter will explore the shadow curriculum and its connection to media literacy, first summarizing the kinds of marketing in schools that have become commonplace, including exclusive sales agreements between school districts and businesses, advertisements posted in schools and buses, and advertising forced on students and teachers through mandated television viewing. It will then move to a more in-depth examination of the shadow curriculum as it affects teachers' decision making regarding curriculum, when such decision making is directly affected by the marketing of curriculum packages to teachers and administrators in public schools. Often the curriculum packages, whether sponsored by corporations intent on promoting a particular point of view or by education companies (who all too often *also* promote a particular point of view), are multimedia productions that include books, CDs, and websites as part of their package. The methodology of looking closely at two specific curriculum packages, Saxon Math and the character education and school discipline program Great Expectations, will use the tools of media literacy, following Thoman's questions for teaching students media literacy (see Thoman & Jolls, Chapter 10, this volume).

The Shadow Curriculum: Business, Schools, and Marketing

Selling to Students

Once upon a time, schools in the United States were not *publicly* assessed using a business model with charts, graphs, competitive comparisons based on the bottom line, and a constant demand for scientifically based "proof" of the benefit of one practice versus another. Less publicly, however, schools and their "outcomes" have long been intertwined with business and corporate interests. One of the goals of education since the late 1800s has been "sorting and training the labor force" (Spring, 1994, p. 18); indeed, back in 1913 one prominent educator complained about what he perceived as unfair criticism by the business community, commenting:

If the various departments of the business world could thus state in specific terms the kind of educational product that it desires in the workers that come to it, it would be performing a far more valuable service than the present method of complaining that the schools are not turning out what they want, when, as a matter of fact, they have never told the schools exactly what they do want. (Bobbitt, 1913, p. 36)

Vocational education, comprehensive high schools, and tracking are all manifestations of corporate influence on American schools. Scientific management based on factory models has held sway over the years (Callahan, 1962). More recently *A Nation at Risk* (1983; see also Berliner & Biddle, 1995) argued that we would lose the global economic war if our schools did not return to a corporate-based rigor, and some today would contend that the No Child Left Behind Act is a direct descendant of the turn of the century scientific management approach.

Business has always had a hand in schooling, but today, corporations and companies are much more upfront about directly expressing educational opinions and shaping educational agendas, via their involvement in business roundtables, civic organizations, and other school reform vehicles. The language of business has now become integral to how we think about schools as words like *value*, *accountability*, *failing schools* (rather than students who fail courses or grade levels), and *cost/benefit ratio* have become part of the national education dialogue.

The more obvious shift is in how businesses have moved directly into schools to conduct business, taking advantage of the continuing limitations of school funding and the increasing needs of students to swap marketing rights for cash. Providing universal education to students through grade 12 is certainly a costly proposition, and the need for weighing financial alternatives that affect school costs and funding is a given. Nonetheless, completely overlaying a business model onto all aspects of education may be inherently flawed. As Kohn (1997) declares:

Ultimately, the *goals* of business are not the same as those of educators. This simple truth . . . is one that educators forget at their peril—or, more precisely, at the peril of their students.

Corporations in our economic system exist to provide a financial return to the people who own them; they are in business to make a profit. . . . Thus, when business thinks about schools, its agenda is driven by what will maximize its profitability, not necessarily by what is in the best interests of students. Any overlap between those two goals would be purely accidental. (p. vi)

The means used by corporate America to determine the viability of for-profit enterprises has gradually been assigned to nonprofit schools. Educators, parents, school board members, the general public, and students themselves now take for granted more and more that the model for a successful business and the model for a successful school are more similar than not, so that increasing numbers of schools engage in practices of marketing and school superintendents frequently refer to themselves as CEOs (Emery & Ohanian, 2004). This, then, is the shadow curriculum.

Direct advertising in schools is so common that we hardly notice it anymore. It takes place through commercials on Channel One's mandated daily 12-minute TV sessions for millions of secondary students, through advertising on sports scoreboards sold to local businesses, through mandated textbook covers provided by local businesses, through printed advertisements posted on the insides and/or outsides of school buses, and through advertising space on school walls sold to various businesses. Such unapologetic marketing goes virtually unnoticed, partly because of its widespread presence. The message is clear: schools need money and equipment and businesses are willing to pay to market to the "captive audience" (Media Education Foundation, 2003) of students.

Marketing in schools in and of itself is not necessarily negative. Rather, it is the failure to scrutinize such decisions using the tools of a media literate society that needs to be called into question. School representatives must ask questions seeking out the underlying message and the potential effect on student thinking, and examining the critical interface between marketing and the goals of education. The benefits of bringing media literacy—for students, teachers, administrators, and parents—into the process of responding to marketing proposals should be exercised.

Schools as Consumers

Districts routinely sign contracts with soft drink companies to offer only designated brands in vending machines and at all school functions. These "pouring rights" agreements and other exclusive contracts between corporations and schools are increasing rapidly. Molnar's (2004) documenting of the number of media references to such exclusive contracts recorded a 122% increase in the past year, with references to such agreements having risen by 858% since 1990 (p. 17). Participating schools see the financial benefit as outweighing the health issues, in spite of the fact that the American Dental Association has taken a public stand against "pouring rights" agreements (American Dental Association, 2003) and the American Academy of Pediatrics has issued a policy statement calling for a ban on soft drink sales in schools altogether (American Academy of Pediatrics, 2004).

Agreements between business entities and schools are now everyday occurrences. For example, in July 2004 two suburban districts in Tulsa signed a contract with a local bank to sponsor the annual football game between the districts' powerhouse high schools. The regular season high school football game typically draws 30,000 fans, and the two districts will receive $5,000 to $7,500 each (to be used for an "academically related entity") in return for naming the game after the bank, in the fashion of National Collegiate Athletic Association bowl games. The winning team will be presented a trophy at midfield by bank executives, and the bank will be free to "display interior and exterior promotional signs and advertising at all or some elementary schools, middle schools, and high schools in the two districts" (Cooper, 2004, p. A–9). These are two of the largest, most affluent school districts in the state, and this agreement could display advertising on school walls to 96,000 students and their teachers at 25 school sites for two years.

The pervasiveness of soft drink availability has become such that some schools allow students to consume their beverages in classrooms. In one case, an Oklahoma high school social studies teacher related that he recently punished a group of students for tardiness by restricting them from bringing soft drinks to his class (S. Jenkins personal communication, July 12, 2004). The teacher was quickly reprimanded by an assistant principal, because prohibiting students from purchasing from the vending machines violated the district's contract with the soft drink company. One media literacy writer points out that while federal officials

worry about marijuana use and keeping liquor and cigarette ads a certain distance away from schools—not necessarily ill-conceived concerns—Pepsi has brazenly walked right in the front door, virtually unnoticed. It has turned your kid's computer into a digital billboard, has succeeded in associating its name with a child's thirst for knowledge, and has made the public educational system that much more dependent on and vulnerable to privately held corporations. (Peters, 1998)

Board members of Tulsa Public Schools, the largest district in the state, are selling advertising space inside school buses. Blake Lund, president of Bullfrog Busboards, Inc., displays banners "like very large bumper stickers" above the windows of Tulsa school buses (Eger, 2003,

p. A–4). The district could make as much as $500,000 per year from the agreement placing ads inside buses ridden by 18,000 students daily.

Schools feeling financial pressure as they seek to increase student and teacher access to updated technology may sign up with Network-Next to receive a mobile computer cart to show PowerPoint and other multimedia presentations. In 2001, 500 schools entered into such contracts, and the hardware and software provided include banner ads on every PowerPoint slide displayed. Products advertised include Rock Star video games, Visa cards, and Wal-Mart (Schor, 2004, p. 89).

A major marketer in schools is Channel One, a daily news and information program broadcasting to public schools that agree to show the broadcast to all students in 6th through 12th grades on 90% of school days. According to the contract, students must be sitting down, attentive to the television, and the sound cannot be muted. In return for requiring students to watch the 12-minute daily broadcasts, including 2 minutes of commercials aimed at teens, schools receive televisions for all classrooms (Channel One, 2004). About 12,000 U.S. secondary schools have signed contracts with Channel One, so eight million students watch.

The insidious effect of marketing in schools is played out in a number of ways, one of the most troubling being students' perceptions of advertising aims. According to a study in two Missouri school districts, ninth graders who watched Channel One did not see commercials as intended to make a profit. Instead, when asked, "Why do professional athletes make commercials?" their answers fell into four categories: 1) It motivates athletes to play better; 2) It's a reward for the athlete; 3) It helps the team; and 4) It enhances the athletes' status among peers" (Fox, 1996, p. 1). Surely some attention to media literacy could help adolescents recognize the financial motive behind commercial advertising.

Marketing in schools is not new. West (1985) surveyed groups of school board members, school administrators, and professors of educational administration and found that educators were "becoming increasingly inclined to adopt a marketing view of education" and that "marketing is one aspect of a total PR [public relations] program" (p. 16). What is changing is the amount of marketing *in* schools. According to Molnar (2003),

The increase in commercialism in schools is taking place as schools confront tight budgets. Because schools across the country face budget shortfalls, they have taken such steps as holding a fundraising telethon (in Jefferson Parish, LA) and hiring full-time fundraisers (Grapevine, TX). (p. i)

Media literacy for teachers and administrators is not keeping pace. As commercialism in schools increases, at least one study indicates that school administrators are becoming less aware of the trend. According to Feuerstein (2001), who surveyed public school principals in Pennsylvania, 74.7% of respondents reported little or no marketing in their schools, though 41.8% reported their schools had contracts with Channel One. Apparently these Pennsylvania administrators, like the Missouri ninth graders, failed to see a connection between commercial advertising and marketing.

Selling to Teachers

A part of the shadow curriculum that often goes unnoticed is commercialism aimed at teachers. Curriculum packages are designed to appeal to teachers who are generally overburdened and underpaid. Promises made by those who market the packages are extensive, while evidence to support their educational worth is often scanty. The popularity of various curriculum packages is in keeping with Giroux's (2000) notion of the business model of education, what he calls *corporate education*, which he asserts is not truly educative:

Corporate education opposes . . . a critical approach because it cannot be standardized, routinized, and reduced to a prepackaged curriculum. On the contrary, a critical and transformative educational practice takes seriously the abilities of teachers to theorize, contextualize, and honor their students' diverse lives. It is far removed from a corporate educational system based on an industrial model of learning that represents a flagrant violation of the democratic educational mission. (p. 91)

Corporations directly sponsor some curriculum materials. A former English teacher who now operates Youth Marketing International is paid by corporations to find them market niches in schools, and she "gets clients by keying in on social trends and current events, especially those she feels are underrepresented among existing school materials, and then approaching those companies whose products are relevant" (Schor, 2004, p. 92). As curriculum is generally slow to change and often does not keep pace with social trends, there are always niches not addressed by traditional curriculum materials, including textbooks. Those sponsoring the creation of such curriculum materials, written by the many authors who compete for the work, include Revlon, Campbell Soup, Gushers snacks, Sunkist oranges, Kellogg's breakfast cereal, American Greetings, Scholastic, *My Weekly Reader*, Court TV, Exxon,

Mobil, Chevron, Procter & Gamble, and the countries of Israel and
Saudi Arabia (Schor, 2004).

Even curriculum materials designed by organizations that appear
purely educational display particular viewpoints and stances. I have
chosen to analyze two: Saxon Math, a widely adopted prescriptive curriculum package in a particular content area, and Great Expectations
of Oklahoma, a regionally popular curriculum package not dealing with
a particular content area, but rather aimed at character education and
school climate. Saxon Math and Great Expectations, like all texts and
curriculum packages, contain messages about what is true, what is right,
and what behaviors and thinking students should engage in. Using a
media literacy approach can help deconstruct the marketing of the
curriculum packages themselves, and Thoman's (Chapter 10, this
volume) five questions provide tools to enable this deconstruction. The
key questions are:

- Who created this message?
- What creative techniques are used to attract . . . attention?
- How might different people understand this message differently
  from me?
- What lifestyles, values, and points of view are represented in, or
  omitted from, this message?
- Why is this message being sent?

Though the questions are designed for students who are becoming
media literate, they can also serve adults seeking to bring their unconscious reactions to media texts and messages into the forefront of their
own thinking, through examining the texts themselves along with information about their creation and their creators. For purposes of this
analysis, three foci presented by Thoman's questions will be used to
examine these two curriculum packages:

- *Apparent purpose*—why was this package created?
- *Attention-getting techniques*—what means are used by the designers to draw the attention of teachers and administrators?
- *Point of view*—what perspectives are represented (or left out)
  about teaching and learning?

Curriculum Package: Saxon Math

Through its website at http://www.saxonpublishers.com, the publisher of several content-specific curriculum packages for kindergarten
through 12th grade claims, "Saxon Math is the nation's best selling and

most thoroughly researched skills-based mathematics program for grades K-12" (Saxon Publishers, 2002–2003). Headquartered in Norman, Oklahoma, Saxon began in 1981 and is now part of Harcourt Achieve Publishing of Austin, Texas. References to the federal No Child Left Behind Act are present on almost every page of the website, and schools can even "apply for grants and funding to assist in the purchase of Saxon products that meet the requirements of [NCLB]." Besides Saxon Math, the website offers materials on its other curriculum packages, including phonics and spelling, early learning, and physics. The publisher claims, "Saxon exclusively employs former educators to sell and service our programs. . . . They are not 'sales people'—they are teachers—and they can relate to the daily challenges educators face in the classroom" (Saxon Publishers, 2002–2003).

Apparent purpose. The apparent purpose for the marketing of the Saxon Math curriculum package to teachers and schools is to sell materials. Before the company's sale to Harcourt Achieve in June 2004, the stated purpose for the company's founding was "to help children learn from an early age" so that "these Saxon students could be tomorrow's astronauts, doctors, scientists or teachers" through "a greater understanding of basic concepts that leads to higher-level thinking, increased self-esteem and greater self-confidence" (Saxon Publishers, 2004). However, since Saxon Publishers became a part of Harcourt Achieve, which is in turn part of the multinational corporation Reed Elsevier, the lofty rhetoric became more market driven, though the curriculum package itself remains unchanged. According to the parent company, the purpose of Harcourt Achieve is to provide "supplemental educational materials" (Reed Elsevier, 2004). Harcourt Achieve is designed to supplement another branch of Reed Elsevier's education initiative, Harcourt School Publishers, which is "the leading U.S. elementary (K-6) publisher with particular strength in the four major subject areas of science, reading, math and social studies" (Reed Elsevier, 2004). Saxon Math has apparently become a supplemental program to Harcourt School Publishers' existing mathematics series.

Attention-getting techniques. Even at first glance the Saxon School Catalog (2004) is traditional. The background of the book's cover is lined paper reminiscent of ruled notebook paper. The contrasting bold text states, "A legacy of proven results, a future of promising success" with the words "proven results" and "success" in significantly larger type than the rest. Three-color photographs of elementary-age children are lined up neatly in a column. Among the four children pictured, there appear to be three ethnic groups represented. All smiling, the children are engaged in classroom work, with textbooks and commercially produced math posters in the background. The largest word on the cover is "Saxon." The catalog includes information on K-12 math, phonics and spelling, and early learning curriculum packages. The overall message of the cover design is that Saxon is serious, but students are happy learners. All the children are wearing solid colors, not uniforms, and all are neatly groomed. Each page inside the catalog contains multiple colors of text, photographs, and graphs—many graphs. The table of contents and introduction pages include a horizontal timeline placed near the bottom of the pages highlighting years of Saxon Publishers events such as the development of the middle grades math series and the completion of the new warehouse and distribution center (complete with a small photograph of a large, well-lit room filled with shelves stacked with materials). Emphasis is on the longevity of the corporation, assuring teachers and administrators that Saxon is not a fad. The large photograph of the Saxon Publishers Corporate Headquarters shows a plain brick three-story building. It looks institutional with little attention to landscaping or ornament of any kind. Featured prominently is a large U.S. flag flying on a very tall flagpole that puts the bottom of the flag well above the top of the building.

The rest of the catalog is also colorful, with a small amount of informational text on each page. All graphs included are vertical bar graphs illustrating increased test scores after the adoption of Saxon programs in various school districts in Nebraska, Colorado, New York, Tennessee, Illinois, and Arizona. Many pages also include text boxes in large fonts with quotes from Saxon users about its benefits. Schools represented by quotes are in California, Washington, DC, New York, Texas, and Florida. Near the end of the catalog is a two-page spread with names and contact information for 58 Saxon educational representatives who cover all 50 states, with more than one representative in California, Florida, New York, and Ohio. Each name is followed by a toll-free phone number and an email address through the saxonpublishers server. At the bottom of alternating pages throughout the catalog are a toll-free number and a web address.

Photographs of groups of Saxon materials are featured throughout, with photos of individual sheets and items used as examples of Saxon materials. Worksheets are titled "Fact Assessments," and assigned a number to indicate order of administration. A sample of an Individual Recording Form is also pictured; the second grade math assessment form is a summary sheet for four written assignments and includes a checklist for mastery of skills such as "shows one half of even number by sharing" and "draws line segment using centimeters" (Saxon Publishers, 2004, p. 17). One large colorful photo displays a jumble of math manipulatives for use in primary grades, including a large clock and several smaller clocks, dice, paper money, buttons, a thermometer, tiles and blocks, geo boards, and calculators. Containers for Saxon materials are pictured throughout the catalog. There are tins, tubs, buckets, folders, binders, boxes, and slip cases. All are apparently color coded, labeled, and stackable. Some have wheels.

Also pictured is a teacher's manual bound with a large spiral so that it can be folded back on itself showing only one page. Providing more than suggested activities, the manual includes detailed information on lesson preparation, vocabulary, learning objectives, instructional notes, and skills tracers that "track math concepts across past, present, and future lessons" (Saxon Publishers, 2004, p. 26). A text box highlights the format of each daily math lesson in grades four through eight: "warm up, new concept, lesson practice, and mixed practice" (p. 27).

New additions to the catalog, labeled with a large gold star with the word "new" in red capital letters, include an "intervention teaching guide," "intervention reference guide," and "test preparation and practice" (pp. 30–31). An optional item available for purchase is a software package labeled a "test and practice generator," compatible with Windows and Macintosh. The heading of this two-page spread is "Everything You Need to Ensure Your Students Succeed in Math!"

Point of view. Saxon Math is designed to comfort teachers and administrators worried about their students' performance on standardized tests and/or worried about their own ability to teach math. Going far beyond a textbook with its explanations of concepts and accompanying problems, purchasing the Saxon Math programs fills classrooms with materials. For example, for each fifth grade classroom in schools purchasing the program, the teacher receives a set of manuals, assessments and classroom masters, a solutions manual, answer key transparencies, test and practice generator software, and instructional transparencies for a total cost of $710. A student edition is $45 and a student workbook is $6 (Saxon Publishers, 2004, p. 37). A set of math manipulatives including protractors and rulers is newly available.

The point of view represented by Saxon Math holds teachers as having (or deserving) little freedom in determining the progress, the pace, or the activities best suited to teaching math. Saxon Math is a unique combination of manipulative materials, which are often associated with child-centered teaching (Moyer & Jones, 2004), together with a daily teacher-proof lesson format. The presence of the manipulatives and the overwhelming amount of material making up the Saxon program may be a co-opting of the notion of child-centered teaching. The scripted nature of the teacher's manual and the prescribed daily lesson format makes it clear that Saxon is a content-centered program, designed to assure teaching conformity. Some teachers and administrators may desire such conformity and uniformity; however, those seeking to adopt a new math program should be cognizant of marketing techniques such as these as they make curriculum decisions. An understanding of media literacy will help teachers look beyond colorful manipulatives with a critical eye toward underlying messages. Media literacy does not promote nor prescribe any particular viewpoint; however, it does promote taking a critical stance toward the purposes of those who would influence teachers, students, administrators, and curriculum.

Curriculum Package: Great Expectations

For teachers and administrators new to the program, the curriculum package called "Great Expectations" begins with a four-day training program held in the summer at several regional institutions of higher education in Oklahoma (Great Expectations of Oklahoma, 2004). Described as "a professional development program that provides teachers and administrators with the skills needed to create harmony and excitement within the school atmosphere" and claiming to improve student scores on norm-referenced tests, the Great Expectations of Oklahoma Foundation claims its teacher training program is "an answer for all schools, regardless of size, geographic location, student demographics, or economic base" (Great Expectations of Oklahoma, 2004; http://www.greatexpectationsok.org). With such a broad, positive claim, it is hard to imagine why the character education program designed to affect school climate has not been more widely implemented in the United States.

Apparent purpose. In examining Great Expectations of Oklahoma (GE), the largest and oldest example of the GE teacher training programs, the stated purpose is visible on every page of the organization's website. The phrase, "transforming education to help students learn," is posted prominently on the left-hand side of each page, while each page ends with a small graphic of the program's logo, an outline of a large tree containing the trademarked "Great Expectations" script text and the phrase, "Tall oaks from little acorns grow . . . ." This graphic is on each page, superimposed over a photo of two globes with a background chalkboard containing a glimpse of vertical arithmetic problems and in the foreground a small stack of books with a pair of wire-rimmed round spectacles on top.

The apparent purpose of Great Expectations is to improve school climate through attention to the role of the teacher; this improvement is linked to "academic excellence," apparently as demonstrated by a 1999 study compiling norm-referenced test scores at the third and seventh grade levels in 31 schools. The study is listed as "Supporting Research," though it is only summarized briefly (Great Expectations of Oklahoma, 2004). Far more attention is devoted to selected quotes from teachers and administrators of GE schools that reflect anecdotally on their students' academic improvement following implementation of GE. The stated mission of GE is, "Great Expectations is dedicated to providing professional growth opportunities for preservice and practicing educators designed to build the knowledge and skills needed to motivate, inspire, and challenge students to achieve excellence in learning and living" (Great Expectations of Oklahoma, 2004).

Founded in 1991 by Charles Hollar, a retired insurance executive from Ponca City, Oklahoma, GE claims not to prescribe the content to be taught, but rather focuses on "the HOW of teaching." GE is characterized by lists—six basic tenets, seventeen classroom practices, life principles represented by "words of the week," the "magic triad" (a smile, a kind touch, and a kind word), a host of inspirational quotations, and even a book list of suggested motivational readings for GE teachers (Great Expectations of Oklahoma, 2004). The six tenets address: (1) high expectations; (2) positive teacher attitude and acknowledged teacher responsibility for student learning; (3) the ability of all children to learn; (4) self-esteem; (5) the importance of mutual respect; and (6) the need for teacher knowledge and skill.

A less obvious purpose for the program is its ability to generate income for the five institutions of higher education that sponsor summer workshops in Great Expectations methodology for teachers and for the GE Foundation. The basic cost per teacher attending the four-day workshop is $350 in Oklahoma and $400 for out-of-state training sessions. The Oklahoma legislature supports GE through state funding of grants to teachers, and in 2003–2004 the funding level for the 118 schools receiving grants was $694,000 (Great Expectations of Oklahoma, 2004). This funding supported teacher scholarships to attend summer workshops along with "two follow-up sessions for teachers and administrators, and the services of a Great Expectations mentor who provide [sic] on-site implementation support" (Great Expectations of Oklahoma, 2004). Of the 118 schools receiving state support during the 2003–2004 school year 12 are high schools, 12 are middle schools or junior highs, and 94 are elementary schools. The GE website also offers promotional products for sale, all prominently displaying the program's logo. Thirteen different items are offered, including various pens, highlighters, cups, notepads, a whistle on a chain, and a teacher sweatshirt with the GE logo on front and a U.S. flag with the words "United We Stand" and "Great Expectations" on the back (Great Expectations of Oklahoma, 2004).

Attention-getting techniques. The GE of Oklahoma website has been frequently updated over the past few years, and its current iteration is colorful, with lavender-trimmed pages and many photos of smiling children and teachers in various school settings. Also included are several photos of teens in caps and gowns, apparently to draw attention to the program's use in secondary schools. On some pages the photo morphs into one of six or eight pictures, so that staying on a page for several minutes will present all photos. The website contains a great deal of text, and pages vary in design, amount of text, and section headings.

The GE website offers a great deal of information but also shows some gaps. For example, there are references to "eight expectations for living" and "life principles" but they are not listed. However, all 17 classroom practices are listed on several different pages within the site, once with a rubric for judging level of teacher implementation (from "model implementer" to "resistant implementer") and once with explanatory text for each of the 17 along with a list of "supporting research" articles in a reference list (Great Expectations of Oklahoma, 2004). Additional information regarding program details is listed on unlinked websites of individual GE teachers or schools (see, e.g., Owens, 2004 for an explanation of the "magic triad—a smile, a kind touch, and a kind word").

Of particular note is the use of "supporting research" on GE on its website. The term "research" is used to mean any related publication whose stance supports GE recommended practices. For example, essays from *Education Digest* and *PTA Today* are included in a list of "supporting research" for classroom practice #13, "A school, class, or personal creed is recited or reflected upon daily to reaffirm commitment to excellence" (Great Expectations of Oklahoma, 2004). For each of the 17 recommended classroom practices the site lists six "supporting research" documents; these include the *Christian Science Monitor*, *Teaching PreK-8*, *Instructor*, *Family Life*, and William Bennett's *The Book of Virtues*.

Probably of most importance to classroom teachers considering attending GE training are the claims for improved student behavior and academic performance. However, in these areas there is very little supporting evidence offered beyond anecdotal statements from teachers and administrators who have implemented GE in their schools. Teachers who are attracted to GE may be unconcerned with the sketchy nature of the research base; this is in keeping with the notion that classroom teachers in general see little connection between their own teaching and educational research (Zeuli & Tiezzi, 1993).

Also designed to attract teachers is the GE combination of traditional practices (like memorized recitations) with constructivist language calling for a classroom environment conducive to student intellectual risk-taking. While teachers are encouraged by GE to act as facilitators, they are also told to "require excellence in every detail" (Great Expectations of Oklahoma, 2004). This dichotomous and philosophically contradictory view may appeal to some teachers for its very eclecticism, as recounted in Cohen's (2001) description of one teacher's adoption of a hands-on mathematics teaching model:

The old and new lay side by side, and so the fabric of instruction was different. However, there seemed to be little mutual adjustment among new and old threads. Mrs. O used the novel concrete materials and physical activities, but used them in an unchanged pedagogical surrounding. Consequently the new material seemed to take on different meaning from its circumstances. (p. 446)

Point of view. The point of view of GE is shaped by an eclectic combination of conservative underlying messages and the child-centered teaching techniques found in many national standards documents (e.g., Bredekamp & Copple, 1997; National Council of Teachers of Mathematics, 1991). GE tenets, for instance, call for several practices associated with child-centered teaching, including the teacher serving as a "facilitator of learning" and one who helps students build self-esteem. The tenets also encourage the teacher to foster a classroom climate conducive to risk-taking by students as they grapple with new material. The climate described in GE materials is one of mutual respect "in which mistakes are seen as opportunities to learn and . . . ideas and efforts are appreciated" (Great Expectations of Oklahoma, 2004). Some of the 17 classroom practices promulgated by GE are similarly progressive in nature, including an emphasis on teaching critical thinking skills and teachers remaining physically active in the classroom, moving around the room continually, in order to engage students in the learning at hand (Great Expectations of Oklahoma, 2004).

However, beneath these nods to learner-centered approaches lies a basic faith in traditional teacher-centered, content-oriented practices. One of the hallmarks of GE is in its requirement of daily recitation of, or reflection on, a creed, written either by a school, a classroom, or an individual. The daily return to the creed is designed to "reaffirm commitment to excellence" (Great Expectations of Oklahoma, 2004). Creeds in GE are serious business, similar to the recitation of the Pledge of Allegiance. Even GE teachers as a group have a creed:

I am a teacher. I accept the challenge to be sagacious and tenacious in teaching every student because I believe that every student can learn. I accept the responsibility to create a learning environment conducive to optimum achievement academically, socially, and emotionally. I actively pursue excellence, for my students and myself. I provide a model of decorum and respect that guides my students as well as honors them. I affirm superlative expectations for my students and myself. I cherish every student. I am a teacher. I change the world, one student at a time. (Great Expectations of Oklahoma, 2004)

Sample creeds from several schools or classrooms also appear on the website. The class of 2000 of Lomega High School in Lomega, Oklahoma, wrote the following creed:

We are the class of 2000. We are loved, and we appreciate our families and teachers. We are proud of our accomplishments. There is no one we would rather be. We believe the choices we make today affect what we will have, what we will be, and what we will do in the tomorrows of life. We are determining what we will become. We have integrity and high moral standards. We stand up for our convictions. We will be good role models for our fellow students at Lomega High School, and we will continue to be leaders in the future. We will never give reason for anyone to doubt our characters. Our futures are our responsibility. The challenge to make the future great for each of us is in our own hands. We accept the challenge. We will succeed. We will utilize every day given to us to the fullest, realizing we will never have another shot at today, right here, right now. We seize the day! (Great Expectations of Oklahoma, 2004)

Even a brief look at these creeds reveals a point of view that reflects a desire for students who accept responsibility for their circumstances, who appreciate adults, and who make personal choices that minimize the likelihood of teen pregnancy, drug use, or violence; likewise teachers will "provide a model of decorum and respect" as they "cherish each student" (Great Expectations of Oklahoma, 2004). Point of view can also be gleaned from what is left out of these creeds. There is no mention of equity or fairness, kindness or justice, open-mindedness or flexibility. There is no mention of forgiveness or individuality.

The fact that the GE program requires creeds may be indicative of a nostalgic wish for bygone days, remembered imperfectly as a time when students were obedient and accepted adult authority. Spring (1994) summarizes the position of 19th-century U.S. educator Horace Mann, who saw schools as places for "the proper training of young children so that they would not desire or perform criminal acts" (p. 13). This position, over a century old, seems analogous to the GE motto, "Tall oaks from little acorns grow." Similarly, Mann's statement, "Manners easily and rapidly mature into morals," is directly connected to the GE emphasis on training students in middle-class manners, requiring each classroom to have a designated greeter—a student who will answer the door to any visitor, shake hands and ask for the person's full name, and then introduce that person to the teacher and the rest of the students (Great Expectations of Oklahoma, 2004).

Schools implementing GE at the highest level and earning the designation "model school" have teachers who "establish procedures for speaking in complete sentences and addressing one another by name" (Great Expectations of Oklahoma, 2004). This stress on manners may be comforting to today's teachers and administrators because of increased reporting of school violence. A similar stance was taken by the Louisiana state legislature in 1999, which passed a law requiring students to address all adult school employees as "ma'am" or "sir" and to use honorific titles when calling adults by name. Louisiana State Senator Don Cravins sponsored the legislation in an attempt to reduce school violence, saying he was impressed by similar rules for state prison inmates: "I've seen how polite and well-mannered the young inmates are" (Baron, 1999, p. 45).

Though the GE program states that it does not prescribe what to teach, but rather how to teach, one content area is specifically addressed: language arts. The seventh GE classroom practice states: "Memory work, recitations, and/or writing occur daily. These enhance character development and effective communication skills while extending curricula. Recitations are exuberant and full of expression" (Great Expectations of Oklahoma, 2004). Even after looking through the "supporting research" for this practice, it is difficult to make a cause–effect link between memory work/recitations and character development. The relegation of writing to an equivalent status with memory work and recitations also indicates a set of beliefs consistent with a conservative approach. In the implementation rubric used by GE mentors to judge a teacher's level of implementation of the program, there are nine observable characteristics related to the seventh class-room practice, but only one of them refers to student writing: "Teacher engages students in journal writing each day." Far more attention is given to the need for teachers to provide students with "character-building poetry and quotes designed to build social competence" and other examples of teachers giving students material to read and discuss rather than encouraging students to write (Great Expectations of Oklahoma, 2004). Teaching phonics is also called for, with activities encouraged by classroom practice #11: "Word identification skills are used as a foundation for expanding the use of the English language" (Great Expectations of Oklahoma, 2004). "Supporting research" for this class-room practice includes articles on phonemic awareness.

Another example of the point of view of Great Expectations is the use of "wisdom literature" drawn from "classic literature, myths, fables, poetry, proverbs, quotes, and other genres" (Great Expectations of Oklahoma, 2004). The philosophy represented is essentialism, in keeping with Hirsch's (1999) explanation of the need for shared knowledge called *cultural literacy*: "No one would claim that possession of main-stream cultural knowledge is a *sufficient* condition for intellectual ability and financial prosperity, but it may often be a necessary condition for them" (p. 12). There are also a list of quotes for use in classrooms, divided into categories such as relationships, mistakes, perseverance, and success and excellence (Great Expectations of Oklahoma, 2004). Many of the quotes are anonymous, while attributed quotes are overwhelmingly from white male Americans from history, including Thomas Jefferson, George Washington, and Benjamin Franklin. There are some quotes from non-Americans and a few from women. Some come from ancient Greeks and Romans, and several are from the plays of Shakespeare. Represented sparingly are quotes related to caring, love, flexibility, or questioning the status quo.

Concluding Thoughts

Selling curriculum packages to schools is big business, and those who are in the business of marketing these packages rely on techniques that speak to their target audience—the teachers and administrators in the schools that buy their materials. Teachers in general do not match the cultural demographics of their students. Gordon, Della Piana, and Keleher (2000) comment on their study of the demographic characteristics of U.S. teachers:

The teaching corps of Chicago and Miami, the only cities where fewer than half the teachers were white (49% and 37% respectively), came the closest to matching their students' demographics. It was not unusual, as in Austin, Texas, for the proportion of African American and Latino students to be double the proportion of teachers of the same race. Of all the cities surveyed, Providence, Rhode Island had the biggest mismatch between students and teachers: almost half the students were Latino, compared to only 5% of teachers. Los Angeles had a striking disparity with only 22% of the teacher corps and 69% of the student body being Latino. (p. 19)

No doubt marketers are aware of this cultural divide between students and their teachers. It is no accident that both Saxon Math and Great Expectations market the promise of student-centeredness with a foundation of conservative, traditional values. The faces of culturally marginalized students appear in the promotional materials, but the values represented by both curriculum packages serve to perpetuate social adaptation, not social transformation.

The role of media literacy for teachers is an important one. Rather than dictating choices to be made when choosing curriculum materials, critical media literacy can help teachers and administrators see beyond the surface messages carefully planned to appeal to teachers (and administrators) as a whole. Media literacy includes not only looking at curriculum materials, but also examining the school environment itself, including the curriculum, the hidden curriculum, and the shadow curriculum. As Horn (2003) notes, teachers should "present their own critical interrogation of the hidden curriculum of selected cultural artifacts" (p. 299). However, teachers should not just ask students critically to interrogate the cultural messages surrounding them, but teachers should themselves engage in such critical interrogation. One aspect deserving of critical attention is certainly the decisions teachers make regarding curriculum packages—their evaluation, their purchase, and their implementation. Using the categories of *apparent purpose*, *attention-getting techniques*, and *point of view* to examine critically the media messages sent by curriculum marketers is a beginning.

REFERENCES

American Academy of Pediatrics. (2004). Policy statement: Soft drinks in schools. *Pediatrics, 113*(1), 152–154.

American Dental Association. (2003, February). ADA weighs in on school vending machines. Retrieved September 28, 2004, from http://www.ada.org/public/media/ releases/0202_release02.asp.

Baron, D. (1999). To sir or ma'am, with love? *Education Week, 19*(1), 45.

Berliner, D.C., & Biddle, B.J. (1995). *The manufactured crisis: Myths, fraud, and the attack on America's public schools.* New York: Longman.

Bobbitt, F. (1913). Some general principles of management applied to the problems of city-school systems. In F. Bobbitt (Ed.), *The supervision of city schools: The twelfth yearbook of the National Society for the Study of Education*, Part I (pp. 7–96). Bloomington, IL: Public School Publishing Company.

Bredekamp, S., & Copple, C. (Eds.). (1997). *Developmentally appropriate practice in early childhood programs* (Rev. ed.). Washington, DC: National Association for the Education of Young Children.

Callahan, R. (1962). Education and the cult of efficiency. Chicago: The University of Chicago Press.

Channel One. (2004). *About Channel One.* Retrieved September 4, 2004, from http:// www.channelone.com/common_about/.

Cohen, D.K. (2001). A revolution in one classroom: The case of Mrs. Oublier. In *The Jossey-Bass reader on school reform* (pp. 440–469). San Francisco: Jossey-Bass Press. (Reprinted from *Educational Evaluation and Policy Analysis, 12*(3), Fall 1990).

Cooper, J. (2004, July 13). Banking on the Jenks-Union grid matchup. *Tulsa World.* pp. A–9, 13.

Eger, A. (2003, October 12). Commercials in buses could "ad" up quickly. *Tulsa World.* pp. A–1, 4.

Emery, K., & Ohanian, S. (2004). *Why is corporate America bashing our public schools?* Portsmouth, NH: Heinemann.

Feuerstein, A. (2001). Selling our schools? Principals' views on schoolhouse commercialism and school–business interaction. *Educational Administration Quarterly, 37*, 322–371.

Fox, R.F. (1996). *Harvesting minds: How TV commercials control kids.* Westport, CT: Praeger.

Giroux, H.A. (2000). *Stealing innocence: Corporate culture's war on children.* New York: Palgrave.

Gordon, R., Della Piana, L., & Keleher, T. (2000). Facing the consequences: An examination of racial discrimination in U.S. public schools. Report of the Applied Research Center, Race and Public Policy Program, Oakland, CA. Retrieved September 6, 2004, from http://www.arc.org/erase/FTC4demo.html.

Great Expectations of Oklahoma. (2004). Great Expectations of Oklahoma: Homepage. Retrieved July 26, 2004, from http://www.greatexpectationsok.org/.

Hirsch, E.D. (1999). *The schools we need and why we don't have them.* New York: Anchor Books.

Horn, R.A., Jr. (2003). Developing a critical awareness of the hidden curriculum through media literacy. *Clearinghouse, 76*, 298–300.

Kelly, T. (2003). Building a sustainable learning community at the University of New Hampshire. *The declaration: Publication of the university leaders for a sustainable future, 6*(2). Retrieved July 13, 2004, from http://www.ulsf.org/pub_declaration _othvol62.htm.

Kohn, A. (1997). The 500-pound gorilla. In A. Kohn (Ed.), *Education, Inc.: Turning learning into a business* (pp. v–xxii). Arlington Heights, IL: Skylight.

Media Education Foundation. (2003). Captive audience: Advertising invades the class-room. [Video production]. United States: Author. Retrieved from http://www.medi-aed.org.

Molnar, A. (2003, October). No student left unsold: The sixth annual report on school-house commercialism trends. Commercialism in Education Research Unit of the Education Policy Studies Laboratory. Report #EPSL-0309-107-CERU. Retrieved from http://edpolicylab.org.

Molnar, A. (2004, September). Virtually everywhere: Marketing to children in America's schools. Commercialism in Education Research Unit of the Education Policy Studies Laboratory. Report #EPSL-0409-103-CERU. Retrieved from http://edpolicylab.org.

Moyer, P.S., & Jones, M.G. (2004). Controlling choice: Teachers, students, and manip-ulatives in mathematics classrooms. *School Science & Mathematics, 104*(1), 16–31.

National Council of Teachers of Mathematics. (1991). *Professional standards for teaching mathematics.* Reston, VA: National Council of Teachers of Mathematics.

Owens, D. (2004). Great expectations: Tall oaks from little acorns grow. Retrieved September 5, 2004, from http://www.angelfire.com/ok4/owens/ge.htm.

Peters, C. (1998). The politics of media literacy: What's this new movement all about? *Z Magazine, 11*(2), 25–30. Retrieved July 13, 2004, from http://www.zmag.org.

Reed Elsevier. (2004). Reed Elsevier-Education. Retrieved from http://www.reedelsevier.com.

Saxon Publishers. (2002–2003). Welcome to the Saxon Publishers website: http://www.saxonpublishers.com.

Saxon Publishers. (2004). Saxon school catalog: 2004 [Electronic version]. Retrieved January 18, 2004, from http://www.saxonpublishers.com/prices/catalog/.

Schor, J.B. (2004). *Born to buy: The commercialized child and the new consumer culture.* New York: Scribner.

Spring, J. (1994). *American education* (6th ed.). New York: McGraw-Hill.

Thoman, E., & Jolls, T. (2005). Media literacy education in the USA: An overview of the Center for Media Literacy. In G. Schwarz & P.U. Brown (Eds.), *Media literacy: Transforming curriculum and teaching. The 104th yearbook of the National Society for the Study of Education, Part I* (pp. 180–205). Malden, MA: Blackwell Publishing.

West, P.T. (1985). To sell or not to sell: Marketing in the public schools. *Catalyst for Change, 15*(1), 15–17.

Zeuli, J.S., & Tiezzi, L.J. (1993). *Creating contexts to change teachers' beliefs about the influence of research.* (Report No. NCRTL-RR-93-1). East Lansing, MI: National Center for Research on Teacher Learning. (ERIC Document Reproduction Service No. ED364540).

Part Two
DOING MEDIA LITERACY IN THE SCHOOLS

<small>CHAPTER 8</small>

The Canadian Experience: Leading the Way

JOHN J. PUNGENTE[1], BARRY DUNCAN[2], AND NEIL ANDERSEN[3]

> Such countries as England, Australia, and Canada are a decade ahead of the United States in training teachers and implementing media literacy across the curriculum.
>
> —(Thoman, 2003, p. 602)

Media literacy educators from the United States regularly pay homage to their colleagues in Canada (see, e.g., Considine, 2002; Ferrington & Anderson-Inman, 1996; Megee, 1997; Minkel, 2002). Canadians have talked about, thought about, taught about, and written about media literacy for many years. Canada first hosted a World Conference in media literacy in Guelph, Ontario, in 1990, and all provinces in Canada now include media literacy in the curriculum. The media literacy movement in Canada has been around since the late 1960s, beginning with stand-alone credits in media study, and taking off in the 1980s as the result of a concerted effort by educators and media creators. Because of Canada's proximity and links to the United States and its leadership in media literacy, we provide in this chapter an overview of the Canadian experience in media literacy from our perspectives as Canadian media educators. Some of the most interesting stories in North American media education are, indeed, Canadian.

To understand Canadian media education, we must first recognize some of our special collective character traits, as well as our relationship

---

[1]John J. Pungente, SJ, is Executive Director of the Jesuit Communication Project in Toronto and President of the Canadian Association of Media Education Organizations. [2]Barry Duncan founded the Association for Media Literacy in Toronto and is currently a media educator in Islington, Ontario. [3]Neil Andersen is an Instructional Leader for the Toronto District School Board, Toronto, Ontario, and a media education consultant.

to our southern neighbor. Former Prime Minister Pierre Trudeau likened living next to the United States to a mouse that sleeps next to an elephant: every time the elephant turns over, the mouse has to run for cover to avoid being crushed. Is it any wonder that Canadians have such a nagging, ambivalent relationship with their American cousins? On the one hand we love American brashness, the sense of adventure and risk taking and, above all, the popular culture. On the other, we occasionally publicly denounce Yankee arrogance and imperialism, and we resist the dominance of American media.

As a country whose population of some 30 million (there are more people in the state of California than in all of Canada) is mostly contained in a narrow band that stretches for some 4,000 miles across a continent, we are painfully aware of the importance of communications. We have made some major contributions to communications technology (the creation of the Anik satellite and Telidon); media theory (Innis, 1952; McLuhan, 1964, 1967; Smythe, 1981); and media production (The National Film Board, the Canadian Broadcasting Corporation, and our film industry, to say nothing of such media exports as Peter Jennings, William Shatner, and Mike Meyers of *Austin Powers*). One of the most multicultural countries in the world, our large cities such as Toronto and Vancouver will soon have more visible minorities than the erstwhile white mainstream population.

The launching of media education in Canada, which has come to include mandated media education in the curriculum, came about for two major reasons: (1) our critical concerns about the pervasiveness of American popular culture, and (2) our system of education across the country, which fostered the necessary contexts for new educational paradigms. This chapter offers an historical overview of the development of media education in Canada, the theory informing Canadian practice, common classroom practices and approaches, comments about some significant resources, and conclusions and implications for future work.

The History

The first wave of media education began in the late 1960s under the banner of "screen education." The Canadian Association for Screen Education (CASE) sponsored the first large gathering of media teachers in 1969 at Toronto's York University. As a result of budget cuts and the general back-to-the-basics philosophy, this first wave died out in the early 1970s; but because scattered small groups of media educators persisted, media education steadily regained momentum in the 1980s and 1990s. Curriculum reform in the 1990s brought collaboration on the development of curriculum frameworks in core subject areas— through the Western Canadian Protocol for Collaboration in Basic Education (WCP) in the West and the Atlantic Provinces Education Foundation (APEF) in the East—resulting in media education being granted official status as part of the curriculum.

During this time, definitions and purposes for media education finally coalesced, and the generally accepted definition of media literacy in Canada was developed for the Ontario Ministry of Education in 1987. Pungente (1996) reports, "According to this definition the media literate person is one who has an informed and critical understanding of the nature, the techniques and the impact of the mass media as well as the ability to create media products" (p. 9). Besides educators, others also sought to bring media literacy to public awareness. The Vancouver-based Media Foundation began publishing *Adbusters* magazine in the 1990s. *Adbusters* not only creates parodies of ads but also established World Buy Nothing Day (the Friday after American Thanksgiving) and TV Turn-off Week (in April). The National Film Board of Canada (NFB), the Knowledge TV Network, Pacific Cinematique, the International Development Education Resource Association, and Media-Watch have all worked to educate Canadians about the media and to encourage Canadian cultural expression in the media. Efforts in the schools accelerated through the 1990s, and by 2000 there was new growth in elementary and secondary school media education, as media education became a mandated part of the English Language Arts curriculum across the country.

Canada's 10 provinces and 3 northern territories are each responsible for their own education system. Snapshots of the histories of Canadian media education from Central Canada, Western Canada, and Atlantic Canada follow. Additional information about the work in the provinces and territories can be found at http://www.media-awareness.ca/english/teachers/media_education/index.cfm, the Media Awareness Network's (MNet) site that describes provincial overviews and media education outcomes.

Central Canada

Ontario. Central Canada (Quebec and Ontario) contains over half of Canada's population. Ontario, where over one-third of Canada's population live, was the first educational jurisdiction in North America to make media education a mandatory part of the curriculum. In 1989 Ontario's Ministry of Education released new curriculum guidelines that emphasized the importance of teaching media education as part of the regular English curriculum. In 1995, the Ontario Ministry of Education more specifically outlined what students are expected to know and when they are expected to know it; these expectations are captured in areas defined as Listening and Speaking, Reading, Writing, Viewing, and Representation, and are primarily found in Language Arts classes. Further revisions to the Language Arts curricula in 1998 extended media education as a required part of the curricula beyond Grades 1–9 to include Grades 10–12.

At the secondary level, an optional stand-alone credit in Grade 11 tends to be taught by teachers keenly interested in media studies, and allows for in-depth exploration of media. This credit proved to be somewhat controversial but survived attempts at elimination by the government in 1996. Currently, the expectations for media study materials are sufficiently broad enough that teachers can insert any relevant examples to cover them.

The Association for Media Literacy. One group, the Association for Media Literacy (AML), is primarily responsible for the continuing successful development of media education in Ontario. There were 70 people at the AML's founding meeting in Toronto in 1978; by the end of the 1980s, the AML had over 1,000 members and a track record of distinguished achievements. For example, in 1986, the Ontario Ministry of Education and the Ontario Teachers' Federation invited 10 AML members to prepare a *Media Education Resource Guide* for teachers. This 232-page guide is used in many English-speaking countries and has been translated into French, Italian, Japanese, and Spanish. It provides a brief overview of media theory, followed by various classroom activities for teachers; the guide also outlines the eight key concepts (see below) that have been adopted by a number of media education enterprises in the United States (see, e.g., Thoman, 2003). Several other provinces used this guide as a foundation for their own media studies documents. In addition, since 1987, AML members have presented workshops across Canada and in Australia, Japan, Europe, Latin America, and the United States.

On their website, the AML publishes *MEDIACY*, a web clearinghouse that updates AML members on events and news, lists new publications in the field, announces speakers and topics for quarterly events, and publishes articles on related topics. The AML has sponsored think tanks and media education conferences since its founding. It also organized the very successful Summit 2000: Children, Youth, and the Media, an international conference held in Toronto in May 2000. For the 1,500 delegates from 55 countries, Summit 2000 was a unique opportunity for media educators to meet and talk with those who produce and distribute media. The AML's efforts paved the way for other provinces to lobby for media literacy and to develop their own curricula.

Quebec. The Quebec Ministry of Education embarked on a multiyear curriculum reform project in the 1990s. The new curriculum, called the Quebec Education Program (QEP), is a blueprint for classroom practices and student learning content for the English, French, and native communities. The QEP is divided into subject areas (Languages, Social Sciences, Science and Mathematics, etc.) and Broad Areas of Learning. Media education is one of these Broad Areas of Learning, and as such is studied across the curriculum and integrated into other subject areas. It is the responsibility of each teacher, regardless of subject or level taught, to integrate media education into his/her teaching.

The goal of media education as a Broad Area of Learning within the QEP (2001) is, "To develop students' critical and ethical judgment with respect to media and to give them opportunities to produce media documents that respect individual and collective rights" (p. 7). QEP acknowledges the omnipresence of both print and electronic media in daily life, as well as student use of media for purposes as diverse as entertainment, education, communication, creation, and work. It recognizes the conscious and unconscious development of individual, societal, and cultural ethics, values, and identity through media, while acknowledging the importance of students' reasoned ability to enjoy media.

Media education in Quebec is student centered, requires students to be active participants in their learning rather than passive receivers of knowledge, and is based on the development of competencies—both subject specific and cross-curricular. Through the development of these competencies, students should experience an integrated curriculum that is also connected to the world outside of the classroom. The QEP aims to develop lifelong learning skills such as problem solving, critical thinking, and the ability to build on and transfer knowledge to new situations and discoveries.

Each year more and more professional development programs and sessions in media education are offered at provincial conferences, school board professional day programs, and as part of in-school cooperative teaching team or team planning sessions in Quebec. Provincial groups offer professional development materials and programs for the support and teaching of media education in the QEP, including the Association for Media Education in Quebec (English); the *Centre de ressources en éducation aux medias* (CREM) (French; http://www.reseau-crem.qc.ca/); and the Réseau Éducation-Médias (French and English; http://www.media-awareness.ca/francais/index.cfm). The Montreal-based Centre for Literacy (http://www.nald.ca/litcent.htm), which maintains an open resources collection on every aspect of media literacy, receives a large number of requests for resources on media education.

Western Canada

British Columbia has emerged as the leader in media education in Western Canada (which also includes Alberta, Saskatchewan, Manitoba, The Yukon, Nunavut, and the Northwest Territories). In 1991, a group in Vancouver formed the Canadian Association for Media Education (CAME). This group has since been active in teacher education and in curriculum development, and created a media literacy framework, the *Conceptual Framework of Media Education*, which was incorporated into British Columbia K-12 curricula. This framework was also made available to the WCP, formed in 1995 for curriculum development by the four Western provinces and two territories (Nunavut joined the WCP in 2000).

The curriculum, known as the Western Canada Protocol Curriculum Framework, includes a mandated unit on media education that differs in content from province to province. Media education is a part of the common essential learnings and one of the supporting domains of the basic Language Arts structure. In core-content English courses, media studies are now required: video in Grade 10, radio in Grade 11, and print journalism in Grade 12. Differences reflect special needs or desired outcomes: Saskatchewan Education has mandated three additional options for Grade 11 English: Media Studies, Journalism, and Creative Writing. In the Northwest Territories, media literacy is a component of Performance Arts, which includes elements of sociology, literature, oral traditions, and the comprehension of different levels of meaning in oral, print, and media texts, for Aboriginal communities. The Territories also offer secondary students a Career and Technology Studies program. Ninety percent of Nunavet students speak Inuktitut/Inuinnaqtun, so the territory is in the process of adapting existing curricula to better suit their needs. Alberta is presently piloting and implementing the senior-high English Language Arts courses. Manitoba's Department of Education has completed a series of Foundation for Implementation documents to accompany their new curriculum. These documents provide teachers with suggestions for instruction, assessment, and learning resources to support the implementation of curricular outcomes and standards. Apart from the 56 specific student learning outcomes for each grade, nothing is prescribed; selection of learning/teaching approaches and learning resources is left to individual schools.

There is enthusiasm for ongoing updating of media studies resources by teachers, but there is a continuing need for formal teacher training. The resources in Western Canada are not as abundant as in Central Canada, and except for Vancouver, the population is also more spread out, making collaboration more difficult.

Atlantic Canada

In Atlantic Canada (Nova Scotia, New Brunswick, Prince Edward Island, Newfoundland, and Labrador) in 1995 an Atlantic Provinces initiative—similar to the Western Language Arts Consortium—developed a common Language Arts curriculum in which media education figures prominently and is mandated as part of every English course at elementary, middle, and high school levels. Learning is felt to be most effective when media education is integrated into a range of curricula, most notably in English Language Arts. The "Foundation for English Language Arts for the Atlantic Provinces" is the blueprint for Language Arts education, and the learning outcomes for each of the provinces are very similar (see http://www.media-awareness.ca/english/teachers/media_education/media_education_overview.cfm for more details on these provinces). Visual, media, and critical literacy are the components of the curriculum; each of these is clearly defined and teachers are offered ideas and suggestions, including encouragement for student production of media, for implementation.

Although media studies courses have been taught in some New Brunswick high schools since 1989, interest in media became more pronounced around 1999. Since then, professional development sessions have been offered on a regular basis at the New Brunswick Teacher's Association (NBTA) Subject Council Days. The New Brunswick Department of Education has sponsored two- and three-day-long summer institutes that also promote media awareness.

Mike Gange, a teacher at Fredericton High School in New Brunswick, a school where early media studies courses were piloted, was elected the first president of the new Association for Media Literacy in New Brunswick (A4ML-NB) in 2001. The members come from the various regions of this small, eastern Canadian province. Getting people together for an A4ML-NB meeting can be problematic, as the population of New Brunswick is quite spread out. Gange acknowledges that it is difficult to reach any kind of consensus among members with distance working against them, and teachers and curriculum specialists need closer collaborative relationships for increased effectiveness (M. Gange, personal communication).

The rise of media education in Canada reflects the determination of individuals and certain groups like the AML out of Ontario, and the importance of a national mandate to include media literacy in the curriculum, but it also reveals some of the problems facing media education. We will return to reflect on this history and what it tells us again at the end of this chapter. Another major player in the growth and development of media education in Canada, however, is the Canadian media themselves. Following is the story of media involvement in Canadian media literacy.

The Canadian Media and Media Education

In 1994 the Canadian media education movement got an important boost from the Canadian Radio-television and Telecommunications Commission (CRTC) and the NFB. At a two-day CRTC session for education and parent groups centered around the issue of children and television violence, representatives suggested that the NFB set up a clearinghouse of resources for media education. The result was the establishment of the MNet, which operated for two years under the aegis of the NFB and incorporated as an independent not-for-profit organization in 1996. The vision was clear: the MNet would be the first Canadian online media education organization. From the beginning, MNet was a bilingual organization, with "sister" websites in English and French. It would support and promote media education through online resources for adults—teachers, parents, librarians, community workers—so that they in turn could help young people develop critical thinking skills to "read" and better appreciate the media messages in their lives.

The Media Awareness Network

In 2002 and 2003, MNet redesigned its website to improve access to its bank of over 4,000 resources. The site attracted over three million unique visits in its first year, with approximately 85% of visitors making repeat visits in a given week. About a quarter of users come from Canada, the rest from the United States and around the world. The *For Teachers* section, produced by Jane Tallim, MNet's Director of Education, includes a searchable *Lesson Library* of nearly 300 teaching units linked to, and designed to fulfill, Canadian provincial media education outcomes K-12. The lessons are supported by the *Media Issues* section, which provides essays and current reference material on media-related topics such as stereotyping, violence, privacy, marketing to children, the portrayal of diversity in the media, and online hate. The section also features *Barry's Bulletin*, a popular culture digest for media educators.

In 2000 and 2001, MNet's research initiative, *Young Canadians in a Wired World* (Phase I), surveyed, for the first time in Canada, 1,100 parents and then 6,000 students on how young people are using the Internet and what they think about this use. In 2003, MNet conducted focus groups in Montreal, Edmonton, and Toronto in order to track the fast transformation of the Internet from a new technology to an accepted and central part of young people's lives. This research continues to inform MNet's education programs (see http://www.media-awareness.ca/english/special_initiatives/surveys/index.cfm for further information on the study). MNet staff members have addressed over 15,000 educators, librarians, parents, and government officials on media-related topics and have been invited to speak at events in Japan, Singapore, Germany, France, Argentina, Mexico, and the United States.

In collaboration with Canada's leading media educators, MNet is embarking on a new program, *Literacies for the 21st Century* (*Media Lit 21*). The aim is to take a cross-cultural, cross-curricular approach to media education, involving media educators, cultural institutions, and media industries, to address the digital media environment and culture. *Media Lit 21* is predicated on the elements required to give media education a "jump start," including a buy-in from Canada's media and cultural industries and governments and a professional development program for teachers (online and on CD). MNet has been fortunate in being financially supported by the public and private sectors, while maintaining complete control over its content.[1]

Concerned Children's Advertisers

Since its founding in 1990, the Concerned Children's Advertisers (CCA; http://www.cca-kids.ca) has developed over 35 child-directed television commercials on topics ranging from substance abuse prevention and active living to bullying and self-esteem, along with study guides to accompany each commercial. CCA offered workshops across the country, and in 1997, in association with the Jesuit Communication Project, produced its first media literacy public service announcement, "Smart as You."

Cable in the Classroom

Canada's *Cable in the Classroom* (http://www.cableducation.ca) provides a very useful resource for teachers from its 35 cable network participants. Each *Cable in the Classroom* program has been copyright-cleared for classroom use for at least one year from the date of original broadcast. Teachers are welcome to tape the commercial-free shows, usually in the early morning, and screen them for their students on an as-needed basis. Many of the broadcasts are accompanied by teachers' guides, often posted on the Internet.

CHUM Television

CHUM Television, a division of CHUM Limited, is one of Canada's leading media companies and content providers, which owns and operates 8 local television stations and 18 cable channels in Canada. CHUM Television's pioneering commitment to support and promote media education, undertaken since the mid-1980s, is unique among Canadian media companies. What began as an effort to make viewers more literate about what they watch by producing programs that explore the nature of screen-based content has grown into a wider support of Canada's media education community and related international conferences, campaigns, and activities. CHUM Television provides commercial-free, copyright-cleared original programming (and related study guides) free of charge for use in the classroom (http://www.chumlimited.com/mediaed), funds media education initiatives, and donates airtime and web space to the issue, in an effort to provide tools and resources to everyone and encourage a heightened awareness about the nature and role of the media.

Several of CHUM Television's conventional and cable channels produce media literacy and social issues programs: Bravo!, Canada's national arts channel, produces *Scanning the Movies*, an analysis of contemporary film hosted by media education scholar Father John Pungente, SJ. *MuchMusic*, Canada's only 24-hour music channel geared specifically to teens and young adults, creates programming that addresses media and social issues from a pop-culture, youth-oriented perspective. Programming examples include *Womaging*, a show about female body image and the media, and *Hip Hop Consciousness*, in which hip-hop artists discuss their efforts to effect positive change in their community and combat the materialism of mainstream hip hop. Citytv Toronto, Canada's largest independent television station serving the

Toronto area, produces *MediaTelevision*, a show providing in-depth analysis and critique of the media process.

Canadian media involved in media literacy efforts operate on the belief that the ability to better understand media should be a primary skill of all Canadians, and that broadcasters can and should play a role in encouraging this literacy as part of good corporate citizenship. They have played an important role in the history of Canadian media education. Educational theorists and scholars have also played a part.

The Theory

Canadian teachers are, like most informed media educators, participating in an eclectic circus. We are enthusiastic pragmatists, selecting from a rich menu of critical, cultural, and educational theories and filtering them for classroom use. Because of the small number of trained teachers, the majority use only snippets from a variety of sources: a few quotes from McLuhan, English studies, a diatribe from Neil Postman, a bit of Noam Chomsky, and the rest culled from resource guides, mass media text books, articles, television documentaries, and news programs.

As a generalization, there seems to be a consensus about contextualizing media education within the frameworks of the British-inspired cultural studies, an interdisciplinary approach to the construction of knowledge that problematizes texts and representations of gender, race, and class. The critical premises behind the *Media Literacy Resource Guide* and our media textbooks are compatible with comparable material emanating from Australia and the United Kingdom Of paramount importance is the influence of the discourses that are attached to the subjects that teachers are trained in, in most cases English/Language Arts. Robert Morgan found, in his 1997 survey of over 100 teachers of media in Ontario, that significant challenges to teacher media literacy effectively included literary biases, elitist or canonical cultural expectations, and traditional English classroom practices. To address these limitations, Morgan recommended that media teachers move beyond simple deconstruction by "acknowledging the individual, ambivalent, contradictory and shifting practices of media use, rather than attempting to suppress them through the assignation of stable and inherent textual meanings" (p. 121). He encouraged teachers to recognize the pleasures of media and reflect media consumption as an empowering rather than a victimizing behavior.

The primary concerns of Canadian media educators include transmission of the common key concepts underlying media literacy; the importance of audience; media and globalization; critical marketing; and media education and digital literacy. The key concepts are:

1. All media are constructions. Media are not simple reflections of external reality. They present productions that are carefully crafted.
2. The media construct versions of reality. Media messages come with observations, attitudes, and interpretations already built in.
3. Audiences negotiate meaning in media. Each of us interacts in unique ways to media texts based on such factors as gender, age, and life experiences.
4. Media messages have commercial implications. Media education includes an awareness of the economic basis of mass media production. The issue of ownership and control is of vital importance.
5. Media messages contain ideological and value messages. Media education involves an awareness of the ideological implications and value systems of media texts.
6. Media messages have social and political implications. Media education involves an awareness of the broad range of social and political effects stemming from the media.
7. Form and content are closely related in media messages. Making the form/content connections relates to the thesis of Marshall McLuhan that "The medium is the message."
8. Each medium has a unique aesthetic form. This enables students not only to decode and understand media texts, but also to enjoy the unique aesthetic form of each.

Audience. Awareness of audience is especially important in understanding the dynamics of youth culture. Audience study has foregrounded the importance of the pleasures of the text. It has helped us conceive of viewers as social subjects with multiple subjectivities. Similarly, texts are now seen as being polysemic—they convey many meanings and hence elicit many different readings. Audience study can lead us to learn about interpretive communities—electronic bulletin boards on North American television programs, websites containing information and gossip on daytime soaps, as well as prime-time programs. Of special interest is the phenomenal success of teen chat rooms for sharing ideas on writing new endings, and adding new characters for films and novels such as the Harry Potter stories.

When teachers examine their students' cultural practices through knowledge of audience theory, they cannot help but change the dynamics of their classrooms. Media can be seen as a symbolic resource that many adults, and probably even more young people, will use in making sense of their experiences, in relating to others, and in organizing the practices of everyday life. The emphasis on finding out what the students already know about media and how they make sense of it should be the starting points for all media teachers. The work of U.K. media educator David Buckingham (1990, 1993) and his colleagues (Buckingham & Sefton-Green, 1994, 2003) have contributed significantly to these understandings.

Globalization. The increasing trend toward globalization of culture has been fueled in part by transnational media corporations and recent mergers. These trends suggest some important theoretical and practical challenges to our notions of cultural sovereignty and democratic citizenship, and a need for new media education paradigms and interdisciplinary partnerships.

In the post-9/11 universe, our global village seems more intimate and at the same time, more frightening. Henry Giroux, an American educator and critical pedagogy advocate, points out, "Critical educators need to take up culture as a vital source for developing a politics of identity, community, and pedagogy. In this perspective, culture is not viewed as monolithic or unchanging, but as a shifting sphere of multiple and heterogeneous borders where different histories, languages, experiences, and voices intermingle amid diverse relations of power and privilege" (Giroux, 1992, p. 32).

Critically examining marketing. Media educators need to have informed perspectives on our right to democratic access to information, especially information that is constructed and disseminated by governments and corporations. In 1995, Len Masterman recommended a new paradigm for media education: teaching critical marketing. With public relations firms and media consultants being hired to create images of and engineer consent for politicians, policies, and programs, we have to be constantly vigilant for ourselves, and help our students see through the spin. An expanded consumerist definition of media literacy looks at the phenomenon of teen and tween marketing, the dynamics of brand images, and the success of organized resistance and culture jamming. Canadian Naomi Klein's (2000) groundbreaking study *No Logo* offers a road map for evolving a new media education paradigm—fighting the corporatizing of public space.

Digital literacy. The new and converging communication technologies have left many media educators behind as the computer and technology departments in our schools have tended to dominate the discourses of technology. Educators and technocrats tend to resort to our old paradigms of thinking borrowed from traditional media, thereby blinding them to new possibilities. The key concepts of media are certainly quite relevant to the digital technologies and the new literacies. Media educators need to critically examine the various discourses being played out, and they should be concerned about the issues around ownership and control, identity formations, and negotiation of meaning (Turkle, 1995).

The Practice

There are several approaches and roles for media education in Canadian classrooms. One of these is an ontological function in which students' relationship with fantasy, reality, one another, and the world can be sorted out. By identifying and examining values messages in media works, students are able to examine and prioritize their own values. Media education can also serve to enhance consumer awareness. Through an understanding of marketing concepts such as psychographics, demographics, and market share, students can come to an understanding of the role that the mass media play in their lives and their roles in the socioeconomic system.

Another perspective served by media education deals with citizenship, particularly as it compares to consumerism. Students can consider the roles of citizenship and how understanding media messages can help them be more effective citizens. A cultural perspective to media messages can be especially powerful. Considering issues of Canadian identity and American identity can further students' understanding of who they are and how they fit into their local and global communities. Whichever approaches are taken, *authenticity* is the key to relevant learning. Authenticity means that the media texts studied have interest and relevance in the students' lives.

There are a variety of classroom practices possible within media education. Whichever is pursued, the deconstruct/construct continuum is always useful: students deconstruct media works, identifying their parts, functions, and structures in the meaning-making process, then proceed with student constructions. Students' construction can be used as the consolidation phase of the units, in that students must have an understanding of form and content, and all that entails, in order to create media. Just as a unit on poetry might conclude with students writing poems, a unit on television news might conclude with students producing their own newscast.

Many teachers are concerned and, in some cases intimidated, by the implications of media production. They do not have studio-quality equipment, nor would they have the expertise and time necessary to set it up and use it effectively. Few schools have the facilities that are necessary to produce professional-quality messages. A television studio, however, is not necessary for the production of television news, just as a printing press is not necessary for the production of a newspaper. A single camcorder, some careful planning and speaking, and in-camera editing are all it takes for students to begin understanding the issues around constructing a newscast. Students' overall familiarity with the media and their experience with technology become real assets.

Overall, there are four main ways of approaching media education in the classroom. In the *medium-based approach*, the characteristics, strengths, and weaknesses of a particular medium are the focus. This may begin with a naming of parts, in which, for example, the parts of a newspaper and a newspaper page are identified and labeled. While this is a useful beginning, the more successful study will consider types of newspapers, for example, dailies, weeklies, tabloids, free distribution, and others. It will also consider the marketing and political roles that newspapers play. The wide choice of publications, especially in urban areas, allows students to compare and contrast newspapers both linguistically and socioeconomically.

A *theme-based study* involves several media. An issue—such as gender representation—can be identified and examined in terms of how it is communicated in a variety of media. Roles and attitudes toward men and women, especially through an area like fashion, can be examined in several media. Students at middle school age are especially sensitive to fashion because it can be a signifier of group acceptance and rejection. Fashion also cuts across newspapers, magazines, and television (in dramas, newscasts, and music videos), and therefore can be the vehicle that provides the unifying theme for studying media.

For many teachers, a media studies unit is a *stand-alone unit* within an English course. This means that they will choose a genre or theme and study it exclusively for up to two weeks. This approach allows them to focus on the media study and teachers can be more confident that their evaluation reflects students' understanding of the media.

Finally, *integrating media studies* into other classroom activities can be beneficial for creating some of the most authentic studies, and for connecting the newer media, such as the Internet or music videos, to older forms of communication such as print or speech.

As in all curricula and teaching, assessment is a key component for implementation and authentication. One particular challenge is that assessment of media concepts in integrated studies can become confounded with assessment of other topics, so teachers must build careful assessment instruments. The AML's Worsnop (1997) has made media assessment an ongoing theme of his study and writing. His book, *Assessing Media Work: Authentic Assessment in Media Education*, is helping many teachers understand authentic media assessment, but the search for appropriate assessment is ongoing.

Ultimately, whatever the theory and practice adopted, at the classroom level the implementation of media education skills has been uneven from school to school and district to district. Some school boards have established media education as a priority and have supported it with ongoing in-service and the appointment of media consultants. Other school boards have left implementation to the individual teacher. During MNet's 2000 research into the status of media education, officials from provincial ministries of education repeatedly stated that although media was strongly integrated into the English Language Arts program as another kind of "text," there was little professional development activity attached to this new discipline, and no money for new resources. Ultimately, the dedication of the individual teacher greatly influences the extent and quality of media education in the classroom. Associations such as Ontario's AML continue to be the strongest ongoing support for teachers pursuing additional expertise and ideas in media education.

Resources

One of the important accomplishments of Canadian media educators has been the development of resources. Without sufficient resources, media literacy cannot be effectively taught in the classroom. Both educational groups and media creators have been part of this resource creation, developing organizations, texts, and other teaching materials; doing research; and creating "alternative media."

Canadian Association of Media Education Organizations

In 1992, representatives from Canadian provincial media education groups met in Toronto to form the Canadian Association of Media Education Organizations (CAMEO). The purpose of the group has been to promote media education across Canada and to link Canadian media education organizations. Over the years, CAMEO has been involved in questions of copyright, in working with the CRTC and other organizations around the issues of violence in the media, and in organizing a countrywide protest that halted plans to bring commercials into public school classrooms in return for free AV equipment. CAMEO's advocacy resulted in media literacy becoming a mandatory part of the Language Arts curriculum at all grade levels across Canada, in 2002.

In 2003, CAMEO's President, John J. Pungente, SJ, participated on an advisory committee, with members of the Canadian Teachers' Federation (CTF), for a national survey on Canadian children and the media. Close to 6,000 Canadian children from every province, aged 8–15, took part. The survey, *Kids' Take on the Media* (Canadian Teachers' Federation, 2003), showed that as children get older, they increasingly appreciate the opportunity to study media in school. CAMEO is continuing to work with the CTF to support professional development for teachers and additional classroom resources to provide high-quality media education in every classroom.

Media Literature

Canadians have written a number of useful media education texts since 1987. The more recent ones include the second edition of *Mass Media and Popular Culture* (Duncan, D'Ippolito, Macpherson, & Wilson, 1996) and *Screening Images* (Worsnop, 1994), which offers many practical ideas for teachers. Concerns about media violence and its effect on children gave rise to a Metro Toronto School Board publication, *Responding to Media Violence* (Metropolitan Toronto School Board, 1996), designed to support Kindergarten to Grade 6 teachers' efforts to help their students makes sense of the violent behaviors they may witness in the media.

More Than Meets the Eye: Watching Television, Watching You (Pungente & O'Malley, 1999) looks at issues of television violence, TV news and prime-time shows, advertising, talk TV, and values. A revised edition of *Scanning Television* (Marcuse & Pungente, 2003) is a media literacy kit that includes 51 short videos and a teacher's guide (Andersen & Tyner, 2003). The subjects of the videos range from the evolution of communications technology and the Internet, to youth advertising, pop culture, culture jamming, international news media, 9/11, and the history of film and television.

Various "alternative" sources for media and media literacy have also contributed to a cultural climate that encourages media education.

Windmill Press in Waterloo, Ontario, is one publishing house that has produced young adult novels built on themes of media literacy. An example is the fantasy/science fiction novel *Racing through Times* by Ron DeBoer (1998) that examines the workings and effects of newspapers. Norton (2001/2002) reports the creation of an ad-free teen magazine, *Reluctant Hero*, begun in 1987. *Reluctant Hero* is a magazine for girls, written by girls, primarily aged 12–16, and is published quarterly out of Toronto and supported by newsstand and subscription sales (http://www.reluctanthero.com).

Conclusions

Canada has been quite active on the world stage in the support and creation of media education. Still, challenges face all who are committed to this work. Our study of media education, given the Canadian experience, shows nine factors that appear to us crucial to the successful development of media education:

1. Media education, like other innovative programs, must be a grass-roots movement, and teachers need to take the major initiative in lobbying for the inclusion of media education in the curriculum.
2. Educational authorities must give clear support to such programs by mandating the teaching of media education within the curriculum, establishing guidelines and resource books, and ensuring curricula are developed and materials are available.
3. Faculties of education must hire staff capable of training future teachers in this area. There should also be academic support from tertiary institutions in the writing of curricula and in sustained consultation.
4. In-service training at the school district level must be an integral part of program implementation.
5. School districts need consultants who have expertise in media education and who will establish communication networks.
6. Suitable textbooks and audiovisual material that are relevant to the country/area must be available.
7. A support organization must be established for the purposes of workshops, conferences, dissemination of newsletters, and the development of curriculum units. Such a professional organization must cut across school boards and districts to involve a cross-section of people interested in media education.
8. There must be appropriate evaluation instruments.

9. Because media education involves such a diversity of skills and
   expertise, there must be collaboration between teachers, parents,
   researchers, and media professionals.

Clearly, teachers themselves are key players in the growth of media
education, and have played a prominent role in carrying the torch for
its inclusion in public schooling. However, in these demanding times
for teachers, outside support, resources, and training must be made
available. It is critical that school administrators and policymakers take
an active and supportive role for success. Professional development
opportunities for school leaders at *all* levels should be the next goal of
media educators, so that more teacher in-service education, more and
better curriculum materials, and the hiring of consultants become
realities.

At the same time, there are risks in mandating media education from
the national level—in moving from the sidelines to the mainstream.
Different provinces and different schools have differing needs, and
these needs must be respected. Major decisions about how media literacy is implemented need to remain in control of educators in schools,
who are familiar with local concerns. Perhaps the most encouraging
development in Canada has been the work of the national AML, a
powerful and vocal support for school-based media education.
Associations and networks that involve teachers, students, families,
school leaders, and media producers may prove the most powerful, and
appropriate, force for media education.

Such networks or organizations need also to think about establishing and publishing refereed, scholarly journals, for two reasons. More
research needs to be done, especially in service of creating useful and
meaningful evaluation tools. Citizens also have the right to know what
media education in the curriculum is actually accomplishing, and policymakers will more likely support funding for education that has proven
benefits. Second, the potential for publishing in a scholarly journal is a
real motivation for university educators' involvement. Media education
needs to be "legitimized" at the university level to attract the interest
of more higher education faculty and to become part of the regular
curricula of colleges and schools of education.

Canada does now possess most of the factors critical to the successful development of media education. However, much work remains to
be done, and this may prove especially hard work in turbulent political
times. Educators can look to Canada for needed experience, ideas, and
collaboration as they pursue media literacy in the United States and

TABLE 1

WEBSITES IN CANADIAN MEDIA LITERACY

Web Address	Site Description
http://interact.uoregon.edu/ MediaLit/CAMEO/index.html	Canadian Association of Media Education Organizations (CAMEO)
http://www.chebucto.ns.ca/ CommunitySupport/AMLNS/ media_literacy.html	Association for Media Literacy-Nova Scotia (AMNS)
http://www.cca-canada.com/	Concerned Children's Advertisers (CCA)
http://interact.uoregon.edu/ MediaLit.it/JCP/	The Jesuit Communication Project
http://www.media-awareness.ca/	Media Awareness Network (MNet)—both French and English links; includes links to Alberta Association for Media Awareness (AAMA), Manitoba Association for Media Literacy (MAML)
http://www.reseau-crem.qc.ca/	*Centre de ressources en éducation aux medias* (CREM)—French
http://www.quadrant.net/Media-Literacy/	Media Literacy Saskatchewan (MLS)
http://www.stf.sk.ca/ prof_growth/ ssc/stela/stela.html	Saskatchewan Teachers of English Language Arts (STELA)
http://www.aml.ca/	Association for Media Literacy (AML)
http://www.chumlimited.com/ mediaed/studyguides.asp	CHUM Television study guides in media literacy including MuchMediaLit and Bravo's *Scanning the Movies* study guides
http://www.crtc.gc.ca/	Canadian Radio-television and Telecommunications Commission (CRTC)
http://ww.amtec.ca/	Association for Media and Technology in Education in Canada (AMTEC)

elsewhere. We close by offering the following websites in Table 1 to assist that collaboration.

NOTE

1. Financial supporters of *Media Lit 21* include Bell Canada, Rogers Cable Communications, AOL Canada, Microsoft Canada, CHUM Television, Canadian Recording Industry Association, National Film Board of Canada, Alliance Atlantis, Bell Canada Enterprises, CanWest Global, and the Government of Canada (Media Awareness Network, 2003).

REFERENCES

Andersen, N., & Tyner, K. (2003). *Scanning television: Teacher's guide* (2nd ed.). Toronto: Harcourt Canada.
Buckingham, D. (1990). *Watching media learning*. Gage, Canada: Falmer Press.
Buckingham, D. (1993). *Reading audiences: Young people and the media*. New York: St. Martin's Press.
Buckingham, D., & Sefton-Green, J. (1994). *Cultural studies goes to school*. London: Taylor & Francis.

Buckingham, D., & Sefton-Green, J. (2003). Gotta catch 'em all: Structure, agency, and pedagogy in children's media culture. *Media, Culture, and Society, 25*, 379–399.

Canadian Teachers' Federation. (2003). Kids take on media. Retrieved October 12, 2004 from http://www.ctf-fce.ca/bilingual/publication/horizons/3/007kidstakeonmedia.pdf

Considine, D. (2002). National developments and international origins. *Journal of Popular Film, 30*(1), 7–15.

DeBoer, R. (1998). *Racing through the times.* Waterloo, Ontario: Windmill Press.

Duncan, B., D'Ippolito, J., Macpherson, C., & Wilson, C. (1996). *Mass media and popular culture* (2nd ed.). Toronto: Harcourt Brace Canada.

Ferrington, G., & Anderson-Inman, L. (1996). Media literacy: Upfront and on-line. *Journal of Adolescent & Adult Literacy, 39*, 656–670.

Giroux, H. (1992). *Border crossings: Cultural workers and the politics of education.* London: Routledge.

Innis, H. (1952). *The bias of communication.* Toronto: University of Toronto Press.

Klein, N. (2000). *No logo: Taking aim at the brand bullies.* New York: Picador.

Marcuse, G., & Pungente, J.J. (2003). *Scanning television: 51 short videos for media literacy studies* (2nd ed.). [DVD]. Canada: Jesuit Communication Project/Face to Face Media.

Masterman, L. (1995, March). *The media education revolution* (Occasional Paper No. 31). Southampton, U.K.: The Centre for Language in Education.

McLuhan, M. (1964). *Understanding media: The extensions of man.* New York: McGraw-Hill.

McLuhan, M. (1967). *The medium is the message: An inventory of effects.* New York: Random House.

Media Awareness Network. (2003). *Advancing media literacies for the 21st century* (Annual Report). Ottawa, Ontario, Canada: Author.

Megee, M. (1997). Students need media literacy: The new basic. *The Education Digest, 63*(1), 31–35.

Metropolitan Toronto School Board. (1996). *Responding to media violence: Starting points for classroom practice.* Toronto: Pembroke Publishers.

Minkel, W. (2002). Media literacy—part of the curriculum? *School Library Journal, 48*(4), 31.

Morgan, R. (1997). Messing with Mr. In-Between: Multiculturalism and hybridization. *English Quarterly, 28*(4), 66–76.

Norton, B. (2001/2002). When is a teen magazine not a teen magazine? *Journal of Adolescent and Adult Literacy, 45*, 296–300.

Quebec Education Program (QEP). (2001). *Preschool and elementary education.* Quebec, CN: Ministry of Education.

Pungente, J.J. (1996). Getting started on media literacy. *Emergency Librarian, 24*(2), 9–12.

Pungente, J.J., & O'Malley, M. (1999). *More than meets the eye: Watching television, watching you.* Plattsburgh, NY: McClelland & Stewart/Tundra Books.

Smythe, D. (1981). *Dependency road: Capitalism, communication, culture, and Canada.* New York: Ablex.

Thoman, E. (2003). Screen-Agers . . . and the decline of the "wasteland." *Federal Communications Law Journal, 55*, 601–609.

Turkle, S. (1995). *Life behind the screen: Identity in the age of the Internet.* New York: Simon & Schuster.

Worsnop, C.M. (1994). *Screening images: Ideas for media education.* Mississauga, Ontario: Wright Publications.

Worsnop, C.M. (1997). *Assessing media work: Authentic assessment in media education.* Mississauga, Ontario, Canada: Wright Communications.

CHAPTER 9

Teachers Need Media Literacy, Too!

SANDRA K. GOETZE[1], DIANE S. BROWN[2], AND GRETCHEN SCHWARZ[3]

He who adds not to his learning diminishes it.

—The Talmud

If media literacy is to become part of the K-12 school experience, enabling transformation in both curriculum and teaching, then teachers need to become literate first. Teachers cannot teach what they have not learned, and learned to value, themselves. Although more American teachers are becoming knowledgeable about media literacy, much remains to be done. A study by Yates (1997) based on over 300 surveys of diverse teachers in a small southeastern city showed that although teachers may believe in the value of media literacy, nearly half (48%) cited lack of training as a barrier to their teaching media literacy, and 84% agreed that future teachers should receive college training in the area. Others in education echo the need for teacher training, including the Assembly on Media Arts, part of the National Council of Teachers of English (NCTE), whose newsletter, *Media Matters* (2000), reported that the Commission on Media "recognizes the need for more formal professional development for in-service teachers and the development of media literacy curriculum at colleges of education" (p. 1). Authors in this volume continue to emphasize the importance of media literacy education for teachers, while others, such as Adams and Hamm (2001), report that when it comes to the new media, "In the last two decades, teachers have often found themselves caught between shifting advice and paltry support for professional development" (p. 6). What is the current state of media literacy in professional development for practicing teachers, graduate university education, and undergraduate preser-

[1]Sandra K. Goetze is an Assistant Professor and the EDTC Program Coordinator in the School of Educational Studies at Oklahoma State University. [2]Diane S. Brown is a teacher at Central Elementary School in Sand Springs, Oklahoma, and a graduate student at Oklahoma State University. [3]Gretchen Schwarz is a Professor in the School of Teaching and Curriculum Leadership at Oklahoma State University.

vice teacher education in the United States? What efforts seem to have the most potential, and what kinds of obstacles threaten the growth of teacher knowledge about and skills in media literacy? This chapter examines the teaching of media literacy to the teachers.

Professional Development

New Mexico Media Literacy Project

A variety of organizations, which may or may not be associated with universities, have become significant in offering practicing teachers professional development in media literacy. One influential resource is the New Mexico Media Literacy Project (NMMLP; http://www.nmmlp.org). Founded in 1993 by veteran newscaster Hugh Downs and his daughter Diedre, the NMMLP is located at a private 6–12 school, the Albuquerque Academy in Albuquerque, New Mexico. Its director is Bob McCannon, an Albuquerque Academy history teacher. The NMMLP is also supported by the New Mexico Department of Education, the New Mexico Department of Health, the McCune Foundation, other public and private donors, and speaking fees earned by McCannon. The NMMLP accepts no funding from the media industry.

Staff members of the NMMLP deliver presentations at conferences, workshops, and in classrooms all over the country, and they produce educational materials including learning activities, CD-ROMs, and videos for classrooms and for professional development purposes. They have also been influential in adding media literacy objectives to the New Mexico state curriculum guides, and in supporting the teaching of media literacy around the state. Two or three times a year, the NMMLP offers four-day "Catalyst Institutes" for teachers and others who come from around the nation to either Albuquerque or to Taos, New Mexico. Workshops include thoughtful readings, discussion, videos, and practice in deconstructing various media messages. In addition, sabbatical visits can be arranged that enable visitors to observe an elective high school class in media literacy at the Albuquerque Academy, and to interview and observe various media literacy educators in New Mexico.

Journalist Rich Shea (2003) captured the intense experience of the Catalyst training that was offered in Las Cruces, New Mexico, in 2002. The power of the media in selling both products and values was emphasized in a contemporary context of corporate corruption, media mergers, and the commercialization of the schools. Trainees studied the messages and information from television ads, reports from the Centers for Disease Control, daily newspapers, and popular movies, augmented by a rereading of *Brave New World* (Huxley, 1932). As McCannon said, "There's nothing you can't *not* study by studying media literacy" (Shea, 2003, p. 29); media literacy becomes a catalyst for the scrutiny of many vital subjects and issues. The NMMLP is characterized by a skeptical orientation toward the media and media purposes. It has reached hundreds of teachers in New Mexico and elsewhere, supplied creative teaching resources, and remains a major voice for media literacy nationwide.

Project Look Sharp

Another resource for educators is Project Look Sharp, a collaborative partnership between Ithaca (New York) College's Department of Teacher Education, Humanities and Sciences, and Communications, and several New York school districts. Services such as the Cable in the Classroom taping service, a media literacy resource library, and individual coaching and consulting are offered free to teachers in partner districts. In addition, Project Look Sharp offers workshops, minicourses, and summer courses such as the Media Literacy Summer Institute, and its website (http://www.ithaca.edu/looksharp) is available to anyone interested in media literacy. The primary goals of Project Look Sharp include providing teachers with pre- and in-service training, developing a model for including media literacy across the school curriculum that addresses new learning standards, and developing and testing tools for evaluating the effectiveness of media literacy education. The executive director of the project is Cyndy Scheibe, a psychology professor who has conducted research on television content and effects for almost three decades. Chris Sperry, a social studies teacher at Ithaca's Alternative Community School, is the project's director of curriculum and staff development. Project Look Sharp has a growing presence in the media literacy movement.

Other Projects

Newer projects are beginning to emerge from coast to coast. Some, like the Connecticut Media Literacy Project, housed in the Neag College of Education at the University of Connecticut, are attached to universities, directed by professors, and offer graduate courses as well as in-service programs (http://www.medialit.uconn.edu). Others are coalitions of teachers, health professionals, parents, journalists, filmmakers, and community members, like the Northwest Media Literacy Center located in Portland, Oregon (http://www.mediathink.org). This project works with schools but also with health departments, radio stations, and the community. The Northwest Media Literacy Center is working on creating a resource library as well as offering outreach to teachers. Perhaps the most influential organization in the United States is the Center for Media Literacy in Los Angeles, described in this volume (Thoman & Jolls, Chapter 10, this volume). The Center for Media Literacy (http://www.medialit.org) is well established; it offers tremendous resources and education; and it has played a vital part in the national media literacy movement. Although similar projects are not located in every state, much of the training information and resources and links of existing organizations are available through their websites, and the fact that teachers will travel across the country to attend training at a place like the NMMLP underscores the dedication of many teachers to learning about media literacy.

Graduate Programs

Appalachian State University

Another major source for in-service teacher education in media literacy is colleges and universities. Several institutions have begun graduate programs in media literacy that are open to teachers. David Considine at Appalachian State University in Boone, North Carolina, has been a leading voice in the media literacy movement, and he and his colleagues' work led to the opening of the first institutionalized graduate program in media literacy for educators in the nation, in 2000. According to Considine (2002), "Housed in the Reich College of Education, the program is the logical outgrowth of a well-documented commitment to media literacy in undergraduate teacher preparation, a long established undergraduate minor in media studies, and a national media literacy reputation." (p. 7). Appalachian State University has assumed a leadership role in developing a Master's program in media literacy based on the following goals:

The media literacy concentration develops the technical and intellectual skills to successfully utilize and critique traditional and emerging mass media formats and information technologies. Programs place emphasis upon the impact and influence of media content and format on school and society, students and citizens. Further, these programs give attention to the subject of media audiences and media ownership. Graduates of the program are prepared to foster media literacy initiatives, projects and curriculum development in a variety of educational settings. (Appalachian State University, 2004)

Appalachian State's master's program is a 36-credit-hour program. The university also offers an 18-credit-hour "Certificate of Completion" in media literacy.

The media literacy master's program at Appalachian State University has a core program of courses with additional hours available through independent study, electives, and in the field of communications. Some courses are taught via the Internet while others are offered in traditional face-to-face formats. Courses include:

- *Media Literacy*, which focuses on what it means to be literate in a media era. Students actively deconstruct media as part of the analysis of the course.
- *Media: Image and Influence* is a course in which students investigate media representations, effects, and audience. This case-based course uses gender, race, and sex as lenses to explore family, adolescence, minorities, and schools, and the social and psychological consequences of media.
- *Media Literacy and Curriculum Development* examines the teaching of media literacy in other countries.
- *Research Methods.*
- *Computers in Educational Settings.*
- *Instructional Technology.* Unlike typical instructional technology courses which focus on the tools of technology, this one focuses on critical thinking. "As an educational innovation, media literacy is contextualized within the culture and climate of the classroom and explored in terms of perceptions and paradigms that have subverted the role of media and technology in our schools." (Appalachian State University, 2004)

Students can take electives in video production, web page design, and photography and digital imaging, but they are required to consider the greater educational and societal goals of these media.

Both the graduate and undergraduate programs at Appalachian State have been well received, as Maynard (2005) discusses in one of this volume's commentaries. The graduate students are largely part time, but the program expects to have six graduates by May 2005 (D. Considine, personal communication, November 16, 2004). This past summer (2004) the graduate program marked its fifth anniversary with the appearance of two guest lecturers, Jean Kilbourne, author of *Can't Buy My Love: How Advertising Changes the Way We Think and Feel* (1999) and media critic, and David Buckingham, Director of the Center for the Study of Children, Youth, and Media at the Institute of Education,

University of London. According to Considine, guest coeditor of the Fall 2004 issue of *Telemedium*, these two lecturers, who represent different paradigms for teaching media literacy, challenged the students (from three countries and 17 states) to evaluate their own ideas. Kilbourne represents the more protectionist attitude toward the media, while Buckingham argues for its positive potential. Considine adds, "Of particular note was how well the week was received by several of the students who are school administrators doing their doctorates in educational leadership" (2004, p. 34).

Center for Media Studies

Robert Kubey, who like Considine has long been a voice in the media literacy movement, is director of the Center for Media Studies at Rutgers in New Jersey. The center, working with the New Jersey Media Literacy Project, provides outreach to the community, while the School of Communication, Information, and Library Studies (SCILS) oversees degree programs.

The center's mission statement identifies the impact of media on contemporary society as a primary concern. "Through research, teaching, public events and outreach, the center seeks ways for the media to better serve the public interest" (Rutgers University, 2004). The center (as articulated in their 1996 Planning Document) provides consultation and information dissemination services to colleges and universities in the New Brunswick region, to citizens of New Jersey interested in becoming more knowledgeable about the media (particularly K-12 teachers), to public officials, and to media professionals. The New Jersey Media Literacy Project helps teachers teach media literacy that aligns with the Core Curricular Content Standards of the state Department of Education. In addition to offering workshops and public events, the center also works with Rutgers in developing distance learning programs and courses.

Coursework for the Master's of Communication and Information Studies (MCIS) requires 36 credits hours, including work in media literacy. Eighteen credit hours of core courses offered through the Department of Communications (COMM) are approached through a scholarly focus by COMM faculty, along with faculty from Journalism and Media Studies and Library and Information Science. Fifteen hours of elective course work, offered by a variety of faculty from the English, Education, Psychology, Visual Arts, and other departments, further enhance the program. Some elective courses are more practical than theoretically based, including a series of internships. These elective choices support the department's "tripartite scholarly focus: social inter-action, mediated communication, and organizational communication" (Rutgers University, 2004). Rutgers also has a Ph.D. program in Com-munication, Information, and Library Studies. Students choose a sub-specialty of Communication Processes, Library and Information Sciences, or Media Studies.

Rutgers also offers outreach to the community and educators. The outreach programs, including workshops, seminars, conferences, and a center library of critical media resources, provide a bridge from the university to the schools and the community. Degree programs may be more practical for full-time students due to the internship courses and would probably appeal to media workers and others in a variety of disciplines such as library science. The broad focus of media literacy at Rutgers University is built on a combination of theoretical inquiry, scholarly research, and areas of public concern.

Other Graduate Programs

Another model for graduate education in media literacy is repre-sented by New School (New York), well known for its contributions in the performing arts. New School offers a 39-hour master's degree in their Department of Communication and Media Studies. The courses are available both onsite and online. Media production is the focus, with courses such as film production; the goal is to equip students to partic-ipate in the media industry and to teach media literacy and media production courses at the secondary or undergraduate levels. This flex-ible program meets the needs of students who work during the day, but it was not designed specifically for teachers (New School, 2004). Other universities offering master's degrees include Webster University, with a master's of Media Communications (Webster University, 2004). At the home campus in St. Louis, Webster offers a Master of Arts in Teaching degree in Communication Arts, with one area of emphasis being media literacy. Webster University also offers an undergraduate degree in media communications with an emphasis in media literacy and an undergraduate media literacy certification program for teachers. Southern Illinois University at Edwardsville also offers a Master of Science in Mass Communications in which students can concentrate in Media Studies. Additionally, they offer a postbaccalaureate certificate in media literacy, requiring 18 hours, designed for secondary education teachers, especially in social studies and English (Southern Illinois Uni-versity, 2004). This program aims to prepare educators with the means to integrate media-related issues into their classrooms.

Renee Hobbs, another leader in media literacy, actually initiated the first field-based master's degree in media literacy for K-12 teachers. Much of the work took place in the public schools. This program (1993–1995) was a joint effort of the Billerica (Massachusetts) Public Schools, the Merrimack Education Collaborative, Fitchburg State College, and the Harvard Institute in Media Education. According to the University of Oregon Umbrella website (http://interact.uoregon.edu/html), which offers current and historical information about media literacy efforts and events, this master's degree (M.Ed.) was the "first systematic district-level initiative to provide educators with the tools, knowledge, skills, and resources to bring media education to public schools in the United States." Teachers took 12 courses, including Analysis of News and Information, Analysis of Advertising and Media Economics, Media Literacy and Arts Education, Storytelling and the Analysis of Mass Media Narratives, Integrating Media Production Activities into the Curriculum, and Global Perspectives in Media Education. Practicum work in curriculum design was also done in the summer at Harvard University (http://interact.uoregon.edu/MediaLit/mlr/courses/mastersbillerica.html). The course work of this program reflects the broader aspects of media literacy, and it was clearly designed for practicing teachers. Hobbs is now at Temple University, working with the doctoral program in Mass Media and Communication and initiating programs for educators such as "media smart seminars" in the Philadelphia metropolitan area (http://reneehobbs.org).

Graduate Courses

Individual university graduate courses are also available at various institutions around the country. Seattle Pacific University offers two courses in media literacy via distance education. These courses, *The Impact of TV and Video on Young Brains: Vital Information for Educators* and *Media Literacy for 21st Century Students*, are available to anyone and confer graduate credit. The courses are taught by Gloria DeGaetano (1996), coauthor of *Screen Smarts: A Family Guide to Media Literacy*. Sometimes media literacy may be embedded in other courses; Ottaviani (1997), for example, designed a project for students enrolled in an urban graduate educational technology course, who were asked to keep journals on prime-time television viewing. The journal assignment pushed teachers to consider such media literacy issues as commercial influence and stereotypes on television.

Media Literacy across the Curriculum is part of an M.Ed. program in Classroom Technology at Bowling Green State University, Ohio, described by Brownell and Brownell (2001). This course, offering considerable hands-on experience in media production, is built on the principle that "media literacy offers a new way to see the world" (p. 8). Bowling Green State University also emphasizes popular culture in its undergraduate programs. A course taught at Oklahoma State University, also called *Media Literacy Across the Curriculum*, is an elective graduate course in curriculum studies. This course was designed both to introduce basic concerns of media literacy—deconstructing TV shows, magazines, and other media; looking at media effects on children; discovering how to integrate media literacy across the disciplines at various grade levels—and to explore various media literacy curriculum models and their philosophical assumptions and implications. The course also explores diverse approaches to educational research in media literacy.

Media literacy may find a place embedded in graduate programs for teachers, and in curriculum studies and social foundations classes, if dedicated media literacy degree programs remain limited.

Undergraduate Education

Media literacy remains difficult to find in undergraduate teacher education offerings. Tyner's (1992) comment rings true today:

There is a desperate need for pre-service teacher training that teaches about media. Students in university education departments, many of whom grew up in a saturated media environment, are clamoring for it. (p. 175)

As we have seen, very few universities have built media literacy into their teacher education programs in the same way Appalachian State University has. While a growing number of states offer certification in educational technology, media literacy remains rare even when the word "media" is used in describing required courses. Most college teacher education programs require courses like *Media and Microcomputers in the Classroom* (offered at the University of Kansas), but such courses involve a mostly technical "how-to" orientation, not critical thinking about the media. This course description is typical:

A study of the use of instructional technology including microcomputers, video, and other forms of technology in the classroom. Students will learn how to select instructional materials and media, to develop and produce a variety of instructional materials, to incorporate the products of technology in their classroom, and to operate and utilize various types of instructional equipment. (http://www.soe.ku.edu/depts./tl/courses.php)

It appears as though it is assumed that the media are simply useful tools that should be used whenever possible; it is difficult to find references to the possible negative impact of new technologies on society or in classrooms.

While students may learn to evaluate educational software, they are generally not asked to evaluate video games, Channel One, or the media conglomerates. Kubey (2000) reports:

My own informal survey . . . has shown all too many education schools concluding that it is still adequate to merely train future teachers to thread a 16 mm projector or encourage them to show students the Civil War documentary by Ken Burns. Some go further in instructing future teachers how to have students develop assignments using multimedia. But there remains precious little emphasis on how to encourage and teach analysis and evaluation of media products and not nearly enough recognition that instruction in the techniques of persuasion and propaganda must extend beyond traditional print media. Further, the issues of source credibility . . . have taken on a new urgency. (p. 33)

The one place preservice teachers may encounter media literacy is in English language arts/literacy course work. The National Council for Accreditation of Teacher Education (NCATE) standards of 2003 (http://www.ncate.org/standards) do include understanding the media's influence on culture, using a variety of approaches for teaching students how to construct meaning from media and helping students compose and respond to film, video, graphic texts, and other media formats. Media literacy may be included in secondary English methods courses or in undergraduate literacy courses for future elementary teachers (although this is by no means a given). Literacy as a field is beginning to embrace media literacy at all levels, and this holds promise for future teachers. As an example, Semali (2000) explains how he includes media literacy in an undergraduate secondary language and literacy teacher preparation program at Pennsylvania State University. Semali's courses involve the problematizing of media texts, requiring research, reflection, and response; major concerns are social justice and equity in education. Roy Fox, media literacy researcher and author of *Harvesting Minds: How TV Commercials Control Kids* (2000), brings media literacy to his work in literacy and English education at the University of Missouri, Columbia. One of his three undergraduate methods courses focuses on the teaching of media, with a secondary emphasis on teaching literature and writing. Students are taught to read and interpret media through several critical lenses, including principles of general semantics, semiotics, feminism, and so on. Students then practice analyzing or deconstructing magazine covers, sitcoms, teen magazines, and other forms of media. After analysis, students move on to exploring the values and cultures represented in diverse texts. Students are also asked to construct teaching plans that pair various media texts with compatible print texts that may present opposing values (R. Fox, personal communication, October 28, 2004).

Multiple Literacies and Beyond in Teacher Education

One of the current themes in literacy scholarship is the concept of multiple literacies, including media literacy. While traditional reading and writing remain essential, students today also need to be able to "read" visual and electronic texts. This concern with multiple literacies is reflected in a regular column on media literacy in the *Journal of Adolescent & Adult Literacy*, written by Lori A. Norton-Meier. Luke (2000) demonstrates how combining media-cultural studies with information technology in a teacher education curriculum offers new approaches for literacy learning. Moreover, Tyner (2003) endorses multiple literacies that involve technology: "Practices that extend the concept of reading and writing to include the viewing and representing of multimedia texts are necessary if digital literacy is to be integrated across the curriculum" (p. 371).

At Oklahoma State University there is currently a great deal of faculty interest in revising the traditional undergraduate educational technology program to include media literacy. Goals for a new program may include media literacy and technology as tools to solve cognitive problems, rather than a simpler focus on technology techniques. Media literacy as a component of the educational technology curriculum brings in the critical thinking element and highlights the ethical and social issues that accompany the expansion of technology into all aspects of human life; the questions raised are not only *how*, but *why* and *when*. Future teachers may learn to analyze and evaluate multimedia curriculum packages sold on TV, along with educational software, and to examine Internet sites for their commercial messages as well as their subject area content. Visuals and sounds and music become as important as written texts; all deserve careful scrutiny in an age no longer dominated by the written word. As Postman (1995) observes:

Technology education is not a technical subject. It is a branch of the humanities . . . Technology education aims at students' learning about what technology helps us to do and what it hinders us from doing; it is about how technology uses us, for good or ill . . . It is about how technology creates new worlds, for good or ill. (pp. 191–192)

The growing acceptance of multiple literacies by literacy and language arts scholars may some day ensure that, at minimum, literacy teachers are taught about media literacy as undergraduates and graduate students. *Literacy and Technology Across the Curriculum* is a graduate course in literacy at Oklahoma State University. This course explores the use of technology as a tool to teach literacy; however, it emphasizes an understanding of the use of technology from sociological and philosophical perspectives. Faculty ask students to develop a critical literacy website based on an area of interest connected to literacy. The critical literacy aspect of the website developed as a way to explore the selected topic from multiple perspectives, utilizing media tools such as Hyperstudio to juxtapose ideas (Hyperstudio, 1993).

Just like media literacy, critical literacy questions how media is utilized to either support or deny access to understanding and to communicating. Critical literacy asks who is being privileged and valued, by asking students to construct meaning through technology tools while questioning values in the media. The course also asks students to think deeply about the motivations of software authors and the ways these authors attempt to position the user. Many students report that they never realized how they were being manipulated in this way; previously, these technology tools were neutral, developed merely to meet *their* needs. Critical literacy, applied to both print and nonprint media, is described as the subversion of meanings in order to critique the underlying ideologies and relations of power that support particular interpretations (Myers, Hammett, & McKillop, 1998). It seems that an understanding of critical literacy enhances one's understanding of media literacy, and vice versa. Literacy programs are a natural place for media literacy to emerge.

Media Literacy and Preservice Programs

Of course, media literacy could well enrich the entire preservice teacher education curriculum. Schwarz (2001) maintains that media literacy is not only necessary content knowledge for future teachers, but "can serve to enliven and to connect teacher education courses, from methods courses and educational psychology to foundations courses and student teaching" (p. 118). The fact that the scholarship underlying media literacy comes from many disciplines points to the interdisciplinary nature of media literacy and its ability to support teacher education as a whole. For example, Schor (2004) reports the results of a survey on children, the media, and consumer culture in her book *Born to Buy*. Her sociological/psychological study demonstrates that "The children who are more involved in consumer culture [largely through the media] are more depressed, more anxious, have lower self-esteem, and suffer from more psychosomatic complaints" (p. 166). These findings could well be utilized in education courses on child and adolescent psychology. In a social foundations course in education, teacher candidates can learn from sociologists (i.e., Putnam, 2000) that habitual television viewing is "especially detrimental to civic engagement" (p. 225). Teachers need to consider the impact of TV on their students and their society. In sum, scholarship on media literacy is pertinent in sociology, psychology, cultural studies, and other areas that contribute to a richer understanding of both students and their educational and social contexts.

Additionally, media literacy fits into specific teaching content and methods courses. In a physical education teaching course, future teachers can consider the effect of TV watching on students' physical health. In a social studies methods course, preservice teachers can study the ways the media interpret history, from film to newspapers to the History Channel, and how students learn from the media. A commentary in this volume (Thier, 2005) shows how media literacy is relevant to science teaching. All content knowledge can be influenced by the mass media. Even future teachers' own notions about teaching may have been partly formed by seeing such films as *Dangerous Minds* or *Mr. Holland's Opus.*

Media literacy has the potential to connect the teacher education curriculum via critical thinking. Project Look Sharp (1999) presents 12 principles for incorporating media literacy across the curriculum; the following apply equally well to a teacher education curriculum (examples have been added):

1. Identify erroneous beliefs about a topic fostered by media content (e.g., Great teachers in the movies do not work in teams. In real life?).
2. Analyze the effect that specific media have had on a particular issue or topic historically and/or across different cultures (e.g., What is the basis for the widely reported concern about an educational crisis in American schools?).
3. Use media to practice general observation, critical thinking, analysis, perspective-taking, and production skills (e.g., Create a video on different ways to handle a discipline problem).
4. Use media as an assessment tool (e.g., Create a multimedia teacher portfolio after student teaching).

5. Use media to connect students to the community and work toward positive change (e.g., Have fieldwork students prepare a presentation on media literacy for the Parent-Teacher Association).

Schwarz (2004) also argues that media literacy incorporated into teacher education may better prepare future teachers for diverse classrooms. She suggests that media literacy can help accomplish four goals for preservice teachers: understanding others who are different; learning to challenge media messages and assumptions that may be demeaning to others; learning alternative teaching approaches that reach students with different learning styles; and learning how to find resources and materials to support diversity in the classroom (pp. 225–227).

Media literacy is interesting to future teachers and provides a means for engaging them in a variety of topics and practices in education. Media literacy familiarizes students with a range of teaching materials and methods, and demands new ways of thinking and respect for multiple points of view. Media literacy has great potential in preservice teacher education.

Obstacles and Possibilities

Media literacy integrated across the teacher education curriculum in the United States is well worth exploring. However, the obstacles are many. The university bureaucracy moves slowly. Few education professors may themselves be conversant, let alone comfortable, with media literacy. Moreover, teacher education programs labor under many curricular demands and must be accountable to outside organizations like NCATE. In some states, like Oklahoma, a growing number of people opt for alternative teacher certification rather than the increasingly laborious university program, and end up taking almost no education courses. Finally, teacher education programs, like the schools, are struggling to deal with federal legislation like the No Child Left Behind Act, which makes no mention of media literacy whatsoever. Incentives for teacher educators to become involved with media literacy are few.

It may be that practicing teachers are the ones most likely to benefit from media literacy, offered through professional development and/or graduate study. It may not be practical nor politically expedient to call for media literacy for all preservice teachers at this time. Professional development and graduate study opportunities remain more amenable to new, varied, and nonlegislated ideas. It is also possible that practicing teachers are more aware of the impact of the media on children and adolescents. As we have seen, various projects and university graduate courses and programs have been successful in bringing media literacy to the attention of a growing number of teachers from public and private K-12 schools, many of whom have become enthusiastic teachers of media literacy. Although their paradigms may differ, these programs, from Project Look Sharp to the master's program at Appalachian State University, seem to have several important characteristics in common: the involvement of dedicated educators, a commitment to media literacy as critical thinking, and a tendency to build creative collaborative partnerships.

Educators who become involved with media literacy often display an almost evangelical fervor for the work. The story of one New Mexico teacher, reported by Shea (2003), is typical:

Damie Nelson, a friendly, petite, gray-haired woman, is a faculty member at the Cliff School, a K-12 public school with fewer than 300 students in rural southwestern New Mexico. For six years, her freshman communications class has included a media lit. unit. This year, she'll be using the CD-ROMs for the first time, in part to train fellow teachers. Seven years ago, her school's librarian attended a Catalyst Institute, then passed its materials on to Nelson. "I started reading through the stuff, and it just electrified me," she explained. "It just fired me up, and I've been doing it ever since." (p. 33)

Several of the commentaries in this volume reflect K-12 educators' enthusiasm for media literacy. Articles by teachers have been appearing in various journals (such as the January 1998 *English Journal*) along with websites on media literacy for teachers. Some teachers become more expert in the field than others, of course. And not every teacher needs to be dedicated full time to media literacy. Involvement with media literacy is renewing for many teachers as they touch on a subject that is so much a part of students' everyday lives. Schor (2004) reports the following:

The average American child is estimated to spend five hours and twenty-nine minutes a day with media, for a weekly total of more than thirty-eight hours . . . Forty-six percent of eight to thirteen year olds report total media exposure (which double counts media being used simultaneously) of more than seven hours per day. (p. 33)

Teachers who acknowledge this reality have the opportunity to connect with their students in new and meaningful ways, and to enliven their own understanding of subject areas while they learn new information and skills.

In addition, no matter what the emphasis of the professional development program or graduate course, media literacy is designed to encourage critical thinking. Graduate coursework, conferences, and workshops explore the representation of minorities in the media, the methods and purposes of advertising, the analysis of the news in different media, and adolescent body image. Media literacy challenges teachers and students to question the status quo, to research diverse issues, to reflect on personal meanings, and to inquire into numerous vital social issues in America today. Although current school reform language, such as that of No Child Left Behind, is notably silent on such issues as critical thinking, inquiry learning, and democratic education, many educators still believe in these goals, and the media literacy movement may well help keep alive a deeper and richer sense of what school is for. Goodson and Norton-Meier (2003) note the democratic ideals for media education in the United States:

Media literacy is more than a curriculum add-on . . . We can build on our students' immersion in media and popular texts, and, in turn, we can use those texts to help students understand the powerful semiotic codes that shape our literacies and our lives . . . A curriculum that includes media literacy gives our students the opportunity to investigate the role of media in society—an essential skill necessary for citizens of a democracy. (p. 261)

Finally, the opportunities for professional development available to in-service teachers through universities and projects like Project Look Sharp are built on collaboration among scholars, educators, government organizations, media organizations, church groups, and private citizens. New partnerships are emerging—partnerships between colleges and school districts, as with Project Look Sharp and the Center for Media Studies at Rutgers; partnerships among college departments as at Appalachian State University and Oklahoma State University; and partnerships among teachers, families, and local community leaders, like at the Northwest Media Literacy project. The wide base of interest in media literacy can be positive, leading to new relationships and community involvement.

Collaboration and partnerships have been major topics in education at all levels for some time (Brabeck, Walsh, & Latta, 2003; Broussard, 2003; Sar & Wulff, 2003). Most would agree that schools benefit from strong working relationships with families, with colleges, with the community, and among educators at all levels. The theme of democracy is one of the major themes in media literacy; teaching media literacy in the schools may well prove a means in itself for increasing democratic practice in the United States in schools. Media literacy could bring people together, creating what Etzioni (1996) calls a communitarian society. Other adults—media creators, TV critics, policymakers, and college professors—can offer their services and resources to the school. The ultimate beneficiaries would be the young who are engaged with media literacy and who are witnessing active collaborative and shared decision making. Schultze and his group (1991) pose the potential:

Creating and performing a rock song or scripting, shooting, and editing a short video takes adolescents out of their consumerist passivity and unleashes their energy and imagination. If combined with research, discussion, writing, and other traditional modes of instruction, producing popular art could refine and advance adolescents' evaluative abilities. This route would also open up a whole new terrain for adolescents to explore with their peers, teachers, and other leaders. And as they explore this new ground, young people will find their own voice in their local settings. (p. 309)

Such projects as the Educational Video Center, described in Chapter 11 of this volume, are proving such possibilities reality.

Conclusion

The effective teaching of media literacy in the schools certainly requires the preparation of K-12 teachers. There remains a need for more opportunities of all kinds for both pre- and in-service teachers to learn about media literacy. Professional development for practicing teachers, whether through projects or through graduate work, may be the most effective route to teaching teachers about media literacy. Some important work has begun across the nation, but teaching teachers remains a significant task.

References

Adams, D., & Hamm, M. (2001). *Literacy in a multimedia age.* Norwood, MA: Christopher-Gordon.

Appalachian State University, School of Education. (2004). Master's in Educational Media. Retrieved May 12, 2004, from http://www.ci.appstate.edu/programs/edmedia/medialit/mlmasters.html

Brabeck, M.M., Walsh, M.E., & Latta, R.E. (2003). *Meeting at the hyphen: Schools–universities–communities–professions in collaboration for student achievement and well being. The 102nd yearbook of the National Society for the Study of Education*, Part II. Chicago: National Society for the Study of Education.

Broussard, C.A. (2003). Facilitating home–school partnerships for multiethnic families: School social workers collaborating for success. *Children & Schools, 25*(4), 211–222.

Brownell, G., & Brownell, N. (2001). After the pilots: Media literacy across the curriculum. In C.M. Crawford (Ed.), *Proceedings of the Society for Information Technology & Teacher Education International Conference* (Orlando, FL, March 5–10). (ERIC Document Reproduction Service No. ED 457828).

Considine, D.M. (2002). Media literacy: National developments and international origins. *Journal of Popular Film & Television, 30*(1), 7–17.

Considine, D. (Ed.). (2004). Buckingham and Kilbourne in Boone: The Master summer sessions at Appalachian State University. *Telemedium, 51*(2), 34.

DeGaetano, G. (1996). *Screen smarts: A family guide to media literacy.* Boston: Houghton Mifflin.

Etzioni, A. (1996). *The new golden rule.* New York: Basic Books.

Fox, R.F. (2000). *Harvesting minds: How TV commercials control kids.* Westport, CT: Praeger.

Garrison, A. (2000). Trends and issues statement. *Media Matters, 11*(4), 1–2.

Goodson, F.T., & Norton-Meier, L. (2003). Motor oil, civil disobedience, and media literacy. *Journal of Adolescent & Adult Literacy, 47*, 258–262.

Huxley, A. (1932). *Brave new world.* Garden City, NY: Doubleday, Doran & Co. Inc.

Hyperstudio [computer software]. (1993). El Cajon, CA: Roger Wagner Publishing.

Kilbourne, J. (1999). *Can't buy my love: How advertising changes the way we think and feel.* New York: Free Touchstone.

Kubey, R. (2000). Media literacy: Required reading for the 21st century. *High School Magazine, 7*(8), 29–33.

Luke, C. (2000). New literacies in teacher education. *Journal of Adolescent & Adult Literacy, 43*, 424–436.

Maynard, C. (2005). Media literacy for a future teacher. In G. Schwarz & P.U. Brown (Eds.), *Media literacy: Transforming curriculum and teaching. The 104th yearbook of the National Society for the Study of Education*, Part I (pp. 281–283). Malden, MA: Blackwell Publishing.

Myers, J., Hammett, R., & McKillop, A.M. (1998). Opportunities for critical literacy and pedagogy in student-authored hypermedia. In D. Reinking, M.C. McKenna, L.D. Labbo, & R.D. Kieffer (Eds.), *Handbook of literacy and technology: Transformations in post-typographic world* (pp. 63–91). Mahwah, NJ: Erlbaum.

New School. (2004). School of media studies. Retrieved June 1, 2004, from http://www.newschool.edu/mediastudies/program/index.html

Ottaviani, B.F. (1997). What about TV? A journal expands the awareness of technology's role in the classroom. *Educational Horizons, 75*(2), 90–96.

Postman, N. (1995). *The end of education.* New York: Alfred A. Knopf.

Project Look Sharp. (1999). *12 basic principles for incorporating media literacy into any curriculum.* Ithaca, NY: Project Look Sharp. (ERIC Document Reproduction Service No. ED 468414).

Putnam, R.D. (2000). *Bowling alone.* New York: Simon & Schuster.

Rutgers University, School of Communication, Information and Library Studies. (2004). The Center for Media Studies Retrieved May 25, 2004, from http://www.scils. rutgers.edu/courses/listing

Sar, B.K., & Wulff, D.P. (2003). Family builders approach: Enhancing the well-being of children through family–school partnerships. *Children & Schools, 25*(4), 241–251.

Schor, J.B. (2004). *Born to buy*. New York: Scribner.

Schultze, Q.J., Anker, R.M., Bratt, J.D., Roamnowski, W.D., Worst, J.W., & Zuidervaart, L. (1991). *Dancing in the dark: Youth, popular culture and the electronic media*. Grand Rapids, MI: William B. Eerdmans.

Schwarz, G. (2001). Literacy expanded: The role of media literacy in teacher education. *Teacher Education Quarterly, 28*(2), 111–119.

Schwarz, G. (2004). Media literacy prepares teachers for diversity. *Academic Exchange, 8*(1), 224–228.

Semali, L. (2000). *Literacy in multimedia America: Integrating media education across the curriculum*. New York: Falmer Press.

Shea, R. (2003, January). Brave new world. *Teacher Magazine, 14*, 29–35.

Southern Illinois University-Edwardsville, School of Mass Communications. (2004). Master's in Mass Communication Retrieved June 15, 2004, from http://www.siue. edu/MASSCOMM/grad/index.html

Thier, M. (2005). Merging media and science: Learning to weigh sources, not just evidence. In G. Schwarz & P.U. Brown (Eds.), *Media literacy: Transforming curriculum and teaching. The 104th yearbook of the National Society for the Study of Education*, Part I (pp. 262–270). Malden, MA: Blackwell Publishing.

Thoman, E., & Jolls, T. (2005). Media literacy education in the USA: An overview of the Center for Media Literacy. In G. Schwarz & P.U. Brown (Eds.), *Media literacy: Transforming curriculum and teaching. The 104th yearbook of the National Society for the Study of Education*, Part I (pp. 180–205). Malden, MA: Blackwell Publishing.

Tyner, K. (1992). The tale of the elephant: Media education in the United States. In C. Bazalgette, E. Bevort, & J. Savion (Eds.), *New directions: Media education worldwide* (pp. 170–176). London: British Film Institute.

Tyner, K. (2003). Beyond boxes and wires: Literacy in transition. *Television & New Media, 4*, 371–388.

University of Oregon Umbrella website. Retrieved from http://interact.uoregon.edu/html

Webster University, School of Communications. (2004). School of Education: Communication Arts (M.A.T.) Retrieved May 25, 2004, from http://www.webster.edu/ gradcatalog/comm.html

Yates, B.L. (1997, June). Media education's present and future: A survey of teachers. Paper presented at the meeting of the National Media Literacy Citizenship Project, Birmingham, AL. (ERIC Document Reproduction Service No. ED424601).

CHAPTER 10

Media Literacy Education: Lessons from the Center for Media Literacy

ELIZABETH THOMAN[1] AND TESSA JOLLS[2]

Literacy for the 21st Century

> The school and the family share the responsibility of preparing the young person for living in a world of powerful images, words and sounds.
>
> —(UNESCO, 1982)

Since the beginning of recorded history, the concept of "literacy" meant having the skill to interpret "squiggles" on a piece of paper as letters which, when put together, formed words that conveyed meaning. Teaching the young to put the words together to understand (and, in turn, express) ever more complex ideas became the goal of education as it evolved over the centuries.

Today information about the world around us comes to us not only through words on a piece of paper, but more and more through the powerful images and sounds of our multimedia culture. Although mediated messages appear to be self-evident, in truth, they use a complex audio/visual "language" which has its own rules (grammar) and which can be used to express many-layered concepts and ideas about the world. Not everything may be obvious at first; and images go by so fast! If our children are to be able to navigate their lives through this multimedia culture, they need to be fluent in "reading" and "writing" the language of images and sounds just as we have always taught them to "read" and "write" the language of printed communications.

In the last 40 years, the field of media literacy education has emerged to organize and promote the importance of teaching this

---

[1]Elizabeth Thoman founded the Center for Media Literacy in 1989 and is a co-founder and current board member of the Alliance for a Media Literate America. [2]Tessa Jolls is the President and CEO of the Center for Media Literacy in Santa Monica, California.

expanded notion of "literacy." At its core are the basic higher-order critical thinking skills—for example, knowing how to identify key concepts, how to make connections between multiple ideas, how to ask pertinent questions, formulate a response, identify fallacies—that form the very foundation of both intellectual freedom and full citizenship in a democratic society.

Indeed, in a time when candidates are elected by 30-second commercials and wars are fought real time on television, a unique role of media literacy is to prepare citizens to engage in and contribute to the public debate.

Media literacy also expands the concept of "text" to include not just written texts but any message form—verbal, aural, or visual—(or all three together!)—that is used to create and then pass ideas back and forth between human beings.

New Ways of Learning

This explosion in information has presented a major challenge to the world of formal education. For centuries, schooling has been designed to make sure students learned facts about the world—which they proved they knew by correctly answering questions on tests. But such a system is no longer relevant when the most up-to-date facts are available at the touch of a button. What students need today is to learn how to find what they need to know when they need to know it—and to have the higher-order thinking skills to analyze and evaluate whether the information they find is useful for what they want to know.

David Berlo, president of the University of Illinois for many years and a noted scholar in the field of communications, presciently identified this educational challenge in the 1975 book, *Communications and Behavior*: "Most of what we have called formal education has been intended to imprint on the human mind all of the information that we might need for a lifetime. Education is geared toward information storage. Today that is neither possible nor necessary. Rather, humankind needs to be taught how to process information that is stored through technology. Education needs to be geared toward the *handling of data* rather than the *accumulation of data*" (p. 8).

Thirty years later, schools are beginning to take up this challenge in several important ways. The tasks are formidable. First, schools and classrooms must be transformed from being storehouses of knowledge to being more like portable tents providing a shelter and a gathering place for students as they go out to explore, to question, to experiment, to discover!

Second, to use a concept originated by the great Brazilian educator, Paolo Freire, teaching must be distinguished from "banking" (Freire, 1970). No longer is it expected that teachers deposit information in students' heads. Recognizing the principles of democratic pedagogy dating back to Socrates, wise teachers realize they do not have to be a "sage on the stage." Instead, their role is to be a "guide on the side": encouraging . . . guiding . . . mentoring . . . supporting   the   learning process. Creative classrooms today are ones where everyone is learning, including the teacher!

Third, curriculum, classes, and activities must be designed that will engage students in problem solving and discovery. And today's multimedia culture, which includes print but goes far beyond it, provides a nearly limitless resource for real world learning—from how to identify "point of view" by exploring how camera angles influence our reaction to the picture on the cover of *Time*, to how to determine whether information on an Internet site is bogus or legitimate.

Questioning the Media

To be a functioning adult in a mediated society, one needs to be able to distinguish between different media forms and know how to ask basic questions about everything we watch, read, or hear. Although most adults learned through English classes to distinguish a poem from an essay, it is amazing how many people do not understand the difference between a daily newspaper and a supermarket tabloid, what makes one website legitimate and another one a hoax, or how advertisers package products to entice us to buy.

Usually the questioning process is applied to a specific media "text"—that is, an identifiable production or publication, or a part of one: an episode of Power Puff Girls, an ad for Pepsi, an issue of *People* magazine, a billboard for Budweiser beer, photos and articles about a bank robbery on the front page of a newspaper, the Super Bowl telecast, a hot new videogame.

Sometimes a media "text" can involve multiple formats. A new animated Disney film, for example, involves not only a blockbuster movie released in thousands of theaters but also a whole campaign of advertising and merchandising—character dolls and toys, clothes, lunchboxes, and so on—as well as a website, storybooks, games, and perhaps, eventually, a ride at one of the Disney theme parks.

Simple questions about the media can be encouraged even at the toddler stage, planting important seeds for cultivating a lifetime of interrogating the world around us. Parents, grandparents, even babysitters can make a game of "spot the commercial" to help children learn to distinguish between entertainment programs and the commercial messages that support them. Even children's picture books can help little ones grasp the storytelling power of images—"And what do you think will happen next?"

As children grow and are able to distinguish the world of fantasy from the real world they live in, they can explore how media are put together by turning the sound off during a cartoon and noting the difference it makes, or even create their own superhero story using a home video camera and easy to use editing software on the family computer. When students begin to use the Internet to research school projects, they can compare different websites and contrast different versions of the same information in order to detect bias or political "spin."

But questions come in many forms. Too often many classroom questions are designed for students to "guess" what answer the teacher already has in mind. True media literacy opens up the possibility that students may come up with insights that the teacher may not have thought of—indeed, may not even agree with. Media literacy consultant Faith Rogow (p. 287, this volume) challenges teachers to clarify their questioning approach with these self-reflective probes:

- Am I trying to tell the students what the message is? Or am I giving students the skills to determine what they think the message(s) might be?
- Have I let students know that I am open to accepting their interpretation, as long as it is well substantiated, or have I conveyed the message that my interpretation is the only correct view?
- At the end of the lesson, are students likely to be more analytical? Or more cynical?

Uncovering the many levels of meaning in a media message and the multiple answers to even basic questions is what makes media education so engaging for kids and so enlightening for adults. There is no doubt that at the heart of media literacy is the principle of inquiry (Thoman & Jolls, 2002).

Although media literacy would seem to be an educational development for the 21st century, the field of media literacy education has a long history, stretching back into the 1800s and the introduction of photography, through the popularization of literature through dime novels and comic books and the birth of movies and eventually television as a popular art form. For much of this time, popular media was considered unworthy of the classroom and ignored, even denigrated, as not suitable for an educated person's time and attention. Such attitudes persist today in the "love–hate" relationship most adults have with media culture and in many of the "media-bashing" movements on the Internet and in the popular press (Fallows, 1996; Sternheimer, 2003).

With the cultural revolution of the 1960s, changing attitudes toward visual and popular culture began to crack some of the highbrow/low-brow resistance. One major influence was the establishment of film as a serious art form, thanks to European filmmakers such as Ingmar Bergman and Federico Fellini. The resulting film discussion groups on college and university campuses educated the next generation of teach-ers and librarians—and parents—to recognize the challenge of under-standing a growing visual culture.

Another important influence was the Canadian philosopher Mar-shall McLuhan, whose prescient analysis of the world as a mediated "global village" was 30 years ahead of the communications explosion created by the Internet. McLuhan's ideas, while exciting to some but frightening to others, were confusing to just about everyone! Never-theless, his theories established a popular, if at times misguided, con-ceptualization of the new "information age" (McLuhan, 1964).

By the 1970s innovative educators in the U.S. were beginning to explore ways to incorporate media issues and activities into the class-room. At first media literacy was seen as teaching children *about* media—how advertising works, how to analyze the nightly news telecast or the visual language of film. Experimentation was extensive and diver-sified and included projects funded by the Ford Foundation and an initiative of the Department of Education in the Carter administration to establish a K-12 "critical viewing skills" curriculum (Tyner, 1991). Tragically, the latter project earned the department a "Golden Fleece" award in 1982 for "wasting tax-payer's money teaching kids to watch TV" (Davis, 1992). The influence of this political misinterpretation of the early goals of media education lasted for decades, by contributing to the notion that media literacy was frivolous and without any educational value.

Throughout the 1980s, entrepreneurial educators, many working alone in their classrooms, struggled with how and what to teach about "the media." Some looked to Canada, Australia, and other countries, where a fledgling media literacy practice was emerging. Unlike these countries, however, the U.S. school system had 50 million students in 16,000 autonomous school districts. And with no serious academic scholarship or leadership from professional teaching organizations, there was simply little momentum for implementing any program of study, even if one could be agreed upon.

In addition, media educator Faith Rogow notes that much of early educational practice, typically influenced by media effects research, resulted in teaching that focused on the potential or presumed "dangers" of media. Pedagogically, the approach is "fatally flawed," she concludes, and students often become cynical instead of intellectually skeptical because a negative approach does not provide them with any sense of agency (Rogow, n.d.)

The formation in 2001 of the Alliance for a Media Literate America (AMLA), a national, grassroots membership organization established to improve and expand the practice of inquiry-based media literacy education, was a significant step forward in professionalizing the media literacy field in America. Through its biennial National Media Education Conference,[1] grassroots teachers rub shoulders with researchers and academics across a range of disciplines and new ideas can be fostered and critiqued. In addition, the Center for Media Literacy (CML) offers both current and historical archives, for teachers, scholars, and others interested in media literacy to draw upon, both at its reference library and online.[2]

Today, the field has matured to a greater understanding of its potential, not just as a new kind of "literacy," but more as the engine for transforming the very nature of learning in a global multimedia environment. "Students will spend all their adult lives in a multitasking, multifaceted, technology-driven, diverse, vibrant world—and they must arrive equipped to do so," notes the Partnership for 21st Century Skills in its report, *Learning for the 21st Century* (2003, p. 4).

The Center for Media Literacy: Making It Easy

One of the core institutional influences in the development of U.S. media literacy is the nonprofit Center for Media Literacy (CML), located in Santa Monica, California. Incorporated in 1989, the center really dates from 1977, when founder Elizabeth Thoman, then a graduate student at the University of Southern California, established *Media & Values* magazine as a thesis project. A former high school English teacher, Thoman created the publication to provide teachers with a link to the knowledge explosion of the emerging information culture and to showcase ways to integrate what she called "media awareness" into schools as well as after-school, community, and religious education programs.[3]

Media & Values, which by the 1990s had a circulation of 10,000, provided a forum for passionate authors to articulate what "teaching the media" was all about. The goal was always to make it easy but keep it solid. Influenced by Freire, and encouraged by media literacy leaders from around the world, Thoman led the magazine to adopt an "empowerment" philosophy centered on informed inquiry in a four-step Awareness/Analysis/Reflection/Action model. Later, the center added to this philosophy by editing Canada's eight "Key Concepts" for media literacy (Pungente, 1989) into *Five Core Concepts*:

- All media messages are constructed.
- Media messages are constructed using creative language with its own rules.
- Different people experience the same media message differently.
- Media have embedded values and points of view.
- Most media messages are constructed to gain profit and/or power.

While traditional educators and publishers toiled to decide the single best media *content* to teach, the CML began to promote media education as *process-oriented inquiry*, using the *Five Core Concepts* with an ever-changing palette of popular culture texts—from Barbie Dolls to tobacco advertising to violence on television. A series of Media Literacy Workshop Kits (consisting of a copy of *Media & Values* magazine with a companion Leader's Guide containing process-oriented lesson plans on a specific theme, such as analyzing the news) modeled the inquiry method for thousands of teachers who purchased the low-cost kits, the first generation of media literacy teaching tools published in the United States (1990–95). In 1994, the Association for Supervision and Curriculum Development commissioned Thoman to write a summary article about media literacy's inquiry method, helping teachers to understand the *Five Core Concepts* and how to teach them. "Skills and Strategies for Media Education" (Thoman, 1999) served for many years as a foundational article, reprinted widely and reproduced for hundreds of workshops and teacher training programs.

In 1999, when Thoman was joined by organizational and change management specialist Tessa Jolls, the two set about to reorient the CML—and its conception of media literacy—for the 21st century. The organization adopted an educational philosophy of "Empowerment through Education," incorporating three intertwining concepts: (1) media literacy is education for life in a global media world; (2) the heart of media literacy is informed inquiry; and (3) media literacy is an alternative to censoring, boycotting, or blaming "the media."

Jolls identified the major challenge for media literacy in the United States as not just making its inclusion in every classroom possible for every teacher, but making it as easy as possible. The stumbling block seemed to be the *Five Core Concepts*—no matter how simply they were phrased, no matter how many examples were given, teachers reported that the concepts were difficult to incorporate easily into everyday classroom activities. It became clear that the *Concepts* were more useful when they were discovered rather than provided; as a result, the 2002 development of a series of *Five Key Questions* to match the long-standing *Five Core Concepts* provided the warp to the woof for a media literacy framework for 21st-century learning and teaching. (The *Questions*, with the corresponding *Concepts*, are examined in more detail beginning on page 191).

The focus of the center's work shifted from interpreting the *Concepts* to teaching teachers to apply each *Question*—and the multiple permutations each one can generate. The vision is for every child to graduate from high school knowing how to ask and apply the *Five Key Questions* to any message in any media. To help organize and unify the many elements of media literacy learning, the CML, in 2002, introduced the CML MediaLit Kit and began to use it as a framework for all its consulting and training. A 28-page Orientation Guide was written, and the remainder of this chapter is based largely on this guide.

CML MediaLit Kit™/A Framework for Learning and Teaching in a Media Age

The transformation of our culture from an industrial age to an information age is why a new kind of literacy, coupled with a new way of learning, is critical in the 21st century. This new kind of literacy is outlined in the CML MediaLit Kit™/A Framework for Learning and Teaching in a Media Age. Resting on a foundation of CML's 25 years of experience in the field plus the thinking of leading practitioners around the world, the CML MediaLit Kit™ was created to help unify the field of media literacy education and establish a common ground upon which to build curriculum programs, teaching materials, and training services.

The bulk of this chapter will explore the six elements of the CML MediaLit Kit™ as an educational framework in depth. This articulation, however, is not an end, but only the beginning of the beginning.

There is significant build-out to be done to address issues such as sequencing—what skills can be taught at what age? And in what order?; integration across the curriculum—what skills work best in what content areas?; and research—each of these questions and many others deserve to be explored through solid research.

To encourage the use and detailed build-out of process skills on pre-K-12 levels, CML has made the CML MediaLit Kit™ available at no charge to teachers for individual classroom use.[4] Teachers are able to use the framework, particularly the *Five Key Questions*, as a starting point for creating lesson plans to teach specific process skills that tie into various curriculum areas. The CML invites others, whether staff development trainers, researchers, or publishers, to adopt the CML MediaLit Kit™ framework on a licensed basis in order to create consistency with larger audiences and pedagogical unity across many disciplines.

Element 1: The Inquiry Process: Analysis/Production

The first element in an inquiry-based media literacy pedagogy is the inquiry process itself. Like two sides of the same coin, the inquiry process is understood to include both analytical (deconstruction) skills as well as creative communications (construction/production) skills. When analysis is combined with creative production, theory unites with application, thereby allowing students to discover and express their learning in an interconnected and natural process. Each enriches the other. As media messages are transmitted through so many different mental processes, the combination of analysis with production also incorporates multiple intelligences in the learning process (linguistic/verbal, logical/mathematical, musical/rhythmic, visual/spatial, body/kinesthetic, intrapersonal/interpersonal). While both activities can happen independently, there is much to gain by meshing the two into one cohesive activity of analysis and production—or as the MediaLit Kit™ expresses it: Free Your Mind! and Express Your View!

Free your mind! Analysis/deconstruction/"reading." To   free   one's mind, students need the skills and abilities to "read" their multimedia world and understand its many layers of messages. The process of taking apart messages, whether print or electronic, is referred to in many ways: analysis, deconstruction, decoding, or "reading" in the traditional terminology of reading/writing literacy.

Media analysis develops critical thinking skills and is an important part of media literacy education because it strengthens observation and interpretation; deepens understanding and appreciation; challenges stereotyping, both misrepresentations and/or underrepresentations; illuminates bias and points of view; uncovers motivations; exposes implicit messages that are less obvious; gives perspective and meaning to the media creators; and enlightens society about the effects and implications of a message.

Express your view!: Production/construction/"writing." In today's multimedia culture "writing" is far more complex than putting pen to paper. Today students may "write" a PowerPoint report for science class, create a persuasive poster about teen smoking for their health project, or draw an original political cartoon. All of these projects require the same core abilities as writing words on paper: organizing thoughts, drafting and redrafting ideas, editing, polishing, and presenting the final project. Education reporter John Merrow (1990–91) notes that "children ought to have access to information about how television is made and to the TV-making equipment itself . . . As they learn to make television, they will also learn most of the other lessons, values and basic skills we want them to."

Student production is an important component of media literacy education for many reasons: it involves the application of multiple intelligences, requires active hands-on learning, increases motivation and the enjoyment of learning, generates new avenues for alternative representations, creates outlets to communicate beyond the classroom, reinforces self-esteem and self-expression, offers real-world practical application of theoretical concepts, and provides a way to assess student understanding of both content and concepts.

Element 2: Media Literacy: A Consistent Definition

One of the most vexing issues in the development of U.S. media literacy is the identification of a clear definition to guide and unify the field. Media literacy education is a wide-ranging discipline and without a clear and consistent definition, it is difficult at times to determine exactly what is being taught under the banner of "media literacy." It has almost been easier to determine what media literacy is *not*:

- It is not media bashing, though it may involve both criticizing media messages and critiquing media institutions.
- It is not simply producing media, though media literacy should include media production.
- It is not teaching *with* videos or CD-ROMs; it is teaching *about* media and society.

- It is more than simply looking for political agendas, stereotypes, or misrepresentations, to understand how these are made to appear "normal."
- It is not based on one perspective only.
- It is not an attempt to censor or limit media consumption; it is an attempt to encourage careful and critical consumption.[5]

Historically, the definition most often cited in the United States is a succinct sentence hammered out by participants at the 1992 Aspen Media Literacy Leadership Institute: "the ability to access, analyze, evaluate and create media in a variety of forms." A dozen years later, it seems that a more robust definition is needed to situate media literacy not as isolated skills but in the context of their importance for the education of students to live and work in a 21st-century media democracy.

CML MediaLit Kit[TM] therefore uses this expanded definition:

Media Literacy is a 21st century approach to education. It provides a framework to access, analyze, evaluate and create messages in a variety of forms—from print to video to the Internet. Media literacy builds an understanding of the role of media in society as well as essential skills of inquiry and self-expression necessary for citizens of a democracy.

What is important to understand is that media literacy is about exploring media culture in a systematic and intelligent way, not about "protecting" kids from unwanted messages. Although some groups urge families to just turn the TV off or forbid the playing of video games, the fact is, media are so ingrained in our cultural milieu that even if you turn off the set, you still cannot escape today's media culture.

Media literacy, therefore, is about helping students become competent, critical, and literate in all media forms so that they control the interpretation of what they see or hear, rather than letting the interpretation control them. To become media literate is not to memorize facts or statistics about the media, but rather to learn to raise the right questions about what you are watching, reading, or listening to. Len Masterman, the acclaimed author of *Teaching the Media* (1985), calls it "critical autonomy" or the ability to think for oneself. Without this fundamental ability, an individual cannot have full dignity as a human person or exercise citizenship in a democratic society where to be a citizen is to both understand and contribute to the debates of the time.

Elements 3 and 4: The Five Core Concepts and the Five Key Questions

As the cornerstone of the media literacy process, the *Five Key Questions* provide a shortcut and an on-ramp to acquiring and applying information process skills in a practical, replicable, consistent, and attainable way. They are an academically sound and yet engaging way to begin. As noted earlier, the *Key Questions* flow directly from *Five Core Concepts* (creator/author/producer; format and techniques of production; influence on the audience; content or message; motive/purpose) that media literacy practitioners around the world have used to explore any rhetorical message.

In the classroom, however, the goal is not to so much to teach the *Core Concepts*, especially with younger students, but, rather, to focus on the *Five Key Questions* in order to help students build the habit of routinely subjecting media messages to age-appropriate inquiry. Teachers, however, need to be thoroughly acquainted with the *Core Concepts* in order to develop classroom activities and curriculum connections that provide students with opportunities to learn and practice the asking of questions about media in their lives.

Let us now look at each *Concept/Question* in more depth. Along the way, we can also begin to identify related questions that can be generated to gain deeper understandings of each *Concept*.

> Core Concept 1: *All media messages are constructed.*
> Key Question 1: *Who created this message?*

The first *Concept/Question* looks at two important aspects of any media message —authorship and "constructedness." We should not think of media texts (newspaper articles, TV shows, and comic books to name just a few) as "natural" things. Media texts are built just as surely as buildings and highways are built. The building materials vary from one kind of text to another. In a magazine, for example, there are words in different sizes and fonts, photographs, colors, varied layout, and page location. TV and movies have hundreds of building blocks—from camera angles and lighting to music and sound effects.

What this means is that whether we are watching the nightly news or passing a billboard on the street, the media message we experience was written by someone, pictures were taken, and a creative designer put it all together. This is more than just a physical process. Whatever is constructed by just a few people then becomes normalized for the rest of us; like the air we breathe, it gets taken for granted and usually goes unquestioned. But as the audience, we do not see or hear the words, pictures, or arrangements that were rejected.

Helping people understand how media are put together or "constructed"—and what was left out—as well as how the media shape what we know and understand about the world we live in is a critical first step in helping them navigate their lives through a global and technological society. *Who created this message?* opens up a whole series of other questions: Who is the author? How many people did it take to create this message? What are their various jobs? What kind of "text" is it? How similar or different is it to others of the same genre? Which technologies are used in its creation? What are the various elements (building blocks) that make up the whole?

> Core Concept 2: *Media messages are constructed using creative language with its own rules.*
>
> Key Question 2: *What creative techniques are used to attract my attention?*

Using *Concept/Question* 2, we can create a checklist for examining the creative components that are used in putting a particular message together. Indeed, each form of communication—whether newspapers, TV game shows, or horror movies—has its own creative "language": scary music heightens fear, camera close-ups convey intimacy, big headlines signal significance. Understanding the grammar, syntax, and metaphor system of media language, especially the language of sounds and visuals that can reach beyond the rational to our deepest emotional core, increases our appreciation and enjoyment of media experiences, while making us less susceptible to manipulation.

We can uncover how this language is used by asking: What do you notice about the way the message is constructed (colors and shapes, sounds and silence, props, sets and/or clothing, movement, and symbols)? Where is the camera? What is the viewpoint? What are the sounds? Music? Words? Narration? Dialogue? Silence? Sound effects? How is the story told? Symbols? Metaphors? What's the emotional appeal? Persuasive devices? What makes it seem real?

One of the best ways to understand how media are put together is to do just that—make a video, create a website, develop an ad campaign about a community issue. The four major arts disciplines—music, dance, theater, and the visual arts—can also provide a context through which one gains skills of analysis, interpretation, and appreciation along with opportunities for self-expression and creative production.

Core Concept 3: *Different people experience the same media message differently.*

Key Question 3: *How might different people understand this message differently from me?*

Audiences play a role in interpreting media texts because each audience member brings to that text a unique set of life experiences (age, gender, education, cultural upbringing, etc.) which when applied to the text—or combined with the text—create unique interpretations. A World War II veteran, for example, brings a different set of experiences to a movie like *Saving Private Ryan* than a teenage boy does—resulting in a different reaction to the film as well as, perhaps, greater insight. Even parents and children watching TV together do not "see" the same program.

This concept turns the tables on the idea of TV viewers as just passive "couch potatoes." We may not be conscious of it but each of us, even toddlers, are constantly trying to "make sense" of what we see, hear, or read. The more questions we can ask about what we are experiencing around us, the more alert we can be about accepting or rejecting messages. Research indicates that, over time, all children can learn age-appropriate skills that give them a new set of glasses with which they can "read" and interpret their media culture.

A good place to start is with the third key question, *How might different people understand this message differently from me?* It may lead to additional questions, including: How well does this text fit with your experience of the world? What did you learn from the media text? What did you learn about yourself from experiencing the media text? What did you learn from other people's responses and experiences? How many other interpretations could there be? How could we hear about them? Are other viewpoints just as valid as mine? How can you explain the different responses?

Core Concept 4: *Media have embedded values and points of view.*

Key Question 4: *What lifestyles, values, and points of view are represented in, or omitted from, this message?*

Media, because they are constructed, carry a subtext of who and what is important—at least to the person or persons creating the construction. Media are also storytellers (even commercials tell a quick and simple story) and stories require characters and settings and a plot that has a beginning, a middle, and an end. The choice of a character's age, gender, or race, mixed in with the lifestyles, attitudes, and behav-

iors that are portrayed, the selection of a setting (urban? rural? affluent? poor?), and the actions and reactions in the plot are just some
of the ways that values become embedded in a TV show, a movie, or
an ad.

It is important to learn how to "read" all kinds of media messages
in order to discover the points of view that are embedded in them and
how to assess those points of view as part of the text rather than merely
accepting them as a given. Only then can we judge whether to accept
or reject these messages as we negotiate our way each day through our
mediated environment.

We can explore the fourth *Concept/Question* with these guiding questions: What questions come to mind as you watch/read/listen? What
political or economic values are communicated in the message? What
judgments or statements are made about personal or social relationships? What is the cultural context or worldview? What ideas or values
are being "sold" in this message? How is the human person characterized? What type of person is the reader/watcher/listener invited to
identify with? What kinds of behaviors/consequences are depicted?
Who or what is left out?

Without the media literacy process, any analysis of a movie, TV
program, advertising, or other media, too often starts—and stops—with
the explicit content of the program. Building on the authorship and
"constructedness" of a message with the first two questions, we achieve
a deeper and more nuanced analysis of what a message is communicating with the fourth.

> Core Concept 5: *Most media messages are constructed to gain profit and/
> or power.*
> Key Question 5: *Why is this message being sent?*

Media messages are made for many reasons. One of them is to make
money. Newspapers and magazines lay out their ad pages first; the space
remaining is devoted to news or features. Likewise, commercials are
part and parcel of most TV watching. What many people do not know
is that what is really being sold through commercial media is not only
the advertised products to the audience—but also the audience to the
advertisers! The real purpose of the programs on television, or the
articles in a magazine, is to create an audience (and put them in a
receptive mood) so that the network or publisher can sell time or space
to sponsors to advertise products—usually in a way that entices us to
want what we really do not need. Sponsors pay for the time based on
the number of people the station predicts will be watching. And they

get a refund if the number of actual viewers turns out to be lower than promised.

But the issue of "message motivation" has changed dramatically since the Internet became an international platform through which groups and organizations—even individuals—can attempt to persuade others to adopt a particular point of view. As an exercise in power unprecedented in human history, the Internet's flood of information underscores the need for users of all ages to be able to interpret rhetorical devices, verify sources, and distinguish legitimate online sources from bogus, hate, or hoax websites.

Clearly, in the media literacy process, the fifth *Concept/Question* goes deeper than the obvious. Examining the purpose of a message also uncovers the structure of media institutions and their role in society as well as the economic and/or political influence of media in a democracy. This may lead to questions such as: Who is in control of the creation and transmission of this message? Who profits? Who pays? Who wins? Who loses? Who decides? Who is served by or benefits from the message?—The public? Private interests? Individuals? Institutions? What economic decisions may have influenced the construction or transmission of this message? Money/sex/power—How is each presented?

Alternate questions for different ages and abilities. Awareness of the developmental stages of students is essential to teachers of media literacy. The *Five Core Concepts* and the *Five Key Questions* are only starting points as inquiry tools; the questions must obviously be simplified for younger children as well as for those with limited language ability or vocabulary. Expansion of the questions allows for more sophisticated inquiry by teens, college students, and adults.

Although some might question the appropriateness of introducing media literacy to preschoolers, this is precisely the age in which it ought to begin. Just like we recognize that learning the alphabet at age 4 is an important building block to being able to analyze a novel at age 16, media literacy has building blocks that provide a foundation for more complex skills. It is important, for example, to encourage children to practice talking about what they see and hear and how it makes them feel. The kit's *Questions to Guide Young Children* provide an entry point for parents, caregivers, and preschool teachers to help young children navigate their media world. Rather than asking "Who created this message?" children can be asked "What is this?" Instead of "Why was this message sent?" children might think about "Is this trying to sell me something?" These simpler questions paraphrase a *Concept* to engage with a child's level of understanding.

Once young people gain mastery with the *Five Key Questions*, it becomes easier to interrelate them and apply them to a media message with far more sophistication. Their growing ability to think abstractly, to solve problems of probability, to generalize, and to express themselves in multiple media platforms also opens up a myriad of scholarly ways to explore a media text. The MediaLit Kit™ suggests three "lenses" for more sophisticated inquiry: messages and values—exploring the *content* of a media message; codes and conventions—exploring the *form* of the message; and producers and consumers—exploring the *purpose* and effects of a message. Each lens promotes an intellectual crossover and encourages unique insights from different perspectives and learning styles.

Element 5: Process Skills: Access, Analyze, Evaluate, Create

In discussing the need for media literacy in 21st-century classrooms, many teachers assert that their classroom plate is already overflowing. "What do I throw out in order to put in media literacy?" is frequently asked. It is reassuring to understand that media literacy is not so much a body of knowledge to be "mastered" as much as an ability to apply increasingly sophisticated questions when one critically engages with any mediated message, from textbooks to the nightly news. It involves posing problems that exercise higher-order thinking skills—learning how to identify key concepts, how to make connections between multiple ideas, how to ask pertinent questions, identify fallacies, formulate a response. It is these "process" skills, not factual knowledge, that form the foundation of intellectual inquiry and workplace productivity, and that are necessary for exercising full citizenship in a democratic society and a global economy. Such skills have always been essential for an educated life and good teachers have always fostered them. But too often they emerged only as a by-product of mastering content areas such as literature, history, the sciences, and mathematics. Learning and process skills were seldom taught explicitly. But as noted in the *Learning for the 21st Century* report, if we are to graduate students who can be in charge of their own continual learning in a media culture, we must "incorporate learning skills into classrooms deliberately, strategically and broadly" (Partnership, 2003, p. 6). By its very nature, media literacy education teaches and reinforces 21st-century learning skills.

Access. When people access messages, they are able to collect relevant and useful information and comprehend meaning effectively. They can read print and multimedia messages with high levels of comprehension; recognize and understand a rich vocabulary of words, symbols, and techniques of communication; develop strategies for locating information from a wide variety of sources; and select an assortment of types of information relevant to the purpose of a task.

Analyze. When people analyze messages, they are able to examine the design of the message's form, structure, and sequence. They can make use of artistic, literary, social, political, and economic concepts to understand a message's context. They do so by using prior knowledge and experiences to predict outcomes; interpreting a message using concepts such as purpose, audience, point of view, format, genre, character, plot, theme, mood, setting, context; using strategies including compare/contrast, fact/opinion, cause/effect, listing and sequencing; and using knowledge about the historical, political, economic, and social contexts in which messages are created and interpreted.

Evaluate. When people evaluate messages, they are able to relate messages to their own experience and make judgments about the veracity, quality, and relevance of messages. They are able to appreciate and take pleasure in interpreting messages in different genres and forms; respond in print and orally to messages of varying complexity and content; evaluate the quality of a message based on its content and form; and judge the value of a message based on ethical, religious, or democratic principles.

Create. When people create (or communicate) messages, they are able to "write" their ideas, using words, sounds, and/or images effectively for a variety of purposes, and they are able to make use of various technologies of communication to create, edit, and disseminate their message. They make use of brainstorming, planning, composing, and revising processes; use writing and oral language effectively with mastery of rules of language usage; create and select images effectively to achieve various goals; and use technologies of communication in the construction of messages (see Hobbs, Chapter 5, this volume).

Element 6: The Empowerment Spiral: How to Organize Media Literacy Learning

Worsnop (1999) has noted that successful media education is more about *how* it is taught, rather than *what* is taught. The final aspect of the basic MediaLit Kit™ framework is the *Empowerment Spiral*, which outlines a way to organize media literacy learning. Also called "Action Learning," the model has proven to be an excellent process for uncorking a spiral of inquiry that leads to increased comprehension, greater critical thinking, and ability to make informed judgments.

Often when dealing with media issues or topics, we can sometimes be intimidated by the complex technological and institutional structures that dominate our media culture. We can feel powerless against the psychological sophistication of advertising messages and pop culture icons.

The *Empowerment Spiral*, based on the work of Brazilian educator Paulo Freire, outlines how to break complex topics or concepts into four short-term learning steps that stimulate different aspects of the brain and enhance our ability to evolve new knowledge from past experience. Teachers or leaders who use these four steps to design lesson plans or organize group activities will find the *Empowerment Spiral* is a powerful matrix that transforms both learning and teaching.

Awareness: Creating the "ah-ha" moment. In the Awareness step, students participate in an activity that leads to observations and personal connections for potential insight: "Oh! I never thought of that before." Youngsters might compare whether their action toys perform like the ones in commercials; teens might time the length of stories on the nightly news to uncover how much is news and how much is nonnews; a class might keep a media journal for just one day (from waking up to falling asleep) to become aware of how many different media they experience in their lives. Awareness activities provide the "ah-ha" moments that unlock a spiral of critical inquiry and exploration that are the foundation of media literacy pedagogy.

Analysis: Uncovering complexity. The next step, Analysis, provides time for students to figure out "how" an issue came to be. Applying the *Five Key Questions* and conducting a close analysis (see page 200) are two techniques that can be used to better understand the complexity of the selected issue. Creative production experiences could also help the group understand "how" and "what" happens in the exchange between a media producer and the audience.

It is important that analysis go deeper than just trying to identify some meaning in an ad, a song, or an episode of a sitcom. Indeed, "why" questions often lead to speculation, personal interpretation, and circular debate, rather than the critical process of inquiry, exploration, and discovery. Instead ask "what" and preferably "how": How does the camera angle make us feel about the product being advertised? What difference would it make if the car in the ad were blue instead of red? What do we know about a character from her dress, make-up, and jewelry? How does the music contribute to the mood of the story being told? The power of media literacy lies in figuring out how the construction of any media product influences and contributes to the meaning we make of it.

Reflection: What seems right or fair? In the Reflection step, the group looks deeper to ask "So what?" or "What ought we to do?" Depending on the group, they may want to also consider philosophical or religious traditions, ethical values, social justice, or democratic principles that are accepted as guides for individual and collective decision making. These may be explored with questions like "Does the First Amendment protect advertising?" and "What are other ways an action hero could have solved a conflict?"

Action: Learning by doing. Finally, the Action step gives participants an opportunity to formulate constructive action ideas, to "learn by doing." It is important to remember that in the media literacy context, action is necessarily equated with "activism" or "advocacy." Media literacy is not about promoting one political view over another, but rather creating a space for examining all points of view. For some topics or groups the action step may indeed involve some kind of public witness or advocacy campaign (protesting sexist advertising, for example) but the most long-lasting actions are often simple activities that symbolize or ritualize increased internal awareness.

- After discovering and reflecting on the amount of violence they saw in one week of children's cartoons, one second grade class decided to write a "Declaration of Independence" from violence on TV. Each child signed his/her name just like the Founding Fathers and they posted their declaration on the bulletin board in the school lobby for all to read.
- To culminate an introduction to media storytelling, a kindergarten class creates their own story and draws it out in a sequence of five or six scenes that the teacher mounts on a long roll of construction paper and hangs on the wall like a giant piece of film.
- High school students concerned about school board budget cuts interviewed their parents and neighbors on video tape and produced a short video about various perspectives on what the cuts

might mean. It was shown every night for a week on the district's closed circuit cable channel.

It should be noted that teachers interested in incorporating media literacy in their classroom do not necessarily need extensive knowledge of media theories or even professional competency in journalism, video production, or film-making. What they *do* need is to be skilled in organizing and facilitating student-centered learning. More than anything else, media education is a "quest for meaning," says Chris Worsnop (1999), one of Canada's media literacy leaders. It is an exploration for both students and teachers. The best preparation is simply an inquiring mind and a willingness to answer a student's question with "I don't know. How could we find out?"[6]

Applying the Framework

So what does media literacy look like in practice? The following scenario illustrates how the inquiry method can lead to deep insight and understanding of a media text.

Close Analysis of a Media Text

While getting caught up in a storytelling experience has been the essence of entertainment since our ancestors told tales around the fire, the relentless pace of entertainment media today requires that at least once in awhile, we should stop and look, really look, at how a media message is put together and the many interpretations that can derive from it. The method for this is called *close analysis*. To learn to conduct this basic media literacy exercise, try it first yourself; then introduce it to a group or class.

Any media message can be used for a close analysis but commercials are often good choices because they are short and tightly packed with powerful words and images, music and sounds. Find a commercial to analyze by recording some during an hour or two of TV watching. Look for a commercial that seems to have a lot of layers—interesting visuals and sound track, memorable words or taglines, multiple messages that call out for exploration. Replay your selection several times as you go through the following steps:

- Visuals: After the first viewing, write down everything you can remember about the visuals—lighting, camera angles, how the pictures are edited together. Describe any people—what do they look like? What are they doing? Wearing? What scenes or images do you remember clearly? Focus only on what is actually on the screen, not your interpretation of what you saw on the screen. If necessary, play it again but with the sound off. Keep adding to your list of visuals.

- Sounds: Replay again with the picture off. Listen to the sound track. Write down all the words that are spoken. Who says them? What kind of music is used? Does it change in the course of the commercial? How? Are there other sounds? What is their purpose? Who is being spoken to, directly or indirectly? (That is, who is the audience addressed by the commercial?)

- Apply Key Questions: With the third viewing, begin to apply the *Five Key Questions* and the Guiding Questions that lead to them. Identify the author(s) and how the specific construction techniques you identified in steps 1 and 2 influence what the commercial is "saying"—values expressed and unexpressed; lifestyles endorsed or rejected; points of view proposed or assumed. Explore what's left out of the message and how different people might react differently to it. What is the message "selling"? Is it the same as the product being advertised? Continue to show the text over and over; it's like peeling back the layers of an onion.

- Review Your Insights: Summarize how the text is constructed and how various elements of the construction trigger our own unique response, which may be very different from how others interpret the text. Try this exercise with other kinds of messages: a story from a newscast, a key scene from a movie, a print advertisement, a website. Are different questions important for different kinds of messages?

Doing a close analysis with a class or group can be exhilarating, with insights coming fast and furiously. After the first showing, start the group exercise with the simple question: "What did you notice?" Different people will remember different things, so accept all answers and keep asking, "What else did you notice?" If the group is having a hard time, show the clip again and invite them to look for something that stands out for them. Continue the brainstorming until you have at least 15 or 20 answers to the question: "What did you notice?" Challenge any attempt to assign interpretation too early. Keep the group focused on identifying only what was actually on screen or heard on the soundtrack. The key to success with this exercise is for the teacher/leader to keep asking questions. Refrain from contributing too many answers yourself.

While no one has the time to subject every media message to this kind of analysis, it takes only two or three experiences with close analysis to give us the insight to "see" through other media messages as we encounter them. It is like having a new set of glasses that brings the whole media world into focus. (Teaching tip: When you find a text that is useful for a close analysis, put it on a videotape six or eight times with five seconds of black between. This makes it easier to show it several times without having to stop and rewind.)

The 21st Century Is Now

In *Playing the Future*, author Douglas Rushkoff (1996) dubs the current youth generation "screen-agers" because their media use is not distinguished specifically as television or movie watching or video game playing or computer use, but simply as a series of screens that are accessed and manipulated in a constantly evolving stream of shared communication. This capability, in turn, is transforming the use and impact of media in everyday life:

- Screen-agers see media not as discrete products that can influence them or their culture but as elements of a multimedia mosaic that *is* their culture.
- Screen-agers "read" and "write" seamlessly using images, sounds, and words.
- Screen-agers experience the world not in physical boundaries but as an instant global network of wireless connections and interconnections.

In this kind of world, the content of a specific media message is no longer all that relevant. It is only one of thousands received every day. What is important is facility with analyzing new information as it's received, evaluating it against one's prior knowledge, formulating a response and ultimately communicating to others your decision or point of view. In other words, what is important is not so much the message itself as how we make sense of the message and by extension, of the mediated world around us. It demands a new kind of literacy, rooted in the real world of instant information, global interactivity, and messages created on multiple media platforms.

Inquiry-based media literacy education provides both the framework and pedagogy for this new literacy needed for living, working, and citizenship in the 21st century. Media literacy cannot wait for the future. It is needed now to assure that our students are equipped to make the decisions and contributions a global economy and a global culture demand of them. We can make it easier for them to attain these critical skills; the tools are waiting to be used.

AUTHORS' NOTE

The CML is grateful for the many contributions to the CML MediaLit Kit™/A Framework for Learning and Teaching in a Media Age by the leading media literacy writers and authors, scholars and researchers named or quoted throughout this article. We are indebted to your rich insights, your thoughtful critique, and your generous collaboration as we worked to develop a collective document that would articulate our common vision.

NOTES

1. Information on AMLA can be found at http://www. AMLAinfo.org

2. The "Reading Room" section of the CML, at http://www. medialit.org, features a chronology of conference reports, articles, and original primary sources that document the history and evolution of media literacy from the early 1970s to the present. CML founder Elizabeth Thoman's personal papers, meeting notes, reports and speeches enrich the site with historical perspective. CML's reference library at its offices in Santa Monica, California, also contains a wealth of historical documents and curriculum resources developed by individual teachers, nonprofit organizations, and publishers from the U.S. and around the world. The library is open by appointment only.

3. An archive of all 63 issues from 1977 to 1993 is online at http://www.medialit.org

4. Teachers can order the kit at http://www.medialit.org/bp_ mlk.html

5. With thanks to Renee Hobbs, Chris Worsnop, Neil Andersen, Jeff Share, and Scott Sullivan.

6. A word about copyright: Issues of copyright enter the media literacy classroom in a variety of ways. Materials produced specifically for educational use and/or purchased from legitimate educational sources are not usually an issue. But what about showing clips from movies rented at the video store? Or students using music from their favorite CD artist as the sound track of a video production? Or copying pictures from the Internet to put into a class PowerPoint presentation or on their own website?

Relevant media "texts," both print and electronic, are necessary for teaching critical analysis in a 21st-century media culture. And the ability to analyze and think critically is the very foundation of both intellectual freedom and the exercising of full citizenship in a democracy. Production projects are integral to learning by experience how media are constructed as well as demonstrating mastery of various media formats and gaining competency in creative self-expression.

The "Fair Use" provision of the 1976 Copyright Law, as amended, states precisely that the use of copyrighted materials is allowed for "criticism, comment, news reporting, teaching (including multiple copies for classroom use), scholarship or research."

However, applying the "Fair Use" standard in specific situations is seldom crystal clear. And as recent headlines about music piracy indicates, new technologies keep shifting the ground for both public discourse and legal interpretation. The following are some organizations/websites to check for the latest guidelines on issues of copyright in educational settings:

- U.S. Copyright Office
- American Library Association, http://www.ala.org/ala/home/copyright.htm
- Free Expression Policy Project, http://www.fepproject.org/

REFERENCES

Berlo, D.K. (1975). The context for communication. In G.J. Hannemann,W.K. McEwan, & D.K. Berlo (Eds.), *Communication and behavior* (pp. 3–18). Reading, MA: Addison-Wesley Publishing Company.

Davis, J.F. (1992). Media literacy: From activism to exploration. Background paper for the National Leadership Conference on Media Literacy. Retrieved November 23, 2004, from http://www.medialit.org/reading_room/pdf/357_AspenBkgnd_Davis.pdf

Fallows, J. (1996). *Breaking the news: How the media undermine American democracy*. New York: Vintage.

Freire, P. (1970). *Pedagogy of the oppressed*. New York: Herder and Herder.

Hobbs, R. (2005). Media literacy and the K-12 content areas. In G. Schwarz & P.U. Brown (Eds.), *Media literacy: Transforming curriculum and teaching. The 104th yearbook of the National Society for the Study of Education*, Part I (pp. 74–99). Malden, MA: Blackwell Publishing.

Masterman, L. (1985). *Teaching the media*. London: Routledge.

McLuhan, M. (1964). *Understanding media*. New York: Mentor.

Merrow, J. (1990–91). Teach kids to make TV! Media & Values (52–53) [electronic version]. Retrieved from http://www.medialit.org/reading_room/article60.html

Partnership for 21st Century Skills. (2003). *Learning for the 21st century*. Washington, DC: Partnership for 21st Century Skills. Retrieved December 13, 2004, from http://www.21stcenturyskills.org/downloads/P21_Report.pdf

Pungente, J. (1989). Media literacy key concepts. In B. Duncan (Ed.), *Media literacy resource guide*. Ontario Ministry of Education, Toronto, ON, Canada. Retrieved December 13, 2004, from http://www.media-awareness.ca/English/teachers/media_literacy/key_concept.cfm

Rogow, F. (n.d.). Shifting from media to literacy: One opinion on the challenges of media literacy education. Unpublished manuscript. Retrieved December 13, 2004, from http://www.nationaledtechplan.org/bb/bb_1/download.asp?file-name=Rogow%20tech-ml%20article.doc

Rogow, F. (2005). *Terrain in transition: Reflections on the pedagogy of media literacy education*. In G. Schwarz & P.U. Brown (Eds.), *Media literacy: Transforming curriculum and teaching. The 104th yearbook of the National Society for the Study of Education*, Part I (pp. 284–290). Malden, MA: Blackwell Publishing.

Rushkoff, D. (1996). *Playing the future*. New York: Riverhead Books.

Sternheimer, K. (2003). *It's not the media: The truth about pop culture's influence on children*. Boulder, CO: Westview Press.

Thoman, E. (1999). Skills and strategies for media education. *Educational Leadership*, *56*(5), 50–54.

Thoman, E., & Jolls, T. (2002). Letter from the founders: Center for media literacy. Retrieved December 13, 2004, from http://www.medialit.org/letter.html

Tyner, K. (1991, Summer). The media education elephant. *Strategies Quarterly*. Retrieved December 8, 2004, from http://www.medialit.org/reading_room/article429.html

United Nations Educational, Scientific and Cultural Organization (UNESCO). (1982, January 22). Grunwald declaration on media education. International Symposium on Media Education, Grunwald, Federal Republic of Germany. Retrieved December 13, 2004, from http://www.unesco.org/education/html/policy_doc.shtml

Worsnop, C. (1999). *Screening images*. Santa Monica, CA: Center for Media Literacy.

CHAPTER 11

The Practice and Principles of Teaching Critical Literacy at the Educational Video Center

STEVEN GOODMAN

We did a documentary about homeless youth . . . It was an important topic for us to learn and research about because it will change not only the way we think about it, but whoever watches the video will also change their way of thinking about it. And it's gonna make a difference in people's lives.

—(Vanessa, EVC Documentary Workshop)

Overall, what I've learned from EVC and what I will take with me, is basically not only working with the camera and things like that and making a documentary, but all in all, how to go out and meet people. And how talk to people.

—(Serena, EVC Documentary Workshop)

Dialogue is the encounter between men, mediated by the world, in order to name the world.

—Paulo Freire (1970, p. 69)

Four high school students walk down a mid-Manhattan street as they talk excitedly about who will conduct the first interview. They have generated good questions to ask concerning the problem of homeless youth in New York City, but are not quite sure if anyone will stop to answer them. They pause at a street corner and work awkwardly to disentangle the cables connecting the digital video camera, microphone, and headphones they are holding. Once they sort out their equipment and their crew roles, the book bag and the camera change hands. The designated interviewer pulls out the notebook from among the extra batteries and videotapes in the bag and opens it to the page with the interview questions scrawled across it. After the third attempt, the scout succeeds in bringing a passerby over to the crew. The interviewer

Steven Goodman is the Executive Director of the Educational Video Center in New York, New York.

explains that they are not from the news, but are students making a documentary project on homelessness. The sound operator slips the headphones on and nods that everything is okay. The cameraperson flips open the viewfinder, zooms in to a medium shot, and pushes the "record" button. The tape starts rolling.

These students are experiencing their first "shoot" out on the street as part of the Educational Video Center's documentary workshop. The Educational Video Center (EVC) is an independent nonprofit media organization that has worked, since it was established in 1984, to build students' skills in documentary production and media literacy while nurturing their intellectual development and civic engagement. These students come from high schools all across New York City and spend four afternoons each week earning academic credit as they learn to collaboratively research, shoot, and edit a documentary on a social issue of immediate importance to them. By the end of the 18-week semester, they will produce *No Home of Your Own*, a documentary exploration of the problem of homeless youth in New York City (Educational Video Center, Producer, 2004). But throughout the process they will learn about much more than the content of this social issue. They will learn about the power of the media to represent ideas, values, and voices, and their own power, as learners and cultural producers, to use media as a tool to educate, inform, and make change in the community.

As founding director of EVC, I have spent more than 20 years working with students and teachers in New York City and have seen how effective the critical literacy method of media education can be. EVC grew out of my combined experience as an independent documentary maker and as a video teacher in an alternative high school in Manhattan's Lower East Side. Since 1984, it has evolved from a single video class into an organization with four main programs: a *high school documentary workshop*; a preprofessional *paid internship program* called YO-TV; a *community engagement program* using EVC documentaries in local neighborhoods to organize for social change; and a *teacher development program* serving K-12 educators throughout New York City as they learn to integrate media analysis and production into their classes. Over the years, funding for EVC has been provided by a range of private foundations, corporations, and government sources including the Open Society Institute, the Time Warner Foundation, the Ford Foundation, the New York Community Trust, the JP Morgan Chase Foundation, the New York State Council on the Arts, the National Endowment for the Arts, and the New York City Department of Education.

The EVC Documentary Workshop annually serves 60 public high school students. They live in predominantly low-income communities and reflect the racial and ethnic makeup of New York City. Each semester, EVC contacts guidance counselors and teachers in high schools throughout the city, requesting that they send students to apply and be interviewed. Students are selected on the basis of equity, level of interest, and counselor recommendation, but not on prior academic record. In fact, most EVC students attend alternative high schools and often struggle with academic skills, family troubles, or worse. At the end of the semester, they present their final group projects in public screenings and they present evidence of their literacy, technical, and critical thinking skills in portfolio assessment roundtables.

The impact that the learning process of EVC workshops has on the individual youth participants magnifies a thousand-fold when the products—EVC's library of over 100 youth-produced documentaries— are distributed and seen by thousands of other students in schools, libraries, and community centers across the country. Teachers can access this library online via the EVC website at http://www.evc.org/screen-ing/catalog.html. The documentaries cover a range of adolescent and community issues including educational equity, media and youth iden-tity, gun violence, AIDS, and environmental pollution. These screen-ings serve as springboards for discussion of the tapes and further inquiry into the issues they have raised.

I use the term *critical literacy* as the unifying concept that animates the methodology of media education at EVC. I define critical literacy in much the same way as theorists Ira Shor, who describes it as a "discourse that foregrounds and questions power relations" (1999, p. 18); Joe Kretovics, who asserts that it "provides students not merely with functional skills, but with conceptual tools necessary to critique and engage society along with its inequalities and injustices" (as quoted in Shor, p. 20); and Gary L. Anderson and Patricia Irvine, who explain the student's process of learning to read and write as part of "becoming conscious of their own experience as historically constructed within specific power relations" (as quoted in Shor, p. 1). However, acknowl-edging the pervasiveness of the mass media and entertainment technol-ogies in our society today, I would expand upon these definitions to include the ability to analyze, evaluate, and produce aural and visual forms of communication. I would argue that developing critical literacy skills enables students to investigate power relations within the social and historical context of their lived experience and within the broader frame of their mediated culture. In this way, students build their capacity to understand how media is made to convey particular messages, and how they can use electronic and print technologies to creatively express themselves, and to document and publicly voice their ideas and concerns regarding the most important issues in their lives. Learning about the world is directly linked to the possibility of changing it (Goodman, 2003, p. 3).

This pedagogy of critical literacy is comprised of three key practices and principles:

1. *Teaching Multiple Literacies*: Students learn to analyze, evaluate, and produce texts across oral/aural, visual, and alphabetic/textual modes of language. Media production (writing) and analysis (reading) are linked. Students develop their capacity to encode and decode meaning in multiple forms of representation through speaking and listening, visualizing and observing, and reading and writing. They learn to use multiple literacies to tell their own stories and through their video production represent themselves as new storytellers.

2. *Teaching Continuous Inquiry*: The students' learning is driven by their own questions about their lived experiences; the social, cultural, and historical conditions that shape those experiences; and the media's representations of those conditions and experiences. The learner-centeredness of this approach develops the students' agency as social, political, and cultural actors in their community. Students learn to work collectively, engaging in a problem-posing dialogue with the individuals and institutions in their community and using their documentary to promote public discussion and action for change.

3. *Teaching Reflection*: Students are given multiple opportunities to reflect on their learning and development over time throughout the production process in journals, in regular critique sessions, and in end-of-semester portfolio roundtables where they present drafts of their video and written work as evidence of their intellectual and artistic development. There is a creative tension between action and reflection to ensure that the students' experience is a rich and sustained *learning process* while they also produce a high-quality *media product*.

In this chapter, I explore these strategies for teaching and learning along with the challenges they present, and examine how they so powerfully develop students' intellectual, cultural, and social capacities. Using EVC's fall 2003 semester Documentary Workshop as a window into these issues, I draw upon tapes recording students at work, as well as on interviews with their teachers and with graduates of the program reflecting back on the long-term impact of their learning. Whenever possible, I listen to the students' voices for insight into the practices and principles of critical literacy.

Teaching Multiple Literacies

A key principle of critical literacy is the notion of "multiple litera-cies": that students need to learn to proficiently analyze, evaluate, and produce meaning in visual, oral, and alphabetic forms of communica-tion. This is in response to a few generally agreed-upon conclusions by media literacy researchers and practitioners: (1) Within our media-saturated culture, television, radio, movies, the Internet, newspapers, magazines, music, video games, and so forth, use particular codes and conventions to tell their stories and teach a particular set of ideas, values, and representations about the world and our place in it; (2) This ubiquitous, informal, and lifelong curriculum combines image, sound, graphic symbol, and alphabetic text in overlapping and increasingly integrated modes of communication; (3) These media messages and narratives are delivered by a global system of ever-expanding digital entertainment and information technologies, concentrated in the hands of an ever-fewer number of corporations; (4) Meaning does not reside in the media text itself. Audiences negotiate meaning from the various media they consume depending on a range of factors including gender, class, race, ethnicity, age, and culture (Bazelgette, 1989; Buckingham, 1990/1992; Duncan, D'Ippolito, Macpherson, & Wilson, 1996; Fisher-keller, 2002; Goodman, 2003; Masterman, 1985; Tyner, 1998).

While teaching multiple literacies may seem to be a worthy educa-tional goal, it is not commonly put into practice. Even though the National Council of Teachers of English (NCTE) and several states have formulated language arts standards that call for students to view and analyze a variety of nonprint media (Martin, 2003), school curricula still tend to privilege print literacy over visual literacy and segregate communication forms according to disciplines such as English, speech, and art classes. Language arts instruction is still generally considered to be synonymous with a written text-centric approach to literacy (Goodman, 2003).

Print-based literacy is rarely connected to the practice of visual arts and spoken word. There is the common idea that reading visual media is different from notational alphabetic texts in that some basic understanding of the rules of grammar and vocabulary has to be learned before meaning can be made from the texts. "Reading" visual texts is more direct, as there is no mediating alphabet to decode. But if the grammar of media arts is not understood—the codes and conventions of close-up shots, dissolves, rolling credits, and all the nuances of editing, sound, lighting, shadow, color, framing, angles, movement, and so forth—a student would be unable to "read" in between the lines of a film. Reading a moving image draws upon the same method of close and repeated observations of all the elements the filmmaker used to construct meaning that an art teacher would employ in reading how a painter created a painting. And an art teacher would also train students to develop multiple readings of a painting much as they would with a written text (Piro, 2002).

In the course of a day, we receive visual, oral, and print messages all jumbled together. We take for granted that sound, image, and text are broadcast simultaneously on television, that a newspaper is a combination of image and text and that much of that text is the spoken word in printed form, that music is increasingly accompanied by image on MTV and in films, and that the sound of radio shows is now accompanied by text and image on the Internet. To teach students to read in between the lines of these modes of language, students first need to become aware that these modes exist as such. Invisible as separate entities, the interwoven threads of sight, sound, and print need to be pulled apart and held up to the light for inspection.

While most of the learning and work at EVC centers around the production of a documentary, learning to deconstruct media critically is essential to the process. Time and attention are given to analyzing still and moving images without sound and to analyzing sound divorced from images. Students are then engaged in video-making activities that link analysis and production and give them opportunities to practice and apply the analytic concepts they have just learned.

To give students a sense of how sound contributes to telling a story, the EVC instructor plays a section of a movie without dialogue. She turns the video screen away from them so the students can hear but cannot see the images. Then she stops the video at various points and asks the students to list the different sounds they notice. In one scene, for example, this may include the screech of breaks, the slam of a car door, footsteps, the wind blowing, a door creaking, silence, a faucet dripping, a dog barking, and violin music.

Students are then asked: What do you imagine is happening in the movie? Why do you think this? What sound clues did you hear that support your prediction? After listening to the section again, the students can revise their notes and then share their ideas. Then the teacher moves the monitor so the students can see the screen and she plays the scene again. They can compare their imagined interpretation of the scene with the visual and aural depiction. They learn the differences between literal sounds that evoke an image of the sound-producing source (such as the car door slam or dog barking) and nonliteral sounds that may create a mood or feeling (such as the violin music that created a sense of tension and anxiety). In addition, they analyze use of dialogue in narrative films and the use of interviews, narration, and sound effects in documentaries and in the news.

To apply this new knowledge regarding the use of sound in telling a story, students are asked to create a simple story with only sound. They practice recording different kinds of sounds using the appropriate microphones and then learn to use different kinds of sound elements to tell a story. Their stories are less than two minutes long and include music, sound effects, and sounds recorded in the classroom or in the street. They edit in sound effects.

A similar activity teaches students to analyze still images. They learn to articulate how the visual elements of composition and framing are used to represent values, ideas, characters, places, or events in a story. They learn how a documentary camera operator employs a similar aesthetic sensibility as a still photographer.

The students are clustered in small groups. Each group is given a different black and white still image to study. All of the photos relate to the topic they are exploring in their documentary; in this case, homelessness. One is a high-angle, vertical framed photo. In the foreground, a boy sleeps on a suitcase on a cracked sidewalk next to some bags piled against the wall of a concrete building. The wall that runs nearly the full length of the right side of the photo has graffiti on it. A woman carrying an infant in a snugli looks down in his direction while one of her hands rests on a stroller with another child in it. Another women stands behind her, holding the hand of a child standing on either side of her. Near the top left corner of the photo, more women, children, and bags are behind her.

The students study their photo and jot down everything they notice. They are asked to consider such characteristics as: the type of shot (close-up, medium shot, long shot); the angle (high angle, low angle); light and shadow; and placement of elements (objects, people, etc.) in the picture (foreground, background, juxtaposition). Then they describe how the image makes them think and feel.

Using an overhead projector, each image is projected for the whole class to see. The students who first analyzed the images present their ideas. After they are finished, others contribute to the analysis. Students collectively explore questions such as:

- Who do you think took the picture?
- How are the people in the photos represented?
- What caption would you write for that photo?
- What kind of message is the photographer trying to convey?
- How do the different elements in the image contribute to get that message across?
- How might the message of the photo change if it were taken from a different angle, or cropped differently?
- Who might be the intended audience for the photo?
- How might different audiences respond to the photo (including the homeless people in the photos)?
- Where do you think the picture appeared?

The aim of this and other similar lesson activities is to develop students' habits of close observation and questioning so that they automatically bring them to bear on all the media experiences they have. Regardless of whether the student is trying to understand a visual, aural, or print-based text, habits of *questioning*, *evaluating*, and *analyzing* distinguish critical literacy from an uncritical literacy.

At the most basic level, the reader, listener, or viewer may learn to simply understand the literal meaning of what is written, said, or visualized. A more experienced "reader" can, as Dale describes (in Tyner, 1998), "draw inferences, understand the limitations of what was written, said or spoken. . . . And finally, we learn to read beyond the lines, to evaluate and apply the material to new situations" (p. 61).

Critical literacy aims to teach students the skills and capacity to read at this most developed level—in between the lines and beyond the lines—whether those lines are alphabetic, painted, videotaped, or spoken. But teachers need to give students repeated opportunities to practice and build upon the micro skills needed to progress through the various levels of development. At each step along the way, students need to practice skills and habits of close and repeated reading, with multiple perspectives, across all textural forms. Students can only initially accomplish this with a great deal of teacher guidance and assistance; gradually, they internalize the skills and finally can perform them independently.

Among the first steps in teaching critical literacy is to make the learning outcomes and levels of proficiency explicit to teachers and students alike. At EVC, the teaching staff develops rubrics that differentiate among the various domains of learning that are embedded in the process of documentary making such as research, camerawork, media analysis, and editing. It is important to see these rubrics as living documents that teachers hold up against their practice in the classroom and based on that experience, review and revise each year. The point is not to have learning standards forever set in stone, but to have ongoing reflection and conversations among the staff about what counts as good teaching and learning and how to collectively get there.

The way that students internalize and apply multimodal critical literacy skills is difficult to quantify. In focus group interviews and surveys distributed to EVC alumni who attended workshops several years ago, Butler and Zaslow (unpublished) began to provide anecdotal evidence of impact.

If I'll be watching something on TV or something in general comes up and something's not right . . . I'll tell somebody about what I'm thinking or what I'm feeling about it. And I don't know, it usually ends up like you're explaining something to them for like an hour but definitely you look more depth at everything.

I spoke to my mom about it. She didn't really understand too much about it but one day we was watching the news and she was like, "These people will say anything on TV." And I'm like, "Well I go to EVC and I don't think they're saying it the way it's meant to be said. I think they're just editing it and making it come out a certain way." And she's like, "What are you talking about?" It took about an hour for me to explain . . . the whole thing to her, but I explained it to her. And she wanted to know if she could go to EVC but I'm like, "You're too old for EVC, Mom." (p. 8)

While their media production skills could not be assessed as not many graduates went on to work as documentary makers, the analytic skills they developed at EVC—while not easily measured—do surface and can be observed "qualitatively through their interpersonal relationships, through the change in attention and focus paid to media messages and production techniques, and in the expectations they have of themselves and of others" (Butler & Zaslow, unpublished, p. 8).

Teaching Continuous Inquiry

Continuous inquiry has been an essential aspect of EVC's educational and cultural practice of critical literacy. The EVC model teaches students to assume a questioning, skeptical attitude; to dig deeply into public problems; and to investigate the connectedness of those problems to the social institutions and historic trends that have shaped them and to the individuals who struggle to overcome them. This approach gives students the opportunity to move between the personal and public spheres, starting with the self-referential and then reaching beyond themselves to study their community at large. Such work sows the seeds for them to grow into what John Dewey called an "organized, articulate Public" (1946, p. 146), civically engaged citizens capable of active social concern.

Dewey is most well known for his writing on school reform and democracy. But he also wrote about the role of the mass media as an educational force in forming public opinion and consequently, its potential to contribute either to a healthy or weak democracy. Observing in the early years of the 20th century both the sensationalist reporting of the press and the rapid growth of communication technologies to distribute those reports, Dewey called for a public journalism of "continuous inquiry":

Telegraph, telephone, and now the radio, cheap and quick mails, the printing press, capable of swift reduplication of material at low cost, have attained a remarkable development. But when we ask what sort of material is recorded and how it is organized, when we ask about the intellectual form in which the material is presented, the tale to be told is very different. . . . Without coordination and consecutiveness, events are not events, but mere occurrences, intrusions. . . . (leading to) the triviality and "sensational" quality of so much of what passes as news . . . Only continuous inquiry, continuous in the sense of being connected as well as persistent, can provide the material of enduring opinion about public matters. (Ratner, 1939, pp. 395–396)

Dewey's commentary is just as relevant today. Much of the news is as remarkable for its instantaneous, 24-hour, global dissemination as it is for its sensational, decontextualized, nonintellectual content. We can hear echoes of Dewey's call for journalists to practice continuous inquiry in the press and for educators to teach students to think and practice such inquiry in school so as to build a more informed public, capable of thoughtful engagement in public problems and in the democratic process.

Continuous inquiry requires skills of observation and imagination and a sense of agency. It requires the careful and repeated observation of the cultural and material world and the ability to create a sense of distance, a defamiliarizing of the familiar. For example, to pose the question: "Why are there homeless teenagers?" the questioner must first take notice of the teens routinely passed by, sitting outside a shelter, or sleeping in a subway car or bus station, and see that there *are* homeless teenagers.

The student must also learn to imagine that which is not present. To pose the problem presupposes that there is a knowable cause, perhaps a solution, and even the possibility of a world where homelessness does not exist. Students must develop the capacity to imagine the world as if it could be otherwise.

The learner must have the self-confidence to find and make sense of answers to such questions, and also believe that a public audience would be interested in hearing what the investigator has found out. In other words, the student must have faith that the search is worth undertaking.

However, too often students come to EVC without such hope. They have not been engaged in this sort of in-depth community research before and do not believe they can complete an inquiry or that their project will make any difference. They seem to be, as Greene (1998) describes, "sunk in the everydayness" of life and so perceive the impoverished social conditions that surrounded them as wholly normal (p. 124). They suffer from what Dewey (1934) called the "anesthetic" in experience that numbs people into an inability to imagine the existence of, much less search for, alternatives. Without the self-confidence to ask questions and search for answers to them, students will be much less likely to develop the other skills needed for successful inquiry.

There are two underlying pedagogical strategies embedded in EVC's inquiry-based approach that make it possible for teachers to actively engage students in the work: the learning process is *dialogue-based* and *student-centered*. From the first day of class, the teacher sets a tone and develops a culture of open honest dialogue and learner-centered participatory decision making. Within this learning environment, students develop a greater sense of empowerment that motivates them to take up the search as well as a respect for themselves and their peers as collaborative learners. Over time, they come to see that their inquiry can make a difference and that through the process the students are becoming teachers and change agents.

Dialogue-Based Teaching

The importance of dialogue in learning is described by Freire (1970): "Only dialogue, which requires critical thinking, is also capable of generating critical thinking. Without dialogue there is no commu-

nication, and without communication there can be no true education"
(pp. 73–74).

In the EVC documentary workshop, dialogue takes place on
several levels. Pairs or small groups of students may have informal
conversations or more formal discussions and debates. They have
multiple opportunities to pose questions and conduct interviews on
video with peers as well as with adults in positions of authority. In
each of these instances, they learn about the subject of their inquiry
in addition to learning on a meta-cognitive level that their ideas and
questions count, and are in fact vital to the success of the entire class
project.

They also learn that the teacher is not the sole possessor of knowledge, and that knowledge is shared and constructed by all the students
and the community members they interview. This shared construction
of knowledge through dialogue constitutes an oppositional shift in
power relations from their traditional school experience where the
teacher, in a dominant role, does the talking and asking of questions
and the student, in the subordinate position, does the listening and
answering. Every community member is a potential resource; every
interview exploring community problems opens up possibilities for
further learning and problem solving. And as such, the entire community can become a laboratory for learning and action.

Several layers of dialogue drive the documentary process: an internal
dialogue between the student and her or his lived experience, and
external dialogues between student and student, student and teacher,
and student and interviewee. A dialogue also takes place between the
teacher, student, and interviewees whose ideas and voices are represented in the documentary and the audience who views it. Finally, it is
important to note that each of these dialogues is grounded in and grows
out of the essential social problem explored in the tape. This process
of inquiry and creative production illustrates Freire's (1970) dictum:
"Dialogue is the encounter between men, mediated by the world, in
order to name the world" (p. 69).

As is evident in this alumnus's powerful reflection on his experience,
students realize that they can engage in dialogue with adults, about
"adult" problems, to "name the world":

One thing that . . . I think is very true to anyone's experience at EVC [is] just
knowing that as a young person you don't have to be older to think about certain
things, think about certain topics, about certain issues and want to talk to older
people to get their opinions. Understand that you are on the same level or

enough of a level that it's OK to have a conversation with an older person about politics or any number of global issues. (Butler & Zaslow, unpublished, p. 15)

Most students, however, do not begin the inquiry with the skills needed to engage in open dialogue and make full use of their "laboratory." The teacher needs to give them a great deal of practice and preparation so they can build the skills along the way. This includes teaching students how to approach a stranger on the street for an interview, how to give and accept constructive feedback from peers, how to use research to develop initial and follow-up questions, and how to turn a formal interview into a relaxed open-ended conversation. Each of these practices at some level involves a blending of oral and print literacies and of social and intellectual skills, and leads to a gradual opening up of students' curiosity and imagination.

The importance of learning "how to talk to people" cannot be underestimated. The documentary inquiry process gives students practice in journalism interviewing techniques that help them to initiate a social encounter in the community and facilitate an intellectually engaging and generative conversation. These are not skills students often learn in overcrowded traditional schools; the investigation of social issues generally falls outside of the academic curriculum and community members are often undervalued as primary sources of information. In addition, as developing skills of oral communication is emphasized less in school than is written work, students have few opportunities to practice the art of dialogue. So gaining such opportunities at EVC is appreciated by them all the more.

In reflecting on their experience at EVC, students seem to remember most the social encounter of the interview, learning to "approach" a stranger to have a conversation, whether on the telephone or on the street:

Overall, what I've learned from EVC and what I will take with me, is basically not only working with the camera and things like that and making a documentary but all in all, how to go out and meet people and how talk to people. We had to do research; we had to find people to talk to. We had to find expert interviews. We had to actually go there, call them and set up the interviews. Things like that. It was a real professionalism. You had to carry yourself in a certain way . . . Interviewing I will take with me. It taught me how to approach someone. (Serena)

Ultimately, the dialogue the students are engaged in is with their audience. They are not only posing questions to their interviewees but are combining the answers they record on video along with imagery, music, special effects, and other elements to tell a story. Their voices are being heard through their tape, making an argument that reflects back a synthesis of the best questions, stories, and wisdom that they collected throughout the course of their inquiry.

The school and community screenings and the question and answer sessions that follow are teachable moments. These are opportunities to present new perspectives, make marginal voices heard, break the silence about injustices witnessed, change audiences' ways of thinking, and even, in some cases, move them to action. As one EVC alum reported, "My experience at EVC and the whole documentary workshop process gave me the whole understanding that there were people out there that valued my opinion and that you can make a difference by just doing a documentary on something." For many students, their EVC experience was a journey out of silence and into dialogue, and from dialogue into action.

The students also spoke about how their thinking changed as a result of their experience producing the homeless youth documentary:

I learned more in this semester about this topic than I have all my life. Before researching this topic, I too had many stereotypical thoughts and I didn't know anything else from what was visible to me, which was just the people sleeping on the streets and subways. As soon as I found out about what's actually going on, and the youth that we usually don't see, my views changed immensely. Now instead of thinking that all homeless people are bad and crazy, . . . I see them as average people, just trying to make it in this world, and people who don't have anyone to turn to. (John)

Another student explained how the video was going to "make a difference" and would change the way audiences thought about the problem.

Homeless youth . . . was an important topic for us to learn and research about because it will change not only the way we think about it, but whoever watches the video will also change their way of thinking about it. And it's gonna make a difference in people's lives. (Vanessa)

Students were no longer only students but teachers, cultural producers, and social activists.

Student-Centered Teaching

The second and related strategy of EVC's inquiry-based approach is grounded in the student-centeredness of the teaching. Throughout the Documentary Workshop, the EVC teachers give students decision-making power in the purposes, content, and direction of their own learning. It would not be sufficient to teach students to conduct neighborhood interviews if the teacher chose all the subjects to be addressed and the questions to be asked. The teacher and not the students would be doing the interesting, challenging intellectual work, and the students would miss out on important learning opportunities. The point is for the students to pose and refine their own authentic questions, find resources and information, weigh evidence, present their findings, and take a vested interest in and ownership of their own learning. The intellectual and emotional rewards are so much greater for the students if they feel connected to, inspired by, and passionate about their subject of choice. Through this experience, they grow to become independent and self-directed learners.

The EVC students consistently report that they feel more positively about themselves, their work, and their community, in contrast to their experiences in traditional teacher-centered classes. A powerful sense of engagement and excitement surrounds them when they are out on the streets, talking with their peers, and talking about subjects of immediate importance to them. They have a sense of ownership about their work when they get to decide the subject of study. And they feel tremendous pride when they present their projects and answer questions at public screenings attended by their friends, family, and teachers. While most schools do not focus on work that has an audience beyond the classroom or school setting, such work leads students to understand the importance of their roles as citizens and social critics. As one student described it:

The single most satisfying moment was at the final screening at EVC. I had my mother there, and my girlfriend at the time, and her mother. Her mother didn't know I could speak that well. She had her perceptions about me based on maybe the way I looked or my appearance. She never got a chance to speak with me or find out how I felt. But when she saw me speaking about the project and how proud I was of it, it touched her. . . . Seeing my mother in the audience and looking at how proud she was. That sticks out as well. (Goodman, 2003, p. 58)

A key principle and strategy of EVC's student-centered class is student choice of the subject of their inquiry. The students' own condition of life becomes their curriculum of study. As a collective, the Documentary Workshop students are given the opportunity to decide what aspect of their life at home, in school, or perhaps in the streets of their community is an important enough issue or problem to explore for nearly the entire 18-week semester. This selection is an involved process that takes several class days to accomplish. Following is a brief description of the process from the fall 2003 semester that resulted in the documentary on homeless youth.

The students first view professionally and student-produced documentaries to become familiar with the genre and the issues they explore, and generate a list of criteria about what they believe makes a "good" documentary. Students then look to the concerns they have in their own lives and in their surrounding community for subjects worth investigating.

Among the topics and questions the students generated were: the representation of women in music, movies, advertisements, and TV and how that affects how they are treated in society; does music impact how we act and how violent we are as a society?; homeless teenagers; the effects of growing up in a broken or an untraditional home; stress; youth rights—why are they not allowed to drink or buy cigarettes but can be tried as adults and go to jail before they are 18; HIV/AIDS and young people; and rats and neighborhoods—why some have more rats than others, and what kinds of diseases they transmit.

The students narrowed the list down from 33 issues to 10 after an hour and a half of discussion about which topics might be redundant, which could be grouped together, and which they felt most strongly about. They then reduced the list to five and carried on the discussion by writing questions and comments to each other on five separate "graffiti boards," each devoted to one of the top five issues.

After reviewing all of the comments scrawled across the graffiti boards, the class more closely considered the pros and cons of each topic using their criteria for a "good" documentary: a clear line of inquiry; multiple voices and perspectives; formal and informal interviews; an engaging story that educates and entertains; and new information, or a different take on what is commonly seen. They were urged to consider the topic that would make the best documentary rather than a personally favored topic. Finally, they voted, choosing homeless teenagers as their focus. As Vanessa explained it, "Homelessness, out of all the topics, seemed to be the most important one—the one that would actually make a difference and that people could relate to 10 years from now."

Teaching Reflection

Critical literacy teaches students to actively reflect on their own work and learning. The skills and habits of reflection are developed through regular journal writing, critiques of a range of documentaries, and rough-cut edit screenings. However, the most intensive time for reflection that is built into the Documentary Workshop is the portfolio roundtable. This learner-centered approach to reflection teaches students to monitor and evaluate their own and each other's growth and learning. The roundtable is a time for student reflection and also a time to reach a collective assessment about the thinking and performance of the student, and by extension, of the teacher as well.

Media educators are constantly making judgments about the quality of camerawork, editing, and research we expect from our students. Often the standards are based on an intuitive sense of what constitutes good work in terms of craft, creativity, and thoughtfulness. Efforts to use less subjective measures such as multiple choice tests tell us less about what the students know than about what she or he does *not* know. These tests do not tell us what students can actually do, or how students think and grapple with problems within the real-life context of a video production. Portfolios and the student exhibitions offer a richer portrait of what students are capable of knowing and doing. They give students an opportunity to publicly show their best work and talk about it with members of the community including parents, other students, teachers, principals, researchers, producers, and artists (Goodman & Tally, 1993, p. 30).

To prepare for the portfolio roundtables, students gather a variety of records and instances of documentation produced during the course of their documentary production. These records include journal entries, rough footage from interviews, rough-cut screenings, edit plans, interview questions, tape logs, and phone logs.

The collection process is well integrated into daily work. But gathering work is not enough; students and staff have to understand how each student is evolving. This includes frequent conversations about the work the students do, making criteria for what constitutes good-quality work explicit.

During the roundtables, students present several drafts of their work to demonstrate their learning and skill development over time. The teachers, parents, media artists, researchers, and community members who sit on the panel are asked not to assign a grade, but to look carefully at the work, look for evidence of student learning, acknowledge the learning evidenced, and encourage that learning through constructive feedback. Ultimately, conversations around portfolios and screenings can help shape a culture of self-reflection and critique that students can internalize. The process of presenting a portfolio to a panel reinforces the self-reflection. Students begin their individual presentation by reflecting on the inquiry process of making their documentary as related to the two skill areas they chose to present. Here is one student's general overview related to interviewing and editing skill areas:

We found people to interview. How we did that was we went online. I looked for shelters, called them and asked them for interviews. They agreed; some didn't. We got interviews. We went to shelters, and we videotaped kids. Then we got to the editing process. That was hard but also I had the most fun doing the editing. It was hard because you had to figure out where you are going and you had to present it in a way that everybody would understand and get your point across clearly. That was definitely the hardest part because—how you gonna go about deciphering through all this information and make it into something coherent that people will understand? (Vanessa)

Students refer to rubrics that provide such criteria. For example, students who chose to highlight camera work might evaluate their learning through the choices of different types of shots to convey a mood; students who present about interviewing might discuss how they learned to ask pertinent follow-up questions to get desired information; and students who present about critical viewing might discuss how they can now identify various points of view in the media. During her roundtable, one student showed a clip of the first street interview she conducted and critiqued her lack of basic skills, such as memorizing questions and paying attention to the interviewee.

That was a bad interview I did. I would say it was a bad interview because I didn't memorize the questions, and I was like "um, um." I was hesitant; I think I made them uncomfortable when I did that. I didn't really pay attention to them . . . I could have come up with a follow up question to that. I wasn't really paying attention; I was just trying to go straight to the next question. That was one of my bad interviews. And also, I was just hesitant. I wasn't confident doing the interview. I was like, "Uh, uh," stuttering and stuff. (Serena)

Then she showed a clip from a later street interview to show her growth and development over time. She proudly showed off the more advanced interviewing skills she demonstrated, such as asking follow-up questions and turning an interview into a flowing conversation:

I had skills! . . . I was kinda like Oprah [gestures with an imaginary microphone in her hand]. You know like, I just kept the interview flowing. And I was able to still get information from her. When she said, "My neighborhood is good," I was like, "Why?" So, I could get a fuller answer. Yeah. I had skills.

She then showed a tape of herself conducting an expert interview and explained how she learned to use research in her interviews:

My research, it really paid off when it came time to do the interviewing. . . . I felt more comfortable interviewing him, 'cause I knew about the topic. I made better questions and was more prepared. . . . Basically, we went to the Health Department and interviewed Mr. Kopel about environmental stress to find out more information about it. He was our expert. . . . This was a good interview because I gave examples about the article we read from the *New York Times.* . . . and I was just more confident. (Serena)

Another student showed her panel tapes of the first interview she conducted with a homeless youth and reflected on how she had improved as an interviewer:

Those were two interviews with the same person. He was nice enough to let me interview him twice. Because the first time, I was so shy . . . I asked him if it was difficult for him to find a job. And he said, "Yes, it was. It was hard to put up a resume." So then, right there. Instead of asking him why was it hard to put up a resume, maybe because he doesn't have an address or a telephone number, I asked him if had a lot of references. Which has nothing to do with the topic! But then the second time I interviewed him, all the questions that I didn't get to ask him, I thought about it the second time, and I kind of put them in there. The second interview was much better than the first one. (Vanessa)

At the end of each presentation, the facilitator asks for questions to clarify anything that was unclear, and allows the panel guests to probe the student's knowledge and understanding. After clarifying questions, the facilitator asks participants for both "warm" and "cool" feedback (McDonald, Mohr, Dichter, & McDonald, 2003). Warm feedback includes only positive comments about the student's cover letter, presentation, and work. What follows is an example of warm feedback given by a guest to Vanessa, one of the student producers of the homeless youth documentary.

I thought that your presentation skills are excellent. Very clear, very thorough. The way you walked us through the information you were presenting . . . I really want to congratulate you, because I think that the interviews that you guys were conducting . . . the ones with the youth themselves, were really challenging. Because these are young people who obviously are dealing with incredibly serious, and in some cases life threatening, situations—not having a place to live . . . So it requires real sensitivity on the part of the interviewer coming to that conversation. And I felt that as much as you thought that the first one wasn't any good. . . . your thoughtfulness and your sensitivity to the person you were talking to, I thought that really came through really clearly. And I'm sure that the interviewee appreciated that. (Tom, EVC staff member panelist)

Then cool feedback, which includes more critical comments and suggestions for the student's future learning, is shared. Students are instructed not to respond to feedback, but just to listen. Here is an excerpt from Vanessa's roundtable:

You have to listen to people before you are talking back to them. And that was definitely something you had to work on all semester. And the same thing when you go to a job interview. When someone starts to give you feedback, you don't want to interrupt them. You want to listen to them and then you speak after they finish. That's my only cool feedback. Other than that, I think you did wonderful work through the whole semester. (Maria, Documentary Workshop teacher)

After the warm and cool feedback has been given, the students can answer any questions that the roundtable participants ask. This exchange took place at Vanessa's presentation:

Participant (Tom): What were the bigger picture challenges of this whole experience of producing a documentary with a group of your peers? For you personally, what were the biggest challenges of doing that?
Student (Vanessa): Working with people.
Participant (Tom): That is the challenge?
Student (Vanessa): That is the challenge. Really. Working with people. Because, when you sit three people together to decide on something, one person is gonna have an opinion. The other one is gonna have a completely different one, and the third one is just gonna be off this earth. And there is no way you can decide on things because people are constantly like, "No, I want this." "I want that." "No, I want this." No matter what you do, everybody is not gonna be happy with it . . . You have to learn to how work with somebody you don't like. . . . And then you grow to love them. You really do.

McDonald et al. (2003), who developed and practiced protocols of assessment and reflection from which EVC's model has been adapted, describe the pedagogical significance of the process:

The point is to reach a different understanding of our students than the kind we're used to, one deeper than what is required merely to keep our teaching and their learning in sync. But this demands a great shift in energy, both practical and organizational . . . we often refer to this great shift of energy with the simple phrase "looking at student work." Here, however, we acknowledge that the "looking" we advocate is simple in the deep and disciplined way that Thoreau's looking was simple at Walden Pond and Annie Dillard's at Tinker Creek. Simple but elemental. Simple but difficult . . . such learning communities foster democracy as well as cognition. They encourage learners—whether they are first graders, graduate students or colleagues in professional education—to appreciate the value of diverse ideas and deliberative communities. (pp. 3, 7)

Long-Term Impact

Critical literacy is both an educational strategy and a cultural practice. It seeks to address Dewey's concerns of developing a civically active "articulate public" that has the intellectual capacity to engage in collective dialogue and inquiry into the most pressing social problems; and Freire's concerns of developing a literate public empowered to "name the world" in order to transform it. Critical literacy as practiced by the EVC further addresses the concerns of Kathleen Tyner, David Buckingham, Cary Bazelgette, and other media literacy researchers and practitioners who aim to teach students to produce and "read" between and beyond the lines of media across a range of communication modes.

The power of this model of teaching and learning is evident in the student work at EVC and opens up important possibilities not only at EVC, but also in school and after-school settings on a much larger scale. But to scale up the teaching of critical literacy requires broad changes in the educational practices, goals, and structures of schools so that language instruction is opened up to include multiple literacies; the locus of instruction shifts from a teacher-centered to an inquiry-based, dialogic, learner-centered model; punitive high-stakes testing gives way to the collective reflection and deliberation of student learning through portfolio assessment forums; and the curricula are expanded beyond the state-mandated academic requirements to embrace the curricula of the students' lives and the media culture and social community in which they live.

Documenting the teaching and learning of critical literacy as it is practiced at EVC gives a snapshot of the impact it has on the students' creative, analytic, and social capacities. Such a snapshot presents the dual challenges of scaling up the work to reach larger numbers of students in schools as well as of scaling it down (McDonald, Buchanan, & Sterling, in press), so the impact continues to be deep and lasting on each individual student. A recent study on the long-term impact of EVC's pedagogy suggests a lasting change in student thinking (Butler & Zazlow, 2004), although more research is needed. However, if focus group interviews with EVC alumni 10 and more years after they took the workshop are any indication, the results are encouraging.

Critical thinking and just thinking, and inquiry. . . . I'm a mom right now of a 5 year old, and I totally use that and teach my daughter that that's very important. You know, questioning why you see something this way. I try to nurture that within her even.

That's what really impacted me with EVC, was it's the place that I could go and . . . not just write something down . . . or read something and regurgitate it for a teacher to look at and that's it. You know, you get a mark if you pass the class or not, no big deal. But here I was getting something. Actually doing it, by yourself, or with a group and it makes so much of a difference to me. . . . And I think that's what this has, it has that feel, you're doing something, you're making these things happen. So it's important to have . . . a place that's keeping an open mind and trying to get young people to speak their mind and I think that young people are very influential and have the most influence over the whole culture and they can just reach so many different people if they're just given that opportunity. (Butler & Zaslow, 2004, pp. 9, 15).

AUTHOR'S NOTE

I'd like to acknowledge the EVC Documentary Workshop students and their gifted teachers Ivana Espinet and Rebecca Renard, whose work together exemplifies the power and possibility of critical literacy explored in this chapter.

REFERENCES

Bazelgette, C. (Ed.). (1989). *Primary media education: A curriculum statement*. London: British Film Institute and the DES National Working Party for Primary Media Education.

Buckingham, D. (Ed.). (1990/1992). *Watching media learning: Making sense of media education*. New York: The Falmer Press. (Republished 1992 by Falmer)

Dewey, J. (1934). *Art as experience*. New York: Minton, Balch, and Co.

Dewey, J. (1946). *The public and its problems: An essay in political inquiry*. Chicago: Gateway Books.

Duncan, B., D'Ippolito, J., Macpherson, C., & Wilson, C. (1996). *Mass media and popular culture*. Toronto: Harcourt Brace Canada.

Educational Video Center (Producer). (2004). *No home of your own: A look at the lives of homeless youth*. New York: Educational Video Center.

Fisherkeller, J. (2002). *Growing up with television: Everyday learning among young adolescents*. Philadelphia: Temple University Press.

Freire, P. (1970). *Pedagogy of the oppressed*. New York: The Continuum Publishing Company.

Goodman, S. (2003). *Teaching youth media: A critical guide to literacy, video production and social change*. New York: Teachers College Press.

Goodman, S., & Tally, B. (1993, August/September). The tape's great, but what did they learn? *The Independent Film and Video Monthly*, 30–33.

Greene, M. (1988). *The dialectic of freedom*. New York: Teachers College Press.

Martin, S. (2003, July/August). Close the book. It's time to read. *The Clearing House*, 76(6), 289–291.

Masterman, L. (1985). *Teaching the media*. London: Comedia Books.

McDonald, J.P., Buchanan, J., & Sterling, R. (in press). Scaling up reform interventions. In S. Bodilly & T. Glennan (Eds.), *The national writing project: Scaling up and scaling down*. Santa Monica: Rand.

McDonald, J.P., Mohr, N., Dichter, A., & McDonald, E.C. (2003). *The power of protocols: An educator's guide to better practice*. New York: Teachers College Press.

Piro, J.M. (2002). The picture of reading: Deriving meaning in literacy through image. *The Reading Teacher*, 56(2), 126–134.

Ratner, J. (Ed.). (1939). *Intelligence in the modern world: John Dewey's philosophy*. New York: Random House.

Shor, I. (1999). What is critical literacy? In I. Shor & C. Pari (Eds.), *Critical literacy in action: Writing words, changing worlds*, (pp. 1–30). Portsmouth, NH: Boynton/Cook, Heinemann.

Tyner, K. (1998). *Literacy in a digital world: Teaching and learning in the age of information*. Mahwah, NJ: Lawrence Erlbaum Associates.

CHAPTER 12

Obstacles, Challenges, and Potential: Envisioning the Future

GRETCHEN SCHWARZ

Media literacy, already practiced in the schools of other nations, has the potential, as the contributors to this volume demonstrate, to transform American curriculum and teaching. The media have themselves been the subject of study in the Academy for some time—in film courses within English departments, among scholars in Cultural Studies who focus on social issues and popular culture, and in other departments such as Political Science, Communications, and Marketing. The standards of the American Library Association now promote the close examination of all kinds of information sources. The media, from films to the Internet, are certainly present in American elementary and secondary schools; however, media *literacy* is still far from a typical part of every young person's educational experience. Moreover, many issues and obstacles to the widespread incorporation of media literacy in schools remain.

Media literacy has all the problems of a young field—becoming visible in the academic world, acquiring credibility among educators and others, developing a strong research base, and finding funding. Scholars and practitioners of media literacy come from diverse disciplines and advocate diverse points of view regarding the purposes and methods of media literacy. Teacher certification in media literacy is rare, almost nonexistent. Implementing media literacy in the schools is especially challenging in the United States, a large, diverse, and educationally isolated country in which curriculum traditionally has not been centralized and in which popular arts have not been taken seriously (Kubey, 1998). In this final chapter, we examine some of the major obstacles and issues that face media literacy educators, and we speculate about the future.

Gretchen Schwarz is a Professor in the School of Teaching and Curriculum Leadership of Oklahoma State University.

Obstacles and Problems

Major and lasting change in American schools comes slowly if at all despite the constant cries for reform that have characterized public rhetoric, especially during the last few decades (Sarason, 1990). Implementing media literacy in the United States is problematic given the political and social contexts of education and the history of school reform; the ongoing practical problems that regularly confront educators; the state of teacher preparation and professional development; and even divisions within the media literacy movement itself. Steyer's (2002) endorsement of media literacy reflects the fact that the implementation of media literacy will not be easy or quick (italics added):

I strongly believe that media literacy ought to be a required part of every student's curriculum, from grade school on up, and that government and the media industry should support a comprehensive program nationwide. *But until that day comes* . . . (p. 249)

Political and Social Contexts and School Reform

Most everyone would agree with the need for students to be literate, to possess knowledge, and to master basic skills. While that can be done through testing and skill-drilling, citizens of a democracy need a deeper and more comprehensive education that allows them to develop the capacity to apply and contribute their knowledge in broader, more creative, and more independent ways. Yet we continue to move away from these powerful kinds of understanding as schools become places of standardized learning. Moreover, the mass media messages that bombard our youth through television, movies, music, and commercials remind them they are important only as consumers and not as citizens. (p. 3)

Glickman's (2004) statement above reflects the difficulty of the current political-social situation for American schooling. Many would argue that current school reform efforts aimed at school performance, especially as captured in the No Child Left Behind (NCLB) Act of 2001 (http://www.nochildleftbehind.gov), are narrow, punitive, and doomed to failure. Some believe that reforms such as NCLB are actually aimed not at improving education, but at ultimately privatizing public education in America (Kohn, 2004; Meier, 2004). In any case, the preoccupation with standardized testing and traditional subject matter traditionally and uniformly taught is disturbing. Van Luchene (2004) warns, "In place of the rich diversity that characterized educational philosophy not so long ago, we find that survival for public schools requires single-minded dedication to a limited set of learning objectives, mastery of which is taken to be established only by multiple choices on a standardized test" (p. 54). Posing questions, discovering new knowledge, and thinking critically—all essential components of media literacy—are not priorities in NCLB and related school reforms; at least one cannot find any mention of these goals in examining NCLB documents.

In the daily life of educators, this reform climate seems to be causing a narrowing of the curriculum (teaching to the test which requires memorization only) (McNeil, 2000; Stecher & Hamilton, 2002); a school culture of stress, fear, and exhaustion for students and teachers (Mathison & Freeman, 2003; Rigsby & DeMulder, 2003); and an avoidance of any subject matter that is controversial or difficult to test. Tucker and Toch (2004), generally supportive of NCLB, acknowledge, "Teachers and parents legitimately complain, for instance, that the simplistic, largely multiple-choice tests that many states use to assess student achievement lead to a dumbing down of what's taught in the classroom" (p. 29). Meier (2004) observes, "The law literally dictates the books we are allowed to use on a national basis, not to mention the pedagogy for teaching literacy and, coming soon, math. Before long, until eighth grade, little else will get taught at all" (p. 6). Bushnell (2003), in a study of New York City school teachers, describes the current climate in terms of Foucault's image of the panopticon, "a physical and social structure designed for the observation and regulation of its residents' activities" (p. 255), in other words, a prison. Bushnell adds, "The use of standardized tests has become a 'tyranny' in which 'teachers find themselves spending more than half the year teaching specifically for the tests; their jobs and the standing of their schools are on the line' (Botstein, 2000, p. A11)" (p. 262). Rubalcava (2004) summarizes, "One of the dangers of NCLB is that all the focus on test scores means that little energy is left for imagination, creativity, intrinsic motivation, intuition, spontaneity, and children" (p. 10). The Rethinking Schools website (http://www.rethinkingschools.org) offers a number of similar critiques of NCLB from their journal, *Rethinking Schools*. Certainly the remarks this writer has heard from a variety of Oklahoma teachers reinforce the finding that teacher autonomy, professionalism, and morale suffer under current reforms, to say nothing of students' classroom experiences.

Assessment demands of the kind NCLB requires discourage tackling controversial issues or striving for outcomes hard to measure by standardized tests. Exploring complicated issues takes time away from test preparation. Furthermore, "taboo topics," controversial topics, seem to disappear in a time of stress, concern over lawsuits and parent complaints, and a focus on specified standard objectives (see Evans, Avery, & Pederson, 2000). The NCLB bias toward "scientifically based research" (selected quantitative studies) adds a chill to the air of educational research, innovation, and inquiry in general, as many qualitative researchers feel their work is no longer supported, even theoretically (see, e.g., Eisenhart & Towne, 2003; Smith, 2003).

The public continues to be concerned about the performance of schools (Rose & Gallup, 2004). Riddell's (1997) portrayal remains accurate today:

Many people speak of a lack of trust in government. . . . U.S. public schools are a prime target of the public's distress . . . The majority of American parents, who do continue to enroll their children in public schools, have become more demanding, with many agitating for improved performance by the schools, for more control over the use of tax dollars. (p. 2)

Despite these concerns, education received little attention in the bitter and divisive presidential campaign of 2004 while, ironically, media coverage (in a country where media literacy is not universal) caused dismay. Columnist Ellen Goodman (2004) observed, "Every issue is covered with maximum aggression and minimum ambivalence. . . . It's high-decibel, low nuance infotainment" (p. G5). The general political climate does not invite open, clear-headed, complex discussion of any issues, let alone education.

In fact, a "back to basics" mindset tends to deny the validity of popular culture or the arts, in general, as classroom content. Kubey (2003) adds that traditionally, "Many Americans see schools as places that will prepare children for jobs, certainly not for leisure and aesthetics . . . When education budgets are under pressure, as they almost always are, music, art, language, dance, and physical education programs and libraries are the first to be hit or cut entirely" (p. 360). Media literacy can be seen as a "frill" in this time of core curriculum, massive testing, and listings of school failures, as competition to the traditional "three R's." Hobbs's (2003) review of case study literature on teachers attempting to implement media literacy leads to her conclusion:

Teachers who are determined to use popular culture in the classroom may develop elaborate strategies to "fly below the radar screen," finding creative ways to use media and popular culture texts in the classroom without attracting attention from colleagues or supervisors that could call these materials into question . . . The use of media and popular culture in the real-world arenas of classrooms is not for the faint of heart. (pp. 106–107)

Finally, the history of school reform is not encouraging. As Eisner (2003) observes, "Schools have a special difficulty in changing their nature" (p. 648). Current reforms are actually, many would argue, an intensification of the school's old ways of doing things, not genuine change. At the same time, there is more rhetoric about meeting individual student needs in new ways; school districts often send mixed messages. Yates (1998) summarizes:

Another barrier to the widespread implementation of media literacy rests with the history of educational reform. History shows that the educational environment creates demands and supports that are used to pressure policymakers to adopt policies favoring the "cause of the moment." There have been so many "causes of the moment" in the educational environment over the years that the educational system's history is marred by disjointed funding and confused teaching practices. (p. 21)

Media literacy may have a difficult time finding a place, given the cynicism and fatigue of educators in light of constant public criticism and the imposition of increasingly laborious, sometimes even contradictory "reforms."

Ongoing Practical Problems

The "usual suspects," of course, also present threats to the growth of media literacy in the schools: time, resources, support, and school inequities. With increasing reform pressures for students to score well on standardized tests in reading and math, teachers are preoccupied with other curricular demands. The school day is full of other mandated content that has been added in recent years, from AIDS education to methods for dealing with bullying. Few schools have resources set aside for teaching media literacy—prepared videos, curriculum materials, books, and so on, and there are few specialists in media literacy to be found in public school systems. Moreover, as Brown (1998) declares, "To succeed, a curricular program of media literacy must be developed through collaboration among teachers, administrators, specialists, and parents, who together must build it into the systematic educational process" (p. 51). Finding time to communicate and work with parents, families, and the community is a continuing challenge for educators; media literacy cannot be fully successful without connecting to the home environment where students are most involved with the media. Finally, increasing inequities among the public schools of America leave especially poor and minority schools at even more disadvantage with less access to the technology and expertise that can support media literacy; such schools will probably have less access to video production equipment, for example, and less access to qualified teachers (see Kozol, 1991; Rethinking Schools, 2001). The problems confronting public school educators in general remain significant; would-be media educators have these same problems and more.

Teacher Preparation and Professional Development

Broad media literacy objectives have been included in the required curriculum of most states now.[1] However, most teachers remain un-prepared to teach media literacy. Such organizations as NCATE (the National Council for Accreditation of Teacher Education; http://www.ncate.org/standards) have shown no apparent interest in media literacy anywhere in its standards (http://www.ncate.org/standard/m_stds.htm); the Interstate New Teacher Assessment and Support Consortium (INTASC) new teacher standards refer only to familiarity with varied media as teaching tools (http://www.ccsso.org/projects/Interstate_New_Teacher_Assessment_and_Support_Consortium/); and few teacher education programs now include media literacy, at any level (see Goetze, Brown, & Schwarz, Chapter 9, this volume, for some that do). Kubey (1998) emphasizes that "with most education schools turning out teachers no better equipped to do media education than was the case 20 years ago, the U.S. situation is one with no, or precious little, formal training" (p. 63); this situation remains true into the 21st century despite increased teacher education requirements in educational technology such as those specified by NCATE.

Professional development for in-service teachers is also likely to remain problematic as the Canadian experience (see Pungente, Duncan, & Andersen, Chapter 8, this volume) shows. Organization and funding are always problems, other concerns compete for teachers' time, and even geography can play a part as many teachers still work in isolated rural schools around the United States. Moreover, school administrators use professional development to attend to the "reform of the moment" in American schools. Currently, with the impact of NCLB, the emphasis is on raising standardized test scores. Given this reality, it seems unlikely that teachers will be supported by the schools in their own efforts to learn about media literacy.

Challenges Within

In addition to politics in general, specific political disagreements complicate the state of media literacy in the United States from within. The media literacy movement has been split in two by differing views of what media literacy is and what it should accomplish. One group, as represented by the Alliance for a Media Literate America (AMLA), situates media literacy as primarily *critical thinking* about the media: analyzing media methods and challenging their messages while acknowledging the pleasures the media offer (see McBrien, Chapter 2, Hobbs, Chapter 5, and Thoman & Jolls, Chapter 10, this volume, as examples of this approach). The newer group, the Action Coalition for Media Education (ACME), founded in 2002 with support from the New Mexico Media Literacy Project (NMMLP) and its director, Bob McCannon, emphasizes media activism, encouraging citizens to take political action against the media. ACME does not find critical thinking sufficient; energies are directed toward such projects as attacking the tobacco industry or negating the value of teen magazines.

Hobbs (1998) identifies two relevant debates: whether media literacy should have a more explicit political and ideological agenda, and whether media literacy initiatives should be financially supported by media organizations. ACME supports a definite political agenda that rejects the financial involvement of media corporations. Its goals are to:

1. inform students and others of the massive censorship that exists in our media today whereby a handful of media monopolies determine the news and culture for most of the globe;
2. reform the system whereby these media monopolies, advertisers and their lobbyists diminish the health of our democracy and people;
3. support the development of activist curriculum that will allow students to explore and help to solve media-related problems. (The New Mexico Media Literacy Project, 2002, p. 1)

The attitude of the NMMLP, as well as ACME, is also reflected in their products. Their CD-ROM, *Understanding Media*, 1998, begins with a song about throwing your TV out the window, for instance. This protectionist or "inoculation" model of media literacy is problematic for other media educators.

Scholars such as Lewis and Jhally (1998) and Semali (Chapter 3, this volume) also endorse the activist model (such as ACME endorses) and perceive any corporate media involvement in media literacy as merely the industry trying to co-opt the movement. This is in contrast to the Canadian experience, where media literacy education has involved media producers along the way. Certainly, there are better and worse examples of how the corporate media can contribute to education. Many argue, for example, that Channel One has no redeeming social or educational value (see Molnar, 1996). On the other hand, Court TV (2004) has produced a useful video about media literacy, *Mind over Media: Voices from the Middle School*. Despite a self-serving prologue that honors media coverage of 9/11 through conversation with the *Today Show* anchors, this video offers a thoughtful introduction to media literacy with interviews of middle school students, educators, parents, and community members. The video may also be supplied free to educators who request it (choices@courtv.com or call 212-973-2867).

The debate over media involvement and ideology has been at times heated, and it is ongoing. Andersen (2003) considers this debate part of the current identity crisis in media education and counsels:

Teachers need to consider where they are comfortable on the spectrum of activism. There is a well-established media education progression from aware-ness to reflection, then to action, but we need to consider what we want "action" to mean. On one end, it might mean personal change, where students' values or consumption patterns are modified; on the other, it might mean participation in the political process to advocate for a change in legislation or policy; for some, it might mean civil disobedience, in the form of culture jamming [like taking to the streets in Seattle to protest the WTO] or hacking. Teachers might also make a distinction between how they are personally active and how they might more safely channel their students' activism—journeying to a protest themselves, but not inviting students to join them. (pp. 82–83)

Basic to the split among American media educators, as reflected in the organizations of AMLA and ACME, is the question of curriculum orientation; different definitions lead to different curriculum models. "Activist" models tend to be almost totally negative about the media, their ownership and purpose, and their influences (see Rogow, this volume). Bragg (2002), on the other hand, declares, "Such protection-ist perspectives and narrow definitions of critical media literacy set themselves against the pleasures the media provide" (p. 41). Bragg explores production work, now a "standard element of British media education," and offers a paradigm in which media literacy "is about enabling participation in media culture rather than learning hostility to it" (p. 42).

Worsnop (2003) also considers this dilemma—how to challenge young people while still respecting their media pleasures. He declares:

Using media education exclusively or even principally as a vehicle or behavior-modifying instrument for some other set of purposes, such as health concerns like drug, tobacco and alcohol use, body image . . . ideological concerns such as the influence of commercial interests . . . [and more] is a forlorn enterprise, an educational blind alley. (p. 180)

Students quickly "get wise" to what the teacher wants in a didactic approach to media literacy; they will play along, attacking all the mass media evils while they still enjoy their movies, music, and other media in their daily lives. Says Wornsop, "If media education is seen exclusively—or even principally—as an instrument to cure things that are seen as being wrong with today's media or with today's students, or with today's society, it won't work . . . it will fail as a subject in the curriculum" (p. 180). On the other hand, as Worsnop also notes, teachers cannot ignore real problems, social concerns like violence or racist stereotypes and moral concerns like teen sexuality or environmental carelessness, and the ways that media influence these. Regarding the political and curriculum split, Worsnop remarks, "The treacherous ground between these two extreme stances is the important territory of media education for the future" (p. 180).

Other Challenges

Other issues also challenge the future work of media literacy educators, including the need for assessment tools; the role of media production in media literacy curriculum; the place of media literacy in the general curriculum; the role of out-of-school versus in-school programs; the need for international conversation in the field to share good teaching practices; and the need for research on many questions, from program efficacy to the thinking processes of students composing in various media.

Assessment

Any legitimate curriculum requires assessment, and yet, Scharrer (2002/2003) argues, "There is surprisingly little discussion of the goals or 'outcomes' associated with participation in a media-literacy program" (p. 354). Increasingly, as Christ and Potter (1998) maintain, "In the U.S., assessment [of the schools, in general] is being advocated by parents, legislative bodies, administrators, and accrediting associations with faculty being asked to articulate what they are doing and to provide evidence that their students are learning" (p. 11). Media literacy educators will have to demonstrate that students actually learn something worthwhile, or that media literacy contributes to overall student achievement, if media literacy is to be accepted as a legitimate part of American curriculum. The discussion of assessment has been slow to develop, however, for several possible reasons: the lack of widespread implementation of media literacy in America—it is hard to assess what is not taking place; disagreements over the purposes of media literacy; and an understandable reluctance to reduce media literacy to multiple choice standardized tests. Still, educators are beginning to share ideas about assessment; Scharrer believes "A number of techniques can measure student learning . . . having students write essays; answer open or closed questions; critique a television show, a song's lyrics, or a commercial; and create their own media content" (p. 358). Quin and McMahon (2003) offer a model of outcomes or standards for different levels of media literacy, and teachers like Krueger (1998) have shared student results in print and on the PBS documentary film *Media Literacy: The New Basic?* (1996). Assessment in media literacy remains in its infancy, however, and much more work on establishing assessment criteria is needed, as well as study of the connections between media literacy and other kinds of academic achievement.

Media Production

Increasingly, the role of media production or creation is a major topic, especially since media creation can be a form of assessment demonstrating what students have learned about media literacy as well as what they have learned about other subject matter. Moreover, media production enables a deeper student understanding of how the media work and why they work the ways they do (how different media use their own "languages," to inform, persuade, and entertain—to connect to people). Media production also enables students to express points of view that have not been common in the mass media monopolies and in new ways that are exciting to many students. Just as traditional literacy includes reading and writing, media literacy must include analysis, evaluation, *and* creation. Tyner (2003) argues for digital production, in particular:

Literate individuals have the ability to use literacy tools and records to their own advantage, including the ability to confront and resist media messages that work against their interests. Digital practices allow individuals and communities to express themselves strategically in a number of discourses, using a wide range of sounds, images, moving images, and texts. Digital tools extend the publishing potential for a broad interchange of critical and independent thought. (p. 374)

The explosive growth of "blogs" (web logs) by widely diverse groups reflects the potential of new media for student exploration and expression.

A few media literacy programs have centered on video production, but acquiring all the essentials for a video/TV "station" is still very expensive. However, current computer technologies combining video, pictures, text, and so on are more widely available and affordable, although as noted, lower-income schools have less access to such resources. Buckingham (2003a) notes that "With digital technology, quite young children can easily produce multimedia texts, and even interactive hypermedia . . . It is in this area that some of the most exciting educational possibilities of digital technology may be found" (p. 6). Frechette (Chapter 6, this volume) points to the exciting future for the digital creation aspect of media literacy. The production of other kinds of media also has value—newspapers, audio recordings, magazines, and graphic novels—increasing media literacy but also improving learning across the curriculum.

Carreiro, Cross, Hewitt, and Santamaria (2004) took part in collaborative projects, called the Media Circus Initiative, with media professionals, university educators, and elementary school students in Toronto, Canada. Through Media Maker Workshops, children were taught video production. The authors conclude that students gained self-reflection, new ways of communicating, and deeper understanding and analysis of the media. The authors felt success in nurturing "a more culturally inclusive approach to media making and media analysis" (p. 47), as well. This work, like that described by Goodman in Chapter 11, indicates how media creation will grow in importance as media production is found to contribute to critical literacies.

The Place of Media Literacy in the Curriculum

Hobbs (1998) suggests that the question of whether media literacy should be taught as a specialty subject or integrated across the curriculum is another of the "great debates" in the media literacy movement. Actually, most media literacy experts, from Aufderheide (1992), an award-winning journalist, author, and professor in the School of Communications at the American University, to Hobbs and others, agree that the integration of media literacy is ideal (see also Manzo, 2000; Semali, 2000). They argue that media literacy is naturally interdisciplinary, that the curriculum is already too full of added shifting mandates, and that media literacy means more in the context of the subject areas. Media literacy may serve to renew curriculum and student interest in the disciplines. Furthermore, the learning and teaching of *anything* are inevitably influenced by the media. Masterman and Mariet (1994) observe that "media materials—films, videos, newspapers, photographs, images [and Internet sites]—are increasingly used in the teaching of all subjects . . . It is a matter of some importance that such material should not be consumed innocently, but read critically" (p. 64). Masterman and Mariet offer such integrated classroom activities as the compilation of oral histories via audiovisual media, the examination of scientific tests and principles used in advertisements, study of popular media representations of different cultures, and creation of popular media texts of literary texts as examples of how media literacy can be integrated across the curriculum (pp. 64–67).

In School or Elsewhere?

Are schools even the best places for media literacy? As Hobbs (1998) asks, "Should media literacy be focused on school-based K-12 educational environments? A fair amount of scholarly and popular writing in media literacy makes little reference to schools, children, teachers, or public education" (p. 22) and instead situates media literacy in other contexts. Grossman and DeGaetano (1999) and Steyer (2002) have aimed their work at parents, for example, stressing the need for activism on the part of parents and civic groups. Certainly, community projects such as Goodman describes in Chapter 11 are successful outside schools. Given the resistance of American public schools to genuine innovation (Sarason, 1990), media literacy may, in fact, be a "hard sell." Hobbs (1998) continues:

Are U.S. public schools likely to change within the next 20 years in the fairly dramatic ways that media literacy would require? For example, instead of reading eight classic novels in the 10th grade, how many communities will accept the practice of students reading four books, studying two films, and analyzing a newsmagazine and a web site? In light of the challenges of making change in public education, the best sites to implement media education may be in after-school programs, summer camps, religious education programs, library and prevention programs, community-based organizations, and at home with parental guidance. Such programs have seen exponential growth in the past 5 years. (p. 23)

However, evaluation of learning in such a range of sites is uncertain—it may or may not occur—and some students would inevitably be left out. As Buckingham (2003b) concludes, "the school curriculum remains a much more significant force in shaping young people's cultural activities and perceptions" (p. 210). He adds, "In order to be effective at a wider level, media educators clearly need to form partnerships with a range of organizations outside formal education" (p. 191). Media literacy must become part of the school's curriculum to prepare all students well, but teachers need to work with groups *outside* school, including various media workers, just as they need to work with other educators in the school such as librarians and special educators. In fact, media literacy may well serve as a useful means of collaboration among many people, inside and outside the school, for the benefit of the students.

International Connections

U.S. educators need to collaborate or at least connect with educators worldwide. The Canadian experience has already been influential; other nations are also doing important work, and shared knowledge can only be helpful. *Visions/Revisions* (Duncan & Tyner, 2003), a special publication for the 50th anniversary of the National Telemedia Council (leading media literacy organization), includes chapters on media literacy in Hong Kong and Japan as well as in New Zealand and Spain. The media affect the world; educators all over the globe are working in media literacy and have ideas, experiences, and resources to share. Graphic novels, for example, called *manga* in Japan, have a rich history in Japan and Europe, and are reaching a wider and largely younger audience in the United States. The graphic novel is a medium that holds educational potential, both for media literacy and other literacies (Schwarz, 2004).

An international vision of media literacy would also aid both teachers and students in understanding the world beyond the United States, a world that is both similar to and different from America. American media are very popular worldwide, for example, and it is important to understand that influence, for better and for worse. Indigenous people do not always benefit from the reach of American media. Mander (2002), for instance, explains how television watching has had a negative effect on Native American cultures in Canada. Young Native Americans are eating more junk food and showing less respect for their elders, two significant, and destructive, changes. American students, for their part, would profit from more familiarity with foreign media, balanced or biased, to understand how the rest of the world sees America today. Media literacy could well prove key to a new global awareness on the part of American youth.

Further Research

Finally, for media literacy to establish itself both as a scholarly discipline and as an integral part of curriculum and teaching in the schools, research is essential. The amount and quality of research on media literacy is growing around the world; however, the need is particularly urgent in the United States as the struggle to introduce media literacy here continues. The United Kingdom has led the way with classroom research by Hart (1994), research on children and the media in a collection edited by Howard (1998), and historical, child- and classroom-oriented research by Buckingham (2003b). Other international examples can also be found in *Visions/Revisions* (Duncan & Tyner, 2003) from the National Telemedia Council (see also the report from Japan by the Study Group on Young People and Media Literacy in the Field of Broadcasting, 2003). Much of the current American scholarship in media literacy is emerging from the literacy field. For example, the *Reading Research Quarterly* includes reports of research exploring adolescent girls' technology-mediated practices (Chandler-Olcott & Mahar, 2003) and the measurement of the acquisition of media-literacy skills (Hobbs & Frost, 2003).

Kubey (2003) believes that, "Media literacy is at a critical point in its history, a time when research into our practice and the efficacy of media education is more important than ever" (p. 109). Hoffmann (1999) also argues that empirical studies are needed; "In an educational climate where all departments and disciplines battle for scarce funds, such studies are often relied on when deciding who gets grants, what is included in recommended curriculum, etc." (p. 165). Kubey suggests that such research—both quantitative and qualitative—will offer the evidence media educators need to be taken seriously by legislators, foundations, schools of education, and the public at large, especially research that links media literacy to positive outcomes like increased student engagement or achievement in various subject areas. Given the many demands being made on teachers and students, education's highly politicized atmosphere, and the uncertain economy, media literacy will need to prove itself if it is to be broadly and quickly diffused. Money and energy will not be invested in innovations that do not improve student learning in some way.

In addition, research is basic for media literacy educators to continue to grow in knowledge and to improve their practice, just as science or history educators must. Doctoral students in a 2004 media literacy seminar at Oklahoma State University—all educators—listed the following research suggestions:

- What is the impact of media literacy at different age levels?
- What kinds of issues or concerns do parents have about media literacy, and how can they be educated about media literacy?
- Does media literacy aid in making students more literate in other ways—in traditional print reading, etc.?
- Does critical thinking about media transfer to other areas?
- Does media literacy motivate nonachieving and low-achieving students?
- How might media literacy broaden students' multicultural awareness?
- Where do you start when trying to form a media literacy curriculum?
- How do teens view connections between media messages and their own values and beliefs?
- Will media literacy change the structure of the classroom?

More topics were suggested, but it is clear from these that educators themselves want answers to important questions about how media literacy fits in the curriculum, meets student, family, and community needs, and can most effectively be taught. Research is essential for living and dynamic curriculum and teaching.

Envisioning the Future

Media literacy in America faces a number of serious obstacles and questions. The times may not be propitious. As Worsnop (2003) reiterates in his consideration of media literacy's future, "Education looks for panaceas—the simpler the better. Complexity is taboo. It can be frustratingly anti-intellectual" (p. 182). Current goals of school reform reflected in the NCLB materials and in school activities that narrow the curriculum to material on standardized tests do not seem encouraging. Media literacy education is itself complicated; difficult to do without sufficient time, support, and resources, and beset by disagreements among its supporters.

However, precedents for educational change coming from outside the usual government mandates or the policymakers exist. The National Writing Project (NWP), for example, is an outstanding example of teachers teaching teachers and improving curriculum and instruction from the bottom up, through changing political climates and diverse federal administrations. The first NWP site was begun as the Bay Area Summer Institute at the University of California Berkeley by Jim Gray in 1974. Since that time the NWP has grown into a network of more than 175 sites in all 50 states and elsewhere. These sites build on university partnerships to offer teachers summer institutes on writing, after which teachers themselves offer in-service programs for other teachers. As Lieberman and Wood (2003) observe in their in-depth study of the NWP, "The NWP professional community provides a powerful context for professional learning and continuous collective inquiry" (p. 102). Student learning has been changed, as well, as many more teachers use diverse ways to teach writing.

Perhaps media literacy educators will create such a network for media education, one committed to the basic principles of media literacy like critical thinking, but one that allows diversity within local organizations. Educators can take advantage of the new media and groups outside schools to develop these networks. Administrative support is also essential, along with a "critical mass" of teachers who provide leadership in their schools. Hobbs (1998) observes:

Most educators who have begun incorporating media literacy concepts into the curriculum have not been part of an organized, systematic, district-wide process...Such momentum from the bottom up represents an important source of energy for the media literacy movement. Though fragmented and often uneven in quality, this approach may be the only pragmatic way. (p. 23)

The growing number of websites (listed in the appendix at the end of this chapter), conferences, books and articles, and opportunities for professional development provide some cause for optimism.

The best hope for widespread acceptance of the need for media literacy is found in the likelihood that citizens, and educators at all levels, will realize, that: 1) serious curricular issues emerge with media literacy—young people using the Internet wisely to support learning; teachers questioning slick, media-supported curriculum packages; and 2) broader social issues follow—questions around voter cynicism and personal privacy and the celebrity culture that Gabler (1998) examines in *Life the Movie*, to name a few. Educators and parents have significant concerns about the media's absorption of teen culture and its repackaging for marketing purposes, selling everything from music to shoes, with the result that "The personae, self-images, ambitions, and values of young people in the United States have been seriously distorted by the commercial frenzy surrounding them" (Quart, 2003, p. 13). At the same time, television contributed to the advancement of the Civil Rights movement and the end of the Vietnam war; the media can influence, in positive ways, social change. Our everyday reality is affected by the media; its ubiquity cannot be allowed to minimize recognition of its impact.

Especially in a postmodern world, media literacy may prove crucial. In a society in which political debate has been reduced to 30-second attack ads and "image is everything," citizens will have to struggle to maintain democracy, to become informed enough and committed enough to make the democratic system work. In a confusing world of blurred boundaries, characterized by "sound bites," "infotainment," and "docudramas," what knowledge is of most worth becomes an even more difficult question; citizens will need to know how to navigate the onslaught of images and sounds to make personal and societal decisions on everything from energy use (should I buy an SUV?) to stem cell research (what should the laws be?). In a media-saturated culture, all of us may need, in fact, to question the very meaning of human life as we now experience it: fragmented, fast-paced, ephemeral, extreme. Gitlin (2001) challenges us to take the media seriously:

In the presence of the media, we may be attentive or inattentive, aroused or deadened, but it is in symbiotic relation to them, their pictures, texts, and sounds, in the time we spend with them, the trouble we take to obtain, absorb, repel, and discuss them, that much of the world happens for us. Media are occasions for experiences—experiences that are themselves the main products, the main transactions, the main "effects" of the media. That is the big story. (p. 10)

Those who believe in the power of media literacy programs believe that media literacy can reenergize disciplines across the curriculum and connect those disciplines, encourage deep inquiry and the creation of new knowledge by young people, and create community and communication among students and adults. Media literacy can involve teachers as coexplorers in topics that really matter outside the classroom. Genuine reform, real transformation in curriculum and teaching, could be propelled by media literacy both in schools and in society. Surely, Americans could agree with Eisner (2003) who declares that what we want is not merely to enable students to do well on tests, but "to provide a curriculum and a school environment that enables students to develop the dispositions, the appetites, the skills, and the ideas that allow them to live personally satisfying and socially productive lives" (p. 651). One of the roots of the word educate is *educere*, "to lead forth." Leading forth can be a frightening and disturbing activity. If enough of the American people have the will to create, or to allow, an educational system that does more than minimal training, media literacy may prove a crucial factor in educating youth in problem solving, critical thinking, thoughtful citizenship, and imaginative leadership.

NOTE

1. A University of Oregon umbrella site offers a chart of all the states and how media literacy objectives are included in various subject areas, at http://www.med.sc.edu:1081/statelit.htm

APPENDIX
TEN WEBSITES FOR MEDIA LITERACY

Media Literacy Online Project http://interact.uroegon.edu/MediaLit/HomePage	This is the umbrella site for links, organizations, other sites, publications, etc., in media literacy.
Center for Media Literacy http://medialit.org	Premier source of resources and basic support. See Chapter 10.
New Mexico Media Literacy Project http://www.nmmlp.org/;	Offers training, information, a few free teacher resources such as handouts on deconstructing the media. Videos and CDs for purchase. See Chapter 9.
Media Literacy Clearinghouse http://www.med.sc.edu:1081/	Resource for lesson plans. Links and downloadable handouts organized by topic.
Project Look Sharp http://www.ithaca.edu/looksharp	Offers links to other media literacy sites and good articles. Long list of resources and links to use when teaching students to evaluate the Internet. See Chapter 9.
PBS (Public Broadcasting) http://www.pbs.org	Source of all kinds of lessons, especially media literacy. Has quizzes, printable activities, etc.
Media Education Foundation http://www.mediaed.org	Has news, handouts, and a great video catalog including videos by Sut Jhally such as *Dreamworlds II* (on MTV and sexism) and *Advertising and the End of the Age*.
Cable in the Classroom http://www.ciconline.org	Offers parent guides, articles, and free videos like *TV Smarts for Kids*.
Films for the Humanities and Sciences http://www.films.com	Look under "Communications" for excellent videos like *Consuming Images* w/Bill Moyers.
Community Learning Network http://www.cln.org	Click under "Subject Area" for media literacy. Find lesson plans, links, and resources.

REFERENCES

Andersen, N. (2003). Ten plus one identity crisis. In B. Duncan & K. Tyner (Eds.), *Visions/revisions: Moving forward with media education* (pp. 74–84). Madison, WI: National Telemedia Council.

Aufderheide, P. (1992). *Media literacy: A report of the National Leadership Conference on Media Literacy*. Washington, DC: The Aspen Institute. (ERIC Document Reproduction Service No. ED 365294).

Bragg, S. (2002). Wrestling in wooly gloves: Not just being critically media literate. *Journal of Popular Film & Television*, *30*(1), 41–51.

Brown, J.A. (1998). Media literacy perspectives. *Journal of Communication*, *48*(1), 44–58.

Buckingham, D. (2003a). Digital literacies: Media education and new media technologies. In B. Duncan & K. Tyner (Eds.), *Visions/revisions: Moving forward with media education* (pp. 2–11). Madison, WI: National Telemedia Council.

Buckingham, D. (2003b). *Media education: Literacy, learning and contemporary culture*. Cambridge, UK: Polity Press.

Bushnell, M. (2003). Teachers in the school house panopticon: Complicity and resistance. *Education and Urban Society*, *35*, 251–272.

Carreiro, P., Cross, J., Hewitt, S., & Santamaria, V. (2004). Media literacy through media making. *Telemedium*, *51*(1), 46–52.

Chandler-Olcott, K., & Mahar, D. (2003). "Tech-savviness" meets multiliteracies: Exploring adolescent girls' technology-mediated literacy practices. *Reading Research Quarterly*, *38*, 356–385.

Christ, W.G., & Potter, W.J. (1998). Media literacy, media education, and the academy. *Journal of Communication*, *48*(1), 5–16.

Court TV. (2004). *Mind over media: Voices from the middle school* [Television broadcast/video].

Duncan, B., & Tyner, K. (Eds.). (2003). *Visions/revisions: Moving forward with media education*. Madison, WI: National Telemedia Council.

Eisenhart, M., & Towne, L. (2003). Contestation and change in national policy on "scientifically based" education research, *Educational Researcher*, *32*(7), 31–38.

Eisner, E. (2003). Questioning assumptions about schooling. *Phi Beta Kappan*, *84*, 648–657.

Evans, R.W., Avery, P.G., & Pederson, P.V. (2000). Taboo topics: Cultural restraint on teaching social issues. *Clearing House*, *73*, 295–303.

Frechette, J.D. (2005). Critical thinking for the cyberage. In G. Schwarz & P.U. Brown (Eds.), *Media literacy: Transforming curriculum and teaching. The 104th yearbook of the National Society for the Study of Education*, Part I (pp. 100–118). Malden, MA: Blackwell Publishing.

Gabler, N. (1998). *Life the movie*. New York: Alfred A. Knopf.

Gitlin, T. (2001). *Media unlimited: How the torrent of images and sounds overwhelms our lives*. New York: Metropolitan Books.

Glickman, C. (Ed.). (2004). Introduction: Straight talk. In C. Glickman (Ed.), *Letters to the next president* (pp. 1–6). New York: Teachers College Press.

Goetze, S, Brown, D., & Schwarz, G. (2005). Teachers need media literacy, too! In G. Schwarz & P.U. Brown (Eds.), *Media literacy: Transforming curriculum and teaching. The 104th yearbook of the National Society for the Study of Education*, Part I (pp. 161–179). Malden, MA: Blackwell Publishing.

Goodman, E. (2004, October 31). Scorched-earth politics in '04. *The Tulsa World*, p. G5.

Grossman, D., & DeGaetano, G. (1999). *Stop teaching our kids to kill*. New York: Crown Publisher.

Hart, A. (1994). Literacy, values, and non-literary texts. *CLE Working Papers*, *3*, 79–93.

Hobbs, R. (1998). The seven great debates in the media literacy movement. *Journal of Communication*, *48*(1), 16–43.

Hobbs, R. (2003). Understanding teachers' experiences with media literacy in the class-room. In B. Duncan & K. Tyner (Eds.), *Visions/revisions: Moving forward with media education* (pp. 100–108). Madison, WI: National Telemedia Council.

Hobbs, R. (2005). Media literacy and the K-12 content areas. In G. Schwarz & P.U. Brown (Eds.), *Media literacy: Transforming curriculum and teaching. The 104th yearbook of the National Society for the Study of Education*, Part I (pp. 74–99). Malden, MA: Blackwell Publishing.

Hobbs, R., & Frost, R. (2003). Measuring the literacy of media-literacy skills. *Reading Research Quarterly, 38*, 330–355.

Hoffmann, G. (1999). Media literacy study. *et Cetera, 56*(2), 165–172.

Howard, S. (Ed.). (1998). *Wired-up: Young people and the electronic media*. London: UCL Press.

Kohn, A. (2004). Test today, privatize tomorrow: Using accountability to "reform" public schools to death. *Phi Delta Kappan, 85*, 568–577.

Kozol, J. (1991). *Savage inequalities*. New York: Crown Publishers.

Krueger, E. (1998). Media literacy does work, trust me. *English Journal, 87*(1), 17–20.

Kubey, R.W. (1998). Obstacles to the development of media education in the United States. *Journal of Communication, 48*(1), 58–70.

Kubey, R.W. (2003). Why U.S. media education lags behind the rest of the English-speaking world. *Television & New Media, 4*, 351–370.

Lieberman, A., & Wood, D.R. (2003). *Inside the National Writing Project*. New York: Teachers College.

Lewis, J., & Jhally, S. (1998). The struggle over media literacy. *Journal of Communication, 48*(1), 109–121.

Mander, J. (2002). TV and the cloning of culture. In B. Bigelow & B. Peterson (Eds.), *Rethinking globalization* (pp. 292–295). Milwaukee, WI: Rethinking Schools.

Manzo, K.K. (2000, December 6). Schools begin to infuse media literacy into the three R's. *Education Week*, pp. 6–7.

Masterman, L., & Mariet, F. (1994). *Media education in 1990's Europe*. Netherlands: Council of Europe Press.

Mathison, S., & Freeman, M. (2003, September 24). Constraining elementary teachers' work: Dilemmas and paradoxes created by state mandated testing. *Education Policy Analysis Archives, 11*(34). Retrieved September 13, 2004, from http://epaa.asu.edu/epaa/v11n34/

McBrien, J.L. (2005). Uninformed in the information age: Why media necessitates critical thinking education. In G. Schwarz & P.U. Brown (Eds.), *Media literacy: Transforming curriculum and teaching. The 104th yearbook of the National Society for the Study of Education*, Part I (pp. 18–34). Malden, MA: Blackwell Publishing.

McNeil, L.M. (2000). *Contradictions of school reform: Educational costs of standardized testing*. New York: Routledge.

Media Literacy: The New Basic? (1996). [Television broadcast/video]. PBS (Corporation for Public Broadcasting).

Meier, D. (2004, June 14). No politician left behind. *Nation, 278*, 6–7.

Molnar, A. (1996). *Giving the kids the business*. Boulder, CO: WestviewPress.

Pungente, J., Duncan, B., & Andersen, N. (2005). The Canadian experience: Leading the way. In G. Schwarz & P.U. Brown (Eds.), *Media literacy: Transforming curriculum and teaching. The 104th yearbook of the National Society for the Study of Education*, Part I (pp. 140–160). Malden, MA: Blackwell Publishing.

Quart, A. (2003). *Branded: The buying and selling of teenagers*. Cambridge, MA: Perseus.

Quin, R., & McMahon, B. (2003). Relevance and rigour in media education: A path to reflection on our identity. In B. Duncan & K. Tyner (Eds.), *Visions/revisions: Moving forward with media education* (pp. 122–140). Madison, WI: National Telemedia Council.

Rethinking Schools. (2001). *The return to separate and unequal: Metropolitan Milwaukee school funding through a racial lens.* A Rethinking Schools Report, 2001. Retrieved November 30, 2004, from http://www.rethinkingschools.org

Riddell, J.B. (1997). The political climate and arts education. *Arts Education Policy Review, 98*(5), 2–9.

Rigsby, L.C., & DeMulder, E.K. (2003, November 18). Teachers' voices interpreting standards: Compromising teachers' autonomy or raising expectations and performances? *Education Policy Analysis Archives, 11*(44). Retrieved November 8, 2004, from http://epaa.asu.edu/epaa/v11n44

Rogow, F. (2005). Terrain in transition: Reflections on the pedagogy of media literacy education. In G. Schwarz & P.U. Brown (Eds.), *Media literacy: Transforming curriculum and teaching. The 104th yearbook of the National Society for the Study of Education*, Part I (pp. 284–290). Malden, MA: Blackwell Publishing.

Rose, L.C., & Gallup, A.M. (2004). The 36th annual Phi Delta Kappan/Gallup poll of the public's attitudes toward the public schools. *Phi Delta Kappan, 86*, 41–56.

Rubalcava, M. (2004). Leaving children behind. *Rethinking Schools, 19*(1), 10.

Sarason, S.B. (1990). *The predictable failure of school reform.* San Francisco: Jossey-Bass.

Scharrer, E. (2002/2003). Making a case for media literacy in the curriculum: Outcomes and assessment. *Journal of Adolescent and Adult Literacy, 46*, 354–358.

Schwarz, G. (2004). Graphic novels: Multiple cultures and multiple literacies. *Thinking Classroom, 5*(4), 17–24.

Semali, L. (2000). *Literacy in multimedia America.* New York: Falmer Press.

Semali, L. (2005). Why media literacy matters in American schools. In G. Schwarz & P.U. Brown (Eds.), *Media literacy: Transforming curriculum and teaching. The 104th yearbook of the National Society for the Study of Education*, Part I (pp. 35–54). Malden, MA: Blackwell Publishing.

Smith, F. (2003). *Unspeakable acts, unnatural practices: Flaws and fallacies in scientific reading instruction.* Portsmouth, NH: Heinemann.

Stecher, B.M., & Hamilton, L.S. (2002). Putting theory to the test: Systems of "educational accountability" should be held accountable. *Rand Review, 26*(1), 17–23.

Steyer, J.P. (2002). *The other parent: The inside story of the media's effect on our children.* New York: Atria Books.

Study Group on Young People and Media Literacy in the Field of Broadcasting. (Unofficial Translation). (2003). Media literacy: Ability of young people to function in the media society. Retrieved December 4, 2003, from http://www.soumu.go.jp/joho_tusin

The New Mexico Media Literacy Project. (2002, Spring/Fall). National Coalition presents ACME summit: A more active kind of media education! *The State of Media Education* (NMMLP newsletter), p. 1. Albuquerque: New Mexico Media Literacy Project.

Thoman, E., & Jolls, T. (2005). Media literacy education in the USA: An overview of the Center for Media Literacy. In G. Schwarz & P.U. Brown (Eds.), *Media literacy: Transforming curriculum and teaching. The 104th yearbook of the National Society for the Study of Education*, Part I (pp. 180–205). Malden, MA: Blackwell Publishing.

Tucker, M.C., & Toch, T. (2004). The secret to making NCLB work? More bureaucrats. *Phi Delta Kappan, 86*, 28–33.

Tyner, K. (2003). Beyond boxes and wires. *Television & New Media, 4*, 371–388.

Understanding Media. (1998). [CD-ROM]. Albuquerque, New Mexico: New Mexico Media Literacy Project.

Van Luchene, S.R. (2004). Rekindling the dialogue: Education according to Plato and Dewey. *Academe, 90*(3), 54–57.

Worsnop, C. (2003). The future of media education. In B. Duncan & K. Tyner (Eds.), *Visions/revisions: Moving forward in media education* (pp. 179–182). Madison, WI: National Telemedia Council.

Yates, B.L. (1998, June). *Media literacy and the policymaking process: A framework for understanding influences on potential educational policy outputs*. Paper presented at the meeting of National Media Literacy and Media Citizenship Conference, Birmingham, AL. (ERIC Document Reproduction Service No. ED424602).

COMMENTARIES

Researching Media Literacy: Pitfalls and Possibilities

ROY F. FOX

Media literacy research is no longer comparable to the early Wright Brothers creations; actually, it is more akin to a jet plane as it taxis toward the runway. Researching media literacy is one of the most important, exciting, and intriguing intellectual experiences available to scholars, regardless of whether they consider themselves to be "text dominant" or "media dominant," and regardless of their disciplinary home, as imagery-laden electronic media and print reach into every corner of every discipline. Research in media literacy luxuriates in rich possibilities, but it also has its pitfalls.

A myriad of differences exist between quantitative and qualitative approaches, and I would like to underscore just how appropriate qualitative approaches are for media literacy research. Qualitative paradigms assume that the phenomena under study *cannot* exist apart from how people perceive it; that researchers can never function in purely objective ways—but that they can, first, admit (and even explore) their own subjectivities. At the same time, they can demonstrate that other experts may share the same or similar interpretations of phenomena. Qualitative researchers try to view their subject through the eyes of the study's participants, so that they reduce carrying preconceived notions into their study, and they seek to conduct their research in the most natural environment and circumstances possible.

Potter (1996) describes several types of qualitative research well suited for media literacy researchers' diverse purposes and topics. These include textual analysis, in which investigators might, for example, analyze one or more episodes of a media text for the director's decisions in how and why she constructed a specific message (e.g., options in scene editing, transitions, camera angles). Media texts can also be analyzed

Roy F. Fox is Professor and Chair of the Department of Learning, Teaching, & Curriculum and directs the Missouri Writing Project at the University of Missouri, Columbia.

for thematic issues (e.g., how Country Western music treats divorce); social issues of race, gender, age, and class (e.g., how does the *Judging Amy* television series define working women?); and genre and intertextuality issues (e.g., how television courtroom dramas "borrow" from the soap opera genre). While these methods can produce results that will inform us about our culture, they are also effective for teachers to use with their students in fostering critical media literacy.

Some studies blend several of these approaches, when they explore how specific people interact with media texts—what Potter (1996) calls *symbolic interactionism*. For example, Postman, Nystrom, Strate, and Weingartner (1987) studied the narrative qualities and mythical patterns found in television beer commercials, which in turn led to an analysis of the ways in which such advertising defined men's roles. One of my studies explored how students responded to Channel One television commercials—how such ads affected students' language, thinking, and behavior (Fox, 1996).

Many other types of qualitative research are appropriate for studying media literacy, given the broad range of critical research to be done. See Table 1 for a list of possibilities for future research in media literacy.

TABLE 1

QUESTION FOR FUTURE RESEARCH IN MEDIA LITERACY

1. *How do students' interactions with media connect to their larger, interpretive communities and cultures?* Every day, individuals interact with multiple messages, from many channels, as they simultaneously interact with ever-increasing circles of people, issues, and cultures. How and why does this occur?

2. *How do students compose media messages? How do composing and comprehending these messages function as reciprocal processes?* We know little about the reciprocal relationships between reading and writing print texts—and even less about students' processing of electronic texts.

3. *How do students understand "media convergence"?* The same or similar messages often converge or appear in a variety of formats and channels. Hence, how do students' perceptions differ, depending upon the particular vessel that carries the message? How do we best teach students to "attend differently" to different media?

4. *How do media affect the development of students' voices?* Developing confident, rational, and articulate "voices" in speech and writing is extremely important for students' identity development, as well as for their success in learning and communicating in any subject. What are the roles and functions of various media in the development of students' voices?

5. *How do students respond to rapid, brief, fragmented, and decontextualized media messages, such as those delivered in television commercials and in "news headlines" programs?* Understanding how such messages persuade students—to vote for someone, to buy something, to believe in some idea—resides at the core of a literate and democratic society.

TABLE 1 (*Continued*)
QUESTION FOR FUTURE RESEARCH IN MEDIA LITERACY

---

6. *How do students interpret media messages that "arouse desire" for intangible qualities, by associating them with tangible products?* Students are immersed in commercial messages that suggest they may, for example, gain increased popularity or sexual appeal by purchasing products that cannot possibly deliver such abstract and human qualities. Do students believe that particular messages promise complete gratification? If so, how and why? If students invest in such messages and products, do they believe their desires have been gratified? If so, how and why do they conclude this?

7. *What is the nature of "HyperDramas" and "memes"—and how do students interact with them?* HyperDramas (e.g., the O.J. Simpson trials, the death of Princess Diana, and the Scott Peterson murder trial) are narratives that suddenly erupt from current headlines and then snowball in media coverage (often by generating "spin-off" narratives), generating workplace conversations and other communication. HyperDramas fuse many genres of media, such as the TV soap opera, Western, talk show, commercial, mystery, news, romance, press conference, cop show, documentary, courtroom drama, and the Super Bowl (Fox, 2001). HperDramas may result or be nurtured by the self-replicating units of culture known as "memes"—images, jokes, jingles, bits of knowledge, etc.—that spread throughout a culture in quicksilver ways, often changing along the way. How can we help students to better understand and process these basic, powerful elements of media?

8. *How do media affect students' physical and mental health?* Researchers in medicine, nursing, nutrition, and psychology, along with such organizations as the Center for Disease Control, the American Academy of Pediatrics, and the National Institute for Children's Health, have only just begun to "connect the dots" between students' media consumption and such issues as obesity, physical activity levels, nutrition, aggression, attention-deficit disorders, anxiety, low self-esteem, and depression. We currently know very little about how specific types of media affect specific types of health.

9. *When teaching media, how effective are certain approaches?* Many media literacy proponents express disdain for the traditional approach to using film in the classroom— that is, showing the movie version of the novel at unit's end on Friday. However, we do not have much evidence of what the effects of even this practice might be, let alone other, more creative approaches to media literacy.

10. *What are teachers' perceptions of the barriers they face in teaching about media?* Teachers often express the fear that media literacy will somehow displace the emphasis on print texts. Others strongly dispute this. What are the other obstacles that teachers feel inhibit or prohibit their engagement with media in their classrooms? Are such perceptions warranted? How do they evolve?

11. *What are the ethical issues within the media literacy movement itself, and how are they resolved?* We need to explore the "situational ethics" involved in key areas, such as (1) media literacy advocates accepting funds from the very sources they claim to research and inform the public about; (2) media literacy distributors or clearing houses of information and curriculum receiving funds from commercial media conglomerates (some organizations have refused to distribute materials they deem to be critical of commercial media); and (3) school districts accepting advertising contracts for machines dispensing "junk food" in the school and/or selling—also within the school—the very products advertised on required, in-school television-viewing.

I am convinced that qualitative approaches are far preferable to statistical analyses when investigating media literacy issues. When we explore the complex interactions within and among individuals, the interpretive communities in which they participate, the abundant signs and symbols communicated within and across messages, the ever-shifting disciplinary perspectives we harbor, and the constantly expanding and contracting circles of culture that envelop us, it makes horse sense to focus on people's thinking about their own experiences. These deep wells are best tapped through the language and other symbols humans use to represent and to reflect on their experiences—which in turn may affect their actions. Effectively tapping these deep wells requires that we at least be aware of some pitfalls in media literacy research.

Pitfalls

The obstacles described in this section do not exhaust the list. They are, however, the obstacles I have found particularly vexing in the past 20 years as I have conducted my own research in media literacy, supervised theses and dissertations focused on media literacy, and helped faculty from diverse disciplines pursue their own research interests, including the securing of external funding. Some of these pitfalls have obvious solutions, while others will likely remain as conundrums for some time.

1. *Media so pervades our lives that it becomes invisible as a field of study.* The density of electronic messages that surrounds us can cheapen the value of any given message, allowing many people to remain unaware of why we should study it in the first place. Nearly 60 years ago, S. I. Hayakawa (1949/2001) argued that we needed to study language because we were immersed in it. He reasoned that the last thing that fish would want to study is water. Today, the same is true of electronic media.

2. *Media literacy resides in numerous, different disciplines.* More than most areas, media literacy, or at least parts of it, resides within numerous disciplines such as cognitive psychology, gestalt psychology, communication, journalism, linguistics, semantics, rhetoric, anthropology, science, engineering, literary criticism, art criticism, film studies, sociology, humanities, and literacy education (Fox 1994b), making it difficult to research thoroughly and nearly impossible for researchers, within any given study, to "cover all the bases."

3. *Federal funding agencies restrict or disallow qualitative research.* In many fields, including the social sciences and humanities, federal agencies will often not accept grant proposals unless they employ "scientifically based research." Other common phrases are "best available evidence" and "evidence-based practice." These terms have often functioned as a kind of euphemism for quantitative methodology. In recent years, such language—first the province of the sciences and business—has been heavily applied to education, especially with the implementation of No Child Left Behind.

4. *The advertising industry is free to use qualitative research in order to increase sales—yet researchers seeking federal funding are not allowed to use these same methods to learn about media literacy.* Granted, there are clear differences here in who pays for what, but excluding qualitative methods from researching media literacy seriously limits the volume, type, and quality of research in this field, as language itself is so intricately integrated into peoples' thinking about media. A marketing firm, for example, can employ qualitative methods for purposes of increasing people's consumption of products (via focus groups, in-home interviews, and even "regression hypnosis"), yet teachers and scholars cannot receive funding to better understand how to teach students to evaluate critically the same messages created from these same approaches. Restricting qualitative methods means that we will learn much less, over time, about the very questions we most need to pursue.

5. *Media literacy research can be confused or combined with computer technology research.* It is easy (and sometimes practical and beneficial) to conflate these two areas. Many media people have a foot in computer technology and vice versa. Both of these broad areas cut across most boundaries—disciplinary, demographic, ethnic, geographic, etc. Despite such broad definitions and despite their similarities, we should remember that media literacy and technology differ in fundamental ways. Media literacy, for instance, is far more concerned with composing and comprehending symbols than are the fields of computer technology and information. Overall, for the past two decades, media literacy has been marginalized by the high-profile, high-dollar computer and technology industries. As a culture, we long ago jumped aboard the computer juggernaut, when we did not understand the current media (or "earlier technologies") of television and film. The point is that today, we understand more about using computers than we do about media literacy, when the opposite should be true.

6. *The "high glitz factor" of media can overshadow equally important elements involved in media literacy.* In Channel One schools, for example, many observers have found that students' heads come up off the desk to view new commercials that reflect an MTV-esque approach of loud, fast music and rapid-fire scene editing—but drop back down when the teacher speaks (Fox, 2001). In this situation, researchers may be sorely tempted *not* to focus on other variables, such as the teacher's attitudes toward advertising, her own past experiences with media, her instructional practices, the state's educational standards, the school district's conditions that led to allowing commercials inside the classroom, or how and why the products being advertised are *also* on sale within the school.

7. *Researchers tend to think of quantitative and qualitative research methods as mutually exclusive.* They are not. Automatically excluding one type of research from the other perpetuates some unnecessary dichotomies between methodologies, researchers, departments, and even disciplines. One can argue that a phenomenon as complex as media literacy demands hybrid and multifaceted approaches. An excellent example is Schor's (2004) study of children and consumer culture, which employed the following methods with both children and advertising agencies: note-taking, interviewing individuals and small groups, observing as a participant, conducting surveys, "shadowing" marketing researchers during their work, attending professional conferences and meetings, examining artifacts such as toys and food, viewing television commercials, and reading reports and marketing data.

8. *Good, qualitative media literacy research is often lengthy.* The sheer bulk and length of qualitative studies militates against their being accepted for publication in the first place, especially in journals, where space is limited. If such reports *are* accepted, there is a greater risk of "boiled down versions" ultimately being sent to press.

9. *Cumbersome approval procedures and censorship can influence media literacy research outcomes.* Some teachers and researchers have changed their focus and direction of research (including the questions they want to ask) due to the bureaucratic intimidations of the human subjects approval process (Zygouris-Coe, Pace, Weade, & Milecki, 2001). Such bureaucratic hurdles can militate against the honest pursuit of truth in research. The same holds true for "prior censorship"; I have known student researchers and teachers who did not collect data involving certain media texts because principals, librarians, and parents *might* object to the titles and/or contents.

These pitfalls are not easy to unravel. Nonetheless, they should not be accepted as more important—or more powerful—than the promises and possibilities of media literacy, explored in the following section.

Possibilities

Some of the following possibilities or recommendations apply to both quantitative and qualitative research approaches, although most of them focus on qualitative. These recommendations range from the backgrounds of investigators, to qualitative methods, to critical lenses for analyzing data. Included in the discussion are broad research methodologies along with consideration of more specific research tools.

1. *Media literacy researchers should be experts in print, as well as visual media.* Having a firm grounding in each symbol system helps ensure that neither will be overlooked and increases the chances that the reciprocal relationships between words and pictures will be effectively analyzed within texts, as well as within students' oral and written language (Fox, 1994a; Paivio, 1991).

2. *Media literacy research needs new and hybrid methodologies.* For decades, media producers—those with vested interests in media—have generated numerous new research methods such as concept testing, viewing and listening studies, market assessment studies, and online surveys. On the other hand, media literacy researchers have developed very few research innovations, other than occasionally adapting case study approaches to media consumers. This must change if the field is to grow. Media literacy researchers need to borrow and adapt methods from other disciplines, as well as to create new ones that are tailored to the researchers' questions, purposes, and contexts.

Perhaps the best example of a new method tailored to the research design is Schor's (2004) study focusing on children and consumer culture, especially the advertising industry. In addition to a host of qualitative methods, Schor surveyed 300 children and used these data to develop a new scale to determine the extent of kids' involvement in consumer culture. This instrument helped her to gauge the influence of consumer culture on psychological variables, such as depression and anxiety (p. 148). Media literacy particularly needs to experiment with methods from other disciplines, especially psychology, anthropology, and marketing, as well as to develop those, like Schor's, that are tailored to educators' research questions and contexts.

3. *Media literacy research should employ more case study approaches.* Media literacy is ideal for case studies in both comprehending and composing media. We especially need case studies that focus on how students negotiate contentious and discrepant events when creating, comprehending, interpreting, and applying media products and events to their own lives. Through case study, we may better understand how young people make sense of media events within their own environments.

4. *Eliciting free and open communication from students is crucial for media literacy research and teaching.* In much media literacy research, we have little choice but to "force verbalization" of students' thoughts, intuitions, feelings, beliefs, and values, because responses to media are often affective in nature and have not been articulated before. "Thinking out loud" is often best elicited by the "combustion" created within focus groups, such as questions, comments, affirmations or denials, requests for more elaboration or examples, and (not to be underrated) innocent laughter. In small groups, thinking and language can snowball, so using several microphones can help researchers when several students speak at once.

5. *Media literacy researchers must carefully select their critical lenses for analyzing results.* Media literacy researchers often grapple with how to analyze their research results most effectively. That is, which set of criteria does one use? While it is largely true that the topic and research design must dictate this, media and critical literacy studies offer an array of possibilities from which to choose—from Marxist analysis, to feminist analysis, to discourse analysis. In a number of studies, I have observed that the critical lens can be misunderstood and hence misapplied, too broad or too narrow in scope, or simply inappropriate for the data to be interpreted.

The most broadly applicable, flexible, and effective critical lens for media literacy researchers, to my mind, is general semantics. Among others, Hayakawa and Hayakawa (2001) clearly describe the basic principles of this system, earlier postulated by Korzybski (1933). Principles of general semantics can be applied to the analysis of media texts (print, visual, and aural elements), as well as to the language that students use to think about and communicate about media. The map/territory construct of general semantics—the notion that peoples' maps or language should at least roughly match their territory or reality—helps researchers focus on some basic questions that often drive qualitative inquiry, such as, "*How* and *why* do participants know what they say they know?" Or, stated another way: "Is the reality of X what participants *believe* it is?"

Conclusion

Once teachers, scholars, administrators, and others better understand the deep, rich nature of media literacy, I suspect that many of the hopes expressed in this commentary will come to fruition. While media literacy has made many gains in the past 25 years, our discipline's collective activities and products have not yet reached that stage of "critical mass" needed for rapid development to occur (see Table 1 for examples of research possibilities). We are not yet able to truly lift off the ground. However, if we engage in some of the processes and directions outlined in this chapter, I hope we will edge just a little bit closer to that painted line on the runway.

REFERENCES

Fox, R.F. (1994a). Introduction. In R.F. Fox (Ed.), *Images in language, media, & mind* (pp. ix–x). Urbana, IL: National Council Teachers of English.

Fox, R.F. (1994b). Image studies: An interdisciplinary view. In R.F. Fox (Ed.), *Images in language, media, & mind* (pp. 3–21). Urbana, IL: National Council Teachers of English.

Fox, R.F. (1996). *Harvesting minds: How TV commercials control kids*. Westport, CT: Praeger.

Fox, R.F. (2001). *MediaSpeak: Three American voices*. Westport, CT: Praeger.

Hayakawa, S.I., & Hayakawa, A. (1949/2001). *Language in thought and action*. New York: Harcourt Brace.

Korzybski, A. (1933). *Science and sanity*. Lancaster, PA: Science Press.

Paivio, A. (1991). *Mental representations: A dual coding approach*. New York: Oxford University Press.

Postman, N., Nystrom, C., Strate, L., & Weingartner, C. (1987). *Myths, men, and beer: An analysis of beer commercials on broadcast television*. Falls Church, VA: AAA Foundation for Traffic Safety.

Potter, W.J. (1996). *An analysis of thinking and research about qualitative methods*. Mahwah, NJ: Lawrence Erlbaum.

Schor, J. (2004). *Born to buy: The commercialized child and the new consumer culture*. New York: Scribner.

Zygouris-Coe, V., Pace, B.G., Weade, R., & Milecki, C. (2001). Action research: A situated perspective. *International Journal of Qualitative Studies in Education, 14*, 399–412.

Merging Media and Science: Learning to Weigh Sources, Not Just Evidence

MARLENE THIER

A true journey of discovery lies not in seeking new shores but in finding new eyes.

—Marcel Proust

Today we are *all* bombarded with powerful images, words, and sounds from various media, designed to win our hearts and minds. As adults, we have life's experiences, the advantages of age, and often higher education as filters to help us navigate these powerful messages. Young people, at very confusing times in their lives, are trying to figure out who they are and what the world is about. How can we, as adults, help young people figure out the impact of media on their decision making, and how can we help them to use the lens of skepticism to be sure they maintain control over their life's choices? An analytical approach to evidence is essential with the mass media. The world is no longer a place where people should blindly trust "experts" to process and provide the information each of us needs to make sound personal decisions about issues involving science and technology, in particular. These days, we all have to be able to think like scientists. That ability includes a habit of healthy skepticism: a scientifically literate person knows to trust evidence when not only the evidence itself, but also *the source it comes from*, passes certain tests of objectivity and completeness.

The science program is perhaps the best venue in school for students to cultivate these critical habits of mind. It is here where they most routinely gather and weigh evidence. There is a range of scientific issues for which the scientific evidence is still under debate. For example, some experts tell us that genetically modified foods are a boon to health while other experts say that eating genetically modified foods is

---

Marlene Thier has been a science materials developer, teacher educator, and leader in the movement to link science and literacy education; she is currently an educational consultant based in Moraga, California.

a foolhardy risk. Some experts tell us that we should take an array of vitamin and mineral supplements to ensure our health while others insist that such supplements largely are a waste of money. By tapping this rich menu of controversy, teachers can help students understand how science evolves while they also sharpen their skills of media analysis.

Inherently, science is a process of probing new ideas and statements for weaknesses, flaws, bias, and hidden meanings. Science courses can encourage students to view data with a scientist's skeptical eye—especially now that so much unrefereed information is available via the Internet, through advertising, and from other media. In developing the skills of media literacy as part of science studies, students learn to dissect advertisements and other more subtle media messages to discern bias and hidden meanings. To analyze contradictory claims and make evidence-based personal decisions, a person must be familiar with the concepts and processes of science. But that person also needs to be able to recognize and understand *how* those facts and processes are being presented and manipulated to put the best light on a given point of view. As Elizabeth Thoman (n.d.), executive director of the Los Angeles-based Center for Media Literacy, points out, "At the heart of media literacy is the principle of inquiry" (http://www.medialit.org/Readingroom/keyarticles/skillsandstrat.htm).

When students view media messages and information analytically, they are cultivating the habit of a "healthy skepticism" that the *National Science Education Standards* considers essential to the nature of science: "Science distinguishes itself from other ways of knowing. . . . through the use of empirical standards, logical arguments, and skepticism" (National Research Council, 1996). A healthy skepticism requires a delicate balance between being open to new ideas and being doubtful of claims for which there is no clear and convincing evidence. In this way, media analysis fosters critical and, therefore, scientific thinking: students learn to rely on evidence to identify arguments—especially those on behalf of unusual claims—as either weak or credible. In doing so, they also learn to differentiate between claims that have scientific validity and those that do not.

The skills of media analysis or media literacy fit the "guided inquiry" approach to science (Thier & Daviss, 2001). In science education, *guided inquiry* can be defined as using a series of structured, sequenced scientific investigations that integrate appropriate processes and information, chosen through research, to fashion meaningful learning experiences for students. Those experiences are effective when they:

- engage students at an emotional level by confronting them with issues or problems that have meaning in students' own lives. Placing scientific ideas and processes in the context of actual issues can suddenly give abstract concepts a personal meaning to students. This is a key element in helping them master knowledge;
- capitalize on students' engagement to lead them to use the concepts, techniques, and information of science to reason their way through a scientific issue to make an informed personal decision about the issue using their data or evidence; and
- help students master sophisticated scientific principles, concepts, and information in ways that will help them to retain the content beyond their final test.

A feature that distinguishes guided inquiry from conventional hands-on science learning is that, after students complete an assigned activity, they are encouraged to design their own projects and investigations to continue exploring the topic. Through these self-selected activities (guided by a teacher), students pursue questions relevant to them about the subject. Working in this way helps students link key ideas, rethink their own theories, and perhaps even satisfy their curiosity in order to achieve a deeper, more enduring level of understanding.

Research has shown that students learn better when they experience something by doing it instead of reading about it in a textbook or hearing about it in a lecture. Students retain only 5–10% of what they read in textbooks, but can recall as much as 80% of the details of something they have experienced (National Training Laboratories, Bethel, MA, n.d.). When students work like scientists, they use language to organize, recognize, and internalize the concepts, principles, and information they encounter through activities. By providing literacy opportunities for students in science, educators enrich the context for both subjects so students can more effectively expand their personal structures of science knowledge by improving their language skills (Thier & Daviss, 2002).

Studies have also shown that true learning takes place only when students engage with information and processes deeply enough to weave that content into their personal views and understandings of how the world works (Harlen, 2000). Clearly, the concept of guided inquiry gives equal weight to knowledge and skills, slighting neither science facts nor science processes. But it also emphasizes concepts more than rote formulas and emphasizes learning science in a personal and social context instead of as discrete sets of compartmentalized abstractions. Many of the areas students study can be found in the media, which further reinforces their interest and engagement. To take students beyond the formulaic aspects of science, teachers must rely on students' language skills. By embedding an inquiry within both the context of students' lives and strong science content, then sequencing investigations as part of a larger curricular design, educators can reach their curricular and instructional goals for science and for media literacy at the same time.

My Sweet Tooth

The following is an example of an activity where teachers can enhance the natural connections between science and literacy in the elementary classroom by applying the principles of guided inquiry (Thier & Daviss, 2002). The activity is called My Sweet Tooth (SEPUP, 1997), which helps students gather evidence and make decisions about the taste, nutritional value, and health implications of sugar and its substitutes.

Students begin the activity by brainstorming ideas about sweeteners in their diets. They might note that sugar is a source of energy and it makes our foods taste better. One student might say, "Sugar makes you fat and gives you cavities, so our family uses artificial sweeteners"; another might respond, "Yuck! That stuff's made out of chemicals." The conversation helps students begin to define the properties of, and differences among, sweeteners.

Next, the activity leads students through three stages. In each, students use language in slightly different forms to gather information, evaluate it, and make evidence-based decisions. In the first stage, students note physical details; in the second, they record personal impressions; in the third, they read to fill gaps in their knowledge.

Working in small groups, students look closely at small samples of sugar and two artificial sweeteners. Students note the details of the materials' physical appearance, first by looking at them unaided and then by looking at the sweeteners through magnifiers. In discussions with their group members, students compare and contrast the magnified and unmagnified appearances of various substances. Then the students make solutions of each of the three, taste each one, and discuss and record their personal preferences along with the reasons behind their choices. (Note: Students with PKU, a genetic condition that makes them sensitive to aspartame, should not taste substances containing this artificial sweetener. In science classes, students should be cautioned not to taste just anything.) The teacher asks students to choose which sweetener they would use at home and to explain to each other their reasons. The discussions help students use spoken language to explore and organize their knowledge and thoughts about sweeteners and to articulate these based on different kinds of evidence. Just as important, they use language to identify information they *do not* have but would need in order to make a better-informed choice.

At this point—when students are motivated to find out more—the teacher asks whether the students would like additional information before finalizing their decisions and, if so, what kinds of information they would like. Students are likely to know which sweetener tastes best to them, but perhaps the discussion has raised concerns; for example, "I like this one best, but is it good for me?" The teacher then distributes a page of background information about different sweeteners for students to read, asks them if their choices have changed, and then offers to help students conduct additional library or Internet research on these and other sweeteners. Working through each stage, students come to learn that decisions can change as the evidence captured in the media grows and changes.

Throughout the activity, students are using many of the reciprocal processes that literacy and science share. Looking at the sweeteners, they note physical details and then compare and contrast the substances' appearances. They gain experience in understanding language operationally—experiencing a concept before learning its abstract name and definition, thereby being able to viscerally associate a term with a concrete meaning. They infer, from scientific studies using animals, how artificial sweeteners might affect humans. They draw evidence-based conclusions about which sweeteners they personally would or would not use. Through their observations and discussions, they use language to sort through evidence and to distinguish facts from opinion. As they read, write, discuss and debate, listen critically to other students, and work through a rudimentary scientific investigation, they also begin to understand that evidence can be a powerful factor in understanding the world.

In addition, the activity's links between science and language can be broadened and strengthened through additional, student-designed investigations. For example, students could conduct a classroom-wide taste test between a regular cola and its low-calorie alternative, then graph the number of students who preferred the taste of each (or found no difference between them). Students also could write reports about the origins, benefits and drawbacks, and health implications of corn syrup, honey, cane sugar, and other sweeteners.

My Sweet Tooth also provides an effective way to sharpen students' response to media. The class can collect advertisements touting products that are "sugar-free," contain "no calories," or made with "all-natural sugar." Students can dissect and compare the products' advertising strategies and even can write their own jingles or raps selling their preferred sweeteners. The activity has direct links to important present-day issues in the media such as childhood obesity, how school menus can reflect better nutrition for students, the effects of dieting on preteen girls, and popular food fads, which are all linked to the pivotal question of "what is good nutrition?" Students encounter these issues in the popular media, which is engaging for them but also highlights the challenge to critically analyze claims using the skeptical lens of inquiry science.

As part of My Sweet Tooth, teachers often encourage students to search the library or the Internet for more information about sweeteners. Usually, students find an array of articles and studies with sometimes-conflicting messages. To interpret the materials' collective meanings as accurately as possible, the students must evaluate the information and presentation strategies of the materials' authors. Was a study declaring a sweetener to be safe for humans paid for or written by the company that makes it? Does the study include negative information about the sweetener's effects on people that a previous report found? If so, how prominently in the study is that negative information featured? What strategies does the writer of the study use to confront (or dismiss) that negative information? This kind of analysis joins conventional reading comprehension—understanding the meaning expressed through the words—to the comprehension of an author's intention and purpose called for by the techniques of media analysis.

This Media Analysis Checklist can be given to students in science classes for them to use as prompts until healthy skepticism becomes a habit:

1. Who is speaking and what is the speaker's purpose? Who has created, published, presented, or sponsored this message and why?

2. Who is the targeted audience? How can I tell? How is this message tailored to that audience?
3. How unbiased is the information or message?
4. Is the information complete? Does the author present enough information for the audience to make an informed decision?
5. Does the author cite sources of factual information included in the message?
6. What techniques are used to attract or hold my attention?
7. What kinds of words are being used? Is the writer using words chosen to stir emotion or sway ideas?
8. How much information does the writer or sponsor think I already know about this topic?
9. Are values or lifestyles being promoted? What does the message present as being good to own, do, or be? What is promoted as being "not good"?
10. Read between the lines. What is implied?
11. What information or points of view are excluded from the message?
12. Are data, statistics, and evidence presented completely? Does the evidence presented help support the ideas in the article?

It is important to understand that in the science classroom, being "media literate" means that students are able to evaluate information about a science issue from a variety of sources—technical reports, television programs, newspapers, websites, and others. It means that students are able to compare information from different media forms and presentations on the same topic. It also means that students know how to use media judiciously as part of an overall exploration of a science topic—for example, that they are able to synthesize new information by drawing on various sources and use a variety of media effectively to get their message across.

Students must understand that a message's author or sponsor shapes the message's stylistic and informational content. A study of tobacco's dangers that is performed by the U.S. Food and Drug Administration is likely to differ in its conclusions from one sponsored by a cigarette company, for example. Similarly, students need to recognize that the choice of language, symbols, images, and sound in a multimedia presentation can all be useful in determining a message's usefulness and credibility. Cigarette advertising directed to young people depicting their peer group engaged in sports, having fun, and surrounded by attractive friends all holding cigarettes sends a powerful subliminal message to the intended audience. The unspoken words speak loudly to the young adolescent craving independence from adults: if you smoke you will be popular, you will be a good athlete, you will be physically attractive, and you will have fun. Young people need to understand on a visceral level that the independence they crave from their parents will be replaced with a long-lasting dependence on tobacco. Similarly, soft drink advertisers on television know the long-term value of having a catchy tune identified with their product so that only the tune needs to be played for people to conjure up a pleasant image of the drink.

Teachers also can help students become aware that different media take different approaches to the same subject. A story about human cloning that appears in a supermarket tabloid must be read differently from an article on cloning in a technical journal. While the article in the supermarket tabloid is most likely absolute and makes all kinds of unsupported and undocumented claims, the technical journal should offer evidence and considered scientific thinking about cloning and its ramifications. Generally speaking, science distinguishes itself from other ways of knowing and from other bodies of knowledge through the use of empirical standards, logical arguments, and skepticism, as scientists strive for the best possible explanations about cloning or other issues. Supermarket tabloids use sensationalism and outlandish claims to sell their product, not to contribute to the scientific discourse.

Regardless of their techniques, most media messages are constructed from language. Language is the primary tool we use to communicate with ourselves as we make sense of our environment. Therefore, students cannot properly interpret media's messages, or resist their manipulative tactics, without a suite of well-developed literacy/language skills. The more questions students know to ask about a media presentation's use of language, the better able they are to develop the healthy skepticism. Indeed, it is incumbent upon all of us to weigh the totality of evidence before accepting the credibility of media information. In fact, we must all ask ourselves how different the world might be if our governments used skepticism and demanded (and respected) evidence and information about environmental concerns or embryonic stem cell research before making policy. When we help our young people in the science classroom view media through the lens of good scientific practice, we prepare them to live in the 21st century—in an age fueled by information and driven by technology. We prepare them to become citizens and adults who can apply a range of scientific skills and knowledge to better understand their world and to live by the words of Albert Einstein: "The important thing is to not stop questioning."

REFERENCES

Harlen, W. (2000). *Building for conceptual understanding in science*. Berkeley: Lawrence Hall of Science, University of California.

National Research Council, Bethel, M.A. (1996). *National Science Education Standards*. Washington, DC: National Academy Press.

National Training Laboratories. (n.d.) *The learning pyramid*. Retrieved September 12, 2004, from http://www.acu.edu/cte/activelearning/whyuseal2.htm

Science Education for Public Understanding Program (SEPUP). (1997). *Chemicals, health, environment, and me (CHEM 2)*. Ronkonkoma, NY: Lab Aids.

Thier, H., & Daviss, B. (2001). *Materials development and the curriculum: A guided inquiry approach*. New York: Teachers College Press.

Thier, M., & Daviss, B. (2002). *The new science literacy: Using language skills to help students learn science*. Portsmouth, NH: Heinemann.

Thoman, E. (n.d.). *Skills and strategies for media education*. Retrieved August 13, 2004, from http://www.medialit.org/Readingroom/keyarticles/skillsandstrat.htm

Media Literacy: A Powerful Tool for Parents and Teachers

CARLA CROCKETT

As both a parent and an experienced teacher, I have found media literacy to be an invaluable tool that I use to teach values and critical thinking skills. I have two preteen daughters whose media consumption is constantly increasing. As their mother, I am deeply concerned about their interpretations of the value messages they receive. I have taught upper elementary and intermediate school for 15 years, with the majority of those years in fifth grade. Like all teachers, I have struggled at times to keep my students motivated and interested in the curriculum. Incorporating media literacy into the curriculum has enabled me to not only keep my students interested, but to also develop their critical thinking skills.

I was first introduced to the concept of media literacy while completing a graduate program at Oklahoma State University. I found the idea of teaching students to think critically about and analyze what they see and hear in the media intriguing. It seemed so obvious! Of course we need to teach children, many of whom spend more time interacting with various forms of the media than they do in school, to think about the images and messages that they receive. I wondered why this issue was not being addressed in the school curriculum. Armed with my enthusiasm for the subject and a commitment to bring media literacy to my students and my children, I was anxious to get started.

Teaching media literacy to my fifth grade students and my impressionable preteen daughters has been both challenging and rewarding. I have seen how media literacy provides them with the tools to think critically about the media and its constant barrage of images and messages. They become empowered through media literacy—because their knowledge of the media makes them less vulnerable. And, because media literacy is relevant to their lives and not just informa-

---

Carla Crockett teaches fifth grade at Hayward Smith Elementary School in Owasso, Oklahoma.

tion they need to hold on to for a later date, they find it motivating and exciting.

McBrien (1999) says, "Students must learn to interpret and understand media messages to make responsible decisions about their media choices" (p. 76). For me, the heart or crux of media literacy is to lessen children's vulnerability and increase their abilities to make responsible media choices. It is about teaching them to think critically.

A Parent's Perspective

As a parent, I am especially concerned about the value messages, unrealistic body images, and false representation of "reality" to which my children are exposed. I am also concerned about their potential vulnerability to advertising targeted directly at them. I want them to recognize values that are important to us as a family, and recognize when those values may be skewed by the media. Their fragile self-images are especially important; I do not want them to feel inferior because they cannot live up to the unrealistic female images they see in the media. And, of course I want them to be able to recognize advertising techniques and the motives behind them.

I have to admit, before taking the media literacy courses I thought I knew what my daughters were being exposed to in the media. However, after completing an assignment to deconstruct one form of media with a child, it became apparent to me that I had only limited knowledge of their media exposure and did not realize the extent of their naiveté.

I chose the website Funschool.com, a site with educational games and activities that my daughters liked to visit, and set out to discover with them the answers to Mann's (1999, p. 6) basic media deconstruction questions:

- Who created this message?
- What techniques are being used to attract my attention?
- Who is profiting from this?
- What information or points of view are not presented?
- What ideologies and value messages are embedded in the media text?

Because it never occurred to them to consider any of these ideas, these questions were difficult for the girls to answer. They were easily able to identify the target audience as children, but they were unable to identify specific techniques used to attract children to the site. The games on this site were for kids and they were fun. What else was there?

As we investigated the site, we found that it was created by a Canadian-based company for the purpose of familiarizing children with its clients' brands and characters. This is achieved through interactive educational games and activities, which incorporate the brand names and characters. Bright colors, movement, animation, and sound are used to attract attention, with most of this coming from the numerous advertisements that are constantly scrolling, blinking, and popping up.

The pervasiveness of the advertising on this site is incredible. A page on the site addressed to potential clients describes the many ways in which Internet advertising can go beyond banner ads to create interactive experiences for the target audience. One pop-up ad, for example, involves using the computer mouse to feed a hungry shark, which happens to be the main character of a new cartoon. Children feed the shark and he then regurgitates the items and invites the children to pursue more "fun" activities with him. A click on the "more fun" button leads to another web page that contains advertisements for other children's television programs. These ads are so cleverly designed that even though they contain small labels that say "ad," it is not always apparent to children that they are advertisements. I was amazed at how difficult it was for my 10-year-old to point out the advertisements. These manipulative techniques are one of the main reasons that I believe media literacy is imperative.

As we continued with the deconstruction, we examined some of the games to determine if there was a balance of perspectives and points of view. The girls guided me on a tour of the site, and we looked for gender and ethnic diversity. Our quest for diversity was unsuccessful. Most characters, adult and child, are white males. For example, an activity designed to teach about different careers and the tools necessary for those jobs depicted the stereotypical careers: doctor, lawyer, engineer, teacher, firefighter, police officer, and so on. All but one of these professionals is male and none are people of color. Another activity, which allows children to mix and match faces and costumes to create their own personal heroes, offers both male and female heroes. However, only white faces or faces that are completely covered are available. Our entire search yielded very little diversity.

Does this lack of diverse representations send an inappropriate message to our children? My own children's responses to our search for diversity helped me to realize that they are underexposed to other cultures. I found this media literacy activity to be an excellent tool for teaching them about diversity.

Deconstructing this site was a learning experience for both my daughters and me. They were challenged to think about issues that they had never before contemplated. They gained some knowledge about advertising techniques and purposes, and they began to think about representation in regard to gender and race. I gained a better understanding of how children perceive the Internet—they question nothing and accept everything, even the annoying pop-up ads (advertising is background noise to them). I learned that I must expose my children to other cultures and help them to develop an appreciation for diversity. And, finally, I concluded that although the amount of advertising and the techniques used to create "interactive experiences" with brand names and characters are major distractions, the site is kid-friendly and many of the activities are educational. I chose not to restrict my children's access to it, but I plan to make them more aware of advertising, its purposes, and the techniques used to market to children.

This process of deconstructing and discussing this website opened an interesting and important dialogue between my daughters and me. It has become an ongoing conversation, and I have seen my daughters begin to apply these questions to other forms of media. Because we now experience so much media together and talk about it, I feel that I am more in tune than ever to my children's media exposure and they have a better understanding of not only the media, but also of our family values. Schwarz (2003) says, "Media literacy means intentional reflection on the media themselves" (p. 45). It is so rewarding for me to see my children reflect and think critically about the media.

A Teacher's Perspective

Deconstructing advertisements and other forms of media has led to similar results in my fifth grade classroom. Students are surprised to learn how biased advertisements are and how much information is *not* given. After deconstructing magazine and television ads, I find that my students are so interested in this topic that they begin to bring in other ads to share with me. They even discuss some of them among themselves. Because they see a real-life application for this information, students enjoy these and other media literacy lessons. As Considine (1995) says, media literacy "connects the curriculum of the classroom to the curriculum of the living room" (p. 41).

Through media literacy lessons that range from technical lessons on the computer to critical thinking lessons that involve deconstructing and constructing media, my students learn to question and analyze what they see. I have found that the most effective way for me to teach media literacy is to use varied teaching approaches and to integrate it into the existing curriculum.

Integrating it into the core subjects, especially language arts and social studies, not only helps me to teach the students to think critically about the media, but because they are so enthusiastic about media literacy, it helps me to keep them motivated about other subjects. For example, instead of just teaching the propaganda techniques and deconstructing advertisements, my students also use their knowledge of the Colonial Era to create advertisements convincing Europeans to settle in the New England, Mid-Atlantic, or Southern colonies. This allows them to demonstrate their knowledge of both American history and media literacy. Students get excited about this assignment, and because they must analyze the historical information about their colonial region and then filter it to create their ads, their knowledge retention is very good. These student-created ads never cease to amaze me!

Having students create their own media is an essential part of media literacy education. It completes the circle. Through creating their own media, students experience firsthand the process of deciding what should be included and/or excluded from their media texts. It not only gives them a voice, but it also helps them to understand the languages and technological aspects of the different media forms. Because the process of creating media involves using other academic skills (reading, research, writing, etc.), creating media is a great way to bring it all together.

Teaching media literacy has been extremely beneficial. It has enabled me to see my students and children become empowered with critical thinking skills, become enthusiastic about learning, and begin to make thoughtful choices about their media consumption. In addition, because the students are so familiar with media, it becomes a common ground for them. Studying media helps to develop a sense of community in the classroom, creating "community within and out from the school, offering young people connection and meaning" (Schwarz, 2000, p. 54).

For me personally, teaching media literacy has renewed and rejuvenated my excitement for teaching. It has not only enabled me to make learning both meaningful and fun for my students, but it has also made *me* think more critically about the media. I believe that in this constantly changing technological age, with the media touching all aspects of our lives, it is imperative that we provide our children with the critical thinking tools that media literacy provides.

REFERENCES

Considine, D. (1995). Are we there yet? An update on the media literacy movement. *Educational Technology, 35*(4), 32–43.

Mann, L. (1999). The aha! of media literacy. *Association for Supervision and Curriculum Development, 4*(7), 1, 6–7.

McBrien, J. L. (1999). New texts, new tools: An argument for media literacy. *Educational Leadership, 57*(2), 76–79.

Schwarz, G. (2000). Renewing teaching through media literacy. *Kappa Delta Pi Record, 37*(1), 8–12.

Schwarz, G. (2003). Renewing humanities through media literacy. *Journal of Curriculum & Supervision, 19*(1), 44–53.

The Library Media Center: At the Center of Media Literacy Education

ANGEL KYMES

Although the media education/media literacy debate has yet to find its way into the majority of classrooms across the United States, school libraries and library media specialists are the exception to this general rule. For a decade or more, librarians have been encouraging students to use multiple media to locate and utilize information. And a prerequisite for effective use is evaluation, based on issues such as timeliness, authority, and relevance. Whether the information is presented in traditional print texts, in graphic novels, in video, on websites, or through other media, library media specialists have assumed the responsibility of teaching students to select and use the items most relevant to their immediate need. Now, as the call for a more critical approach to literacy has surfaced in education, the library media specialist is in a position to continue assisting students in utilizing and processing information from a variety of media.

When students begin by realizing that only specific items are included in the collection in their local library media center, they are ready to begin to think about why those items are included, and about what significance they can attribute to the information they are able to locate. As the Internet has allowed library media collections to multiply exponentially, students are in even greater need of critical media awareness by which they may analyze and evaluate the information they are able to find. We teach students to evaluate websites by asking questions regarding the production of the information, the bias and validity of the information, and the multiple media involved in the transmission of the information. We must also teach students to be thoughtful and critical about the media, for its influence is so pervasive. There is value in requiring students to question issues of power and subjection based on representation, misinformation, and existing social structures that may inaccurately reflect society. Because students enjoy media and find

Angel Kymes was a school library-media specialist and is now a full-time graduate student at Oklahoma State University.

useful ways to incorporate it into their lives and their identities, they must learn to realize that they have power and they have rights. They can use media, in many forms, to establish views and a stance that is consistent with their own values and personality. They do not have to succumb to media propaganda without thinking. They do not have to mindlessly accept what they are told, without questioning who is providing the information, what that person/company has to gain, and what implications their acceptance of that information has on their world and their personal worldview.

The library positions itself in society and in the school as a place for everyone. The librarian respects all persons and all informational needs. Purves (1998) points out that new technologies are forcing us to ask questions of new [online] texts that we perhaps should have been asking of print sources all along; I would argue that librarians have been requiring and encouraging students to ask those questions of *all* sources of information. In the library, we are in a slightly different business than our colleagues in the classroom. Lemke (1998) notes that classrooms are dominated by a "curricular learning paradigm" in which information is presented in a predetermined manner, in a fixed order on a fixed schedule. The curriculum is central to the learning, not the learner. He claims that this system is "widely refused and resisted by students" and provides little example of usefulness, as it is "failing disastrously in the United States today" (p. 293). Many teachers would agree that in classrooms where student experience is undervalued and there is little connection to what the student considers "real life," there is a resistance to methods and content alike. In contrast, libraries operate under what Lemke calls an "interactive learning paradigm" (p. 294). This constructivist paradigm assumes that students determine what they need to know, learn in an order that suits them, select media appropriate for their task, and make use of what they learn. In the library, we are in the business of creating lifelong learners. We want students who are able to find the information they need at the point of need. We want them to be at least a little critical, and somewhat skeptical of what they are able to locate. We want them to then use their information in a personally and socially meaningful manner. Though we are generally and historically considered to be only in the business of books, the modern library media center is a place of dynamic technological revolution. As Tyner (1998) notes, libraries are perfect settings for encouraging and implementing media education.

The library media center operates in conjunction with all of the other instructional programs at work within a school. It may be through the collaborative efforts of the library media specialist that the media literacy skills necessary for student success are most effectively developed. The library media specialist can help the classroom teacher select appropriate videos and websites to emphasize critical awareness in the development of a skills unit. The librarian may additionally have more technical experience and know-how to assist the classroom teacher in the development of a lesson or series of lessons that culminate in student media production. Traditional themes and topics of study can be revived with the infusion of a new perspective and new materials. In many schools, the library media specialist is responsible for the delivery of student-based news programs viewed school-wide through a closed circuit video feed. The library media specialist often has audiovisual expertise that can be utilized by students and teachers for creating media messages and projects that allow students to demonstrate their knowledge, express their point of view, and learn valuable lessons about the role of the media producer.

The function of the library and the role of the librarian continue to change as technology and media revolutionize information retrieval and information use. Luke (2003) questions how "banks of touch-screen computers changing students' research practices" and how the "social and spatial organization" of the library will change what students do and how they do it (p. 401). For students to continue to be successful in the world of technological advancement, they must be able to explore media, understand media, think critically about media, and produce and use media for their own advantages and purposes. Modern school library media centers are being transformed into spaces where students can learn, use, and create media with the support of educators who value such abilities. Students who are given a vocabulary through which to critique media, skills, and tools needed for analysis, and outlets through which their voices can be heard will be able to make a difference in the society in which they live. It is the responsibility of educators—library media specialists and classroom teachers alike—to provide these skills, tools, and outlets for students. As Stephens (1998) argues:

Don't we have a responsibility to these same young to find fresh approaches to the conundrums that seem to have left a residue of nihilism in much of their music and in many of their minds? Can we continue to submit our responses to Nirvana songs and Nike commercials only in print? As equipment for shooting and editing plummets in price, are we to continue to leave video, with all its power, to rock stars and advertising agencies? When the strains inherent in a revolution like this become evident, retreat seems an increasingly attractive alternative: Publish some more celebrations of reading. Grumble about "the menace of unreality." Suggest to some green-haired, body-pierced, fast-eyed, image-bedazzled young persons that all their answers await them in books. I don't think this is, in the end, an acceptable alternative. I think we must push on. (pp. 228–229)

When library media specialists join with classroom teachers to incorporate media literacy into the school's curriculum, they recognize the transformative power of media in the lives of young people and the abilities of those young people to be agents of change in their world. Students are invited into the modern library media center where ideas, experience, equipment, and philosophy are woven together. By providing them with tools and skills through which they may better understand, critically evaluate, and produce media, educators empower students to be shareholders in a world where literacy, in its broadest, most inclusive form, is available to all.

References

Lemke, J.L. (1998). Metamedia literacy: Transforming meanings and media. In D. Reinking, M. McKenna, L.D. Labbo, & R.D. Keifer (Eds.), *The handbook of literacy and technology: Transformations in a post-typographic world* (pp. 283–301). Mahwah, NJ: Lawrence Erlbaum Associates.

Luke, C. (2003). Pedagogy, connectivity, multimodality, and interdisciplinarity. *Reading Research Quarterly, 38*, 397–403.

Purves, A.C. (1998). The web of text and the web of God: An essay on the third information revolution. New York: Guilford.

Stephens, M. (1998). *The rise of the image the fall of the world*. New York: Oxford University Press.

Tyner, K.R. (1998). *Literacy in a digital world: Teaching and learning in the age of information*. Mahwah, NJ: Lawrence Erlbaum Associates.

Media Literacy for a Future Teacher

CHERI MAYNARD

As a middle-level education major at Appalachian State University in North Carolina, I was required to take a media literacy class called *Media and Young People* during the spring semester of 2004. I really had no idea why it was so important for middle school education majors to have an entire semester class on media. I have a teenaged son; he could teach me more about technology than I would ever be able to learn in a lifetime. What was I supposed to teach my middle grade media-technology-using superiors?

My instructor for this class was Dr. David Considine. He had the classroom full of future middle school teachers thinking and talking about the influences of the media—in their many forms—on young people. For one assignment we were asked to recall our own childhood and adolescence and to write about how we were affected by media. I was a child of the 1960s and an adolescent of the 1970s, when *Bonanza* and *I Dream of Jeannie* were popular and David Cassidy became a teenage heart-throb. There were only two television channels in my hometown—ABC and NBC affiliates. There was certainly no such thing as the Internet. Still, slowly, as I looked back, I could see how the music I chose to listen to and the television programs I watched shaped my perception of reality. Adolescents today are bombarded by even more media messages through even more kinds of media. It is no wonder that today's youth need help in comprehending the kinds of messages being sent to them, as well as how and why these messages are being sent.

Another project we did that could be used in my own classroom is one in which we examined stacks of magazines (from *Teen People* to *Hot Rod*). First, we looked at the cover page and discussed what was being presented to spark the interest of young readers. We then sifted through the magazines and read several articles and ads. We were challenged to determine what was being sold to the readers and by what means. Also,

---

Cheri Maynard is a senior at Appalachian State University, majoring in middle school education.

we analyzed what the priorities were. Sex and beauty rated highest; education and family life rated lowest. This kind of lesson gives middle school students, too, the opportunity to interact and exchange ideas about the media they enjoy. At the same time they can become aware of the messages being conveyed and the ways those messages work on the reader. Consciousness raising is an important part of media literacy.

Dr. Considine was not satisfied solely with educating us regarding media literacy materials and techniques; he emphasized that we must first learn to know the young people we are going to teach. He could not have known how much I—a "nontraditional student" and mother of a teenaged son—could have needed to learn this lesson.

At 17 years old, my son was going through the phases described by Ron Taffel in a book we were assigned to read called *The Second Family* (2001). Taffel reintroduces parents to their children who have, almost overnight, seemed to turn into people the parents neither recognize nor understand . . . nor like very much. Taffel helps teachers and parents understand how to get over the wall that so often divides adolescents from adults so they can communicate, and so that adults can guide them. My son had developed what Taffel calls a "second family." He lived on the Internet, talking to friends until very late at night. They often contacted him for advice. I was amazed and disheartened to see how wise he could be with friends from school—his second family— when he was always defensive and impatient with his family at home. My son communicated positively with his second family far more than he did with his first family. I did not know this was common. When I read the Taffel book, I breathed a sigh of relief. I wasn't the only one after all!

At first, "playing second fiddle" in my son's life hurt my feelings terribly. We had always been close. It was as if he had woken up one morning and was someone else. In place of my child was a tall, lanky teen with long hair and headphones permanently connected to his ears. The laughter we used to share, he now shared exclusively with his friends. I actually began to resent those friends, and their technology, for taking my son away from me. But then I started thinking back as I read *The Second Family*.

My son was an only child and I had been a stay-at-home mom. When he came home, I was refreshed and eager to hear how my son's day had been. I had been there to keep the house clean and organized, to cook hot meals, and to help him with his homework. Things changed when I returned to college. While I was once Ozzie and Harriet all rolled up into one, I now hardly had time to do my own homework.

There was precious little time to help him with his. I had become an absentee mother. I realized that my son had found the support of and connection to a "second family."

A light came on that made me see/consider life from my son's perspective. I began to understand that he wanted to be in a world with me—not *my* world and not exactly *his* world either—but somewhere in the middle. The night I invited him to join me with his electric bass while I played my acoustic guitar was that "somewhere in the middle." I had my son back, playing music with me, and laughing again with me. I also began to comprehend how the media could have such an influence over children and adolescents. In our fast-paced society, with both parents working to make ends meet, our children are often left to negotiate information and values that come to them from the very media that keep them occupied. Barring them from the TV, radio, or computer is not the answer. Becoming involved in those major media-influenced elements of their lives in an educated manner is an answer, maybe the only answer. It is the responsibility of parents and teachers to know what is filling the time and the heads of the young people who look to us for guidance and education. Media literacy is essential in the process.

As a college student, future teacher, and now mother of two, I realize that if I am ever going to "reach" my sons and students, then I must meet them in the middle and I must gain insight into the many sources of media messages that come to them every day, as well as help develop their own insight. As I prepare to teach English language arts and social studies to young adolescents, I intend to integrate media literacy into my curriculum. I no longer wonder why a future teacher should take a whole course in media literacy.

REFERENCE

Taffel, R. (2001). *The second family*. New York: St. Martin's Griffin.

Terrain in Transition: Reflections on the Pedagogy of Media Literacy Education

FAITH ROGOW

Witnessing History

We are living in incredible times. For only the second time in human history a major piece of the concept of what it means to be literate is shifting. The first major shift involved the "who," as in "who should be literate?" That shift began in the 16th century with the invention of the printing press. Because the printing press made mass media possible, it ultimately changed expectations about who needed to be literate. We went from a world where no one expected more than a few professional scribes and clerics to be able to read and write, to our current world, where we assume that everyone needs to master those skills.

We are now witnessing a second shift. This one is about the "what," as in "what does it mean to be literate?" In our society simple print literacy is, by necessity, giving way to media literacy.

As an education consultant who, among other things, has done a lot of work with producers of children's educational television, I have been riding the leading edge of this literacy shift for more than two decades. As the founding and immediate past president of the Alliance for a Media Literate America (AMLA), the United States's first membership organization for media literacy educators and advocates (http://www. AMLAinfo.org), I have seen first hand the rather convoluted path media literacy has taken in the United States. In these pages, I return to my roots as an historian and take a step back to consider the influence of where we have been on where we are going.

Why the Shift?

The reason for reconceptualizing literacy is multifaceted and flows from the sheer pervasiveness of media in our culture. When I was a

---

Faith Rogow is the past President of the Alliance for a Media Literate America and now heads Insighters Educational Consulting.

child, the phone wasn't a media technology. In contrast, today's cell phones function as computers, game terminals, cameras, radios, and more. In a related change, space that was once civic is now commercial. Rather than honoring notables, we sell naming rights. On our school sports fields, signs for soft drinks are as prominent as the team logo. Media is everywhere.

Even traditional print media aren't what they used to be. Compare a newspaper or a textbook with their counterparts from 50 years ago. In the current versions, illustrations, photographs, graphs, and charts abound. Students who are trained to take away information only from print are missing significant content. The unassailable fact is that, in the United States, most people now get most of their information about the world from image-based sources. Given that reality, it doesn't make sense to continue to relegate media literacy to a nice but optional classroom enhancement. To the contrary, the most promising way to address the changes with which we live is to integrate media literacy into existing core subject areas across the curriculum and at all grade levels.[1]

Ironically, given that much of the media saturation we live with is generated in the United States and drives our economy, our educational system is still heavily, sometimes exclusively, focused on print. Every year a student is in school, from pre-K through undergraduate education, students are required to spend time learning to decipher, analyze, and write print. That requirement will and should remain. But people who are not conversant in all forms of media are not prepared for basic citizenship. So we have to expand traditional concepts that limit literacy to print skills. Today, the question about media literacy is no longer "should we?" but rather, "*how* should we?"

What Media Literacy Education Is and Is Not

As it developed in the United States, media literacy education has often been defined as teaching about media *impact*. This approach to media literacy, championed by those who were concerned about media effects, especially on children, used methods that sometimes didn't (and don't) make much sense pedagogically.

For example, people who believe that media cause harm often suggest that responsible adults keep children away from media. Hence initiatives like TV Turnoff Week. As a one-time awareness exercise, turning off media can provide useful insight. But as an overriding educational strategy, it makes little sense. It would be absurd for an educator to argue that we attempt to make a person print literate by keeping them away from books. Likewise, we can't make students media literate by keeping them away from media.

The assumption that media are a source of harm has been so common[2] that it has crept into educational materials in subtle ways. For example, many media literacy texts routinely use the definite article in conjunction with the word "media," implying that "*the* media" is a monolithic whole, a singular entity, or worse, some kind of connected conspiracy. Would we use "the" if we were seeing the complexity of media experiences, reading the word as it should be read, as plural? Would we be as quick to use "the" if the grammatically correct plural form of the word was "medias" instead of "media"?

Educators cannot succeed by simply reporting the conclusions of researchers, media analysts, or cultural critics who suggest that audiences are being manipulated by media. Because this approach does not provide students with any sense of agency, such instruction often leaves students cynical rather than skeptical. How do we convey respect to students if our subtle message is, "you are too naïve (or young or dumb) to know this for yourself so I am going to clue you in"?

This is not a call to abandon media criticism or media reform efforts. To the contrary, we can make the entire citizenry media literate and if they don't have access to a wide range of high-quality media options, it won't matter. But political approaches cannot succeed by themselves. People don't act on what they don't understand. Media literacy education is an essential component of efforts to ensure that American media serve the interests of the public and democracy and not just the financial interests of a few corporations.

Nevertheless, creating media literacy techniques based primarily on a concern about media impact is essentially a Puritan approach in which children are viewed as inherently weak and prone to sin, and the goal of education is to save kids from themselves. Progressive education suggests a different model, where students are presumed to have ability and the goal of education is to develop that ability.

We certainly want to continue to teach about media. Effective media literacy education cannot be credible and also ignore the impact of media (both positive and negative). Nor can it fail to acknowledge the powerful commercial interests that control much of the media to which we have access. But, as educator Kevin Maness (2004) has pointed out, teaching *against* media is not the same as teaching *about* media. Teaching students to be critical of media is not the same as teaching them to think critically.

If Media Literacy Is Not About Critiquing Media, What Is It?

Above all else, media literacy is about teaching students to think critically.[3] It is a skill set encompassing the abilities to analyze, access, and produce media. Telling students what an ad (or film or music video or whatever) means might peak interest and even provide new insight, but it is not the same thing as teaching students to analyze for themselves. After all, how can you teach students to think for themselves if you have already predetermined the message?

Given the power dynamics of typical classrooms, when we as teachers present our own views, they are often received as if they are fact, or as too many exam-savvy students have learned, an excuse to simply memorize and repeat rather than analyze texts for themselves. Certainly educators need to be able to share their own perspectives. However, media literacy education that *begins* by or is limited to the presentation of our own (or anyone else's) analysis of media—especially if we imply, either subtly or overtly that our view is the "correct" interpretation— undermines our ability to teach skills.[4]

Moreover, the approach contradicts a basic tenet of media literacy, that is, that people always interpret what they see, hear, and read through the lens of their own experience. When we provide students with the skills to analyze for themselves, we must be prepared to accept the possibility that they may come to conclusions that differ from our own—evidence-based conclusions to be sure, but not automatic echoes of our own perspectives or ideology. Once we provide students with the tools to think for themselves, we must allow them the chance to do just that. And that may be the single greatest challenge for educators who are working in a system that demands memorization of single "right answers" that can be regurgitated on standardized tests.

To think more deeply about the pedagogy of media literacy approaches, educators might want to evaluate their lessons using the following questions:

1. Am I trying to tell the students what the message is, or am I giving students the skills to determine what they think the message(s) might be?
2. Have I let students know that I am open to accepting their interpretation, as long as it is well substantiated, or have I conveyed the message that my interpretation is the only correct view?
3. At the end of this lesson, are students likely to be more analytical or more cynical?

Where Do We Go from Here?

Summarizing the approach to media literacy that focuses on critical thinking rather than media effects is no easy task. Four years ago, the founding Board of Directors of the AMLA tried to do just that. Here is what we came up with:

Media literacy is an essential life skill for the 21st century. It is the process of applying literacy skills to media and technology messages, learning to skillfully interpret, analyze, and create messages. As communication technologies transform society, they impact our understanding of ourselves, our communities, and our diverse cultures. Media literacy empowers people to be both critical thinkers and creative producers of an increasingly wide range of messages using images, language, and sound.

A slightly different version of this same definition is available on the AMLA website at http://www.amlainfo.org/medialit/index.php. It is one of three (!) versions that the AMLA uses, each one tailored to the priorities of different audiences. That the AMLA's definition of media literacy lacks brevity attests to the process of creating definitions by committee. More importantly, it reflects the diversity of the field. That diversity has been an excuse for division in the past, but in reality, it is a strength.

No single person can comprehensively cover all there is to teach in any subject area, including media literacy. By definition, media literacy is interdisciplinary, covering issues as wide-ranging as the functioning of democracy, the credibility of websites, the identification of stereotypes, the evaluation of "scientific" claims about the nutritional value of various foods, and much, much more. In this way, media literacy is very much like multicultural education. It includes core content and competencies, but it is also a shift in worldview. It can be as complex as engaging students in major video productions or as simple as asking, "What are the sources of your information?" whenever we ask, "What do you already know about this topic?"

The critical next step is media literacy efficacy research. Evaluation will enable us to gather the most promising practices and approaches into a unified, multidisciplinary field. I predict that such research will reveal that media literacy's inherently interdisciplinary nature is the best way to teach critical thinking across the curriculum and link subject areas. In other words, where once we shouted just to get media literacy included someplace in the curriculum, it is now well within the realm of possibility that media literacy will not only be included, but will actually be central to what is taught in American schools, as the glue that holds everything together. Key coalitions such as the Partnership for 21st Century Skills and the National Forum on Information Literacy have accepted media literacy as essential to their vision for education in the future. Organizations like the National Council of Social Service and National Council of Teachers of English have acknowledged the importance of media literacy education, and, of course, the National Society for the Study of Education has devoted this volume to the topic.

In addition to high-quality research, teachers will need training. Too often those who oppose media technologies in the classroom lament that teachers use video as a babysitter or computers as a reward. But few administrators or education schools provide pre- or in-service training that would help teachers learn to do anything else. So the withholding of training becomes a self-fulfilling prophecy for the failure of technology to improve instruction. Learning to use media effectively is not difficult, but neither is it self-evident. Educators will need the time and training to integrate media and media literacy into what they do, or they will continue to use media the way they generally use it at home, that is, for entertainment.

Finally, organizations like the AMLA, which convenes the National Media Education Conference to provide a space for educators to engage in cross-disciplinary conversations and strategy sharing, need support. To have clout with policymakers, the field needs numbers. We need a media literacy education organization with 10,000 members. We need every education organization to adopt an official platform endorsing media literacy education. And we need educators in the field willing to take a chance on something new.

Conclusion

We know a lot about how people learn. We need to be sure that we apply what we know to media literacy education. When we do, we will inevitably create strategies that go well beyond teaching about media impact. They will be at least as much about "literacy" as they are about "media."

Visibility will be a key to the future of media literacy. There are thousands of educators doing media literacy, but their work isn't always recognized as such. Different people are using different labels. This commentary uses the term media literacy. Library media specialists are calling it "information literacy." Computer scientists are calling it "technology literacy." Critics are calling it "cultural literacy" or "critical literacy." Health educators are calling it "life skills." But make no mistake—we are all touching part of the same proverbial elephant. The more that each of us can listen to the others, and reach across disciplines, the more our own work will be improved. The more that we can join together to make ourselves visible, the more powerful will be our voice and our ability to bring permanent and universal media literacy education to the United States.

NOTES

1. For a model of how this integration can be accomplished, see the work of Project Look Sharp: http://www.ithaca.edu/looksharp

2. For examples of media literacy work based on the assumption that media are harmful, see the New Mexico Media Literacy Project, Media Education Foundation, Action Coalition for Media Education, Common Sense Media, American Academy of Pediatrics, National Institute on Media and the Family, etc.

3. For a more comprehensive and historical examination of the "critical thinking" approach to media literacy, see Kathleen Tyner's *Literacy in a Digital World* (Lawrence Erlbaum, 1998).

4. For example, educators and cultural critics like Jean Kilbourne or Sut Jhally have created compelling films that share their analysis of advertising and commercial media. These films are widely used in high school and college classes across the United States. When referenced as if they are fact rather than opinion, or as if the films' conclusions are beyond question, they foster memorization or passive acceptance of the filmmaker's ideology rather than skill-building. To be clear, this is not a critique of Kilbourne's or Jhally's work. Both have created valuable tools. This discussion is about how we use those tools to engage in effective media literacy education.

REFERENCE

Maness, K. (2004). Teaching media-savvy students about the popular media. *English Journal, 1*, 46.

Name Index

Note: This index includes names associated with a theory, concept, program, experiment or other work with a substantive description. It does not include names given in examples or passing references.

Subject Index